PRESTON'S VICTORIAN RED LIGHT DISTRICT

For Nina, Ruth and Beth

First published in 2023
by Palatine Books
Carnegie House
Chatsworth Road
Lancaster LA1 4SL
www.palatinebooks.com

Additional illustrations by Penny Cameron

British Library Cataloguing-in-Publication data
A catalogue record for this book is available from the British Library

Paperback ISBN 13: 978-1-910837-47-4

Designed and typeset by Carnegie Book Production
www.carnegiebookproduction.com

Printed and bound by Ashford Colour Press Ltd

Preston's Victorian red light district:

into the Sandhole

John Garlington

'Have we not a "Sandhole", a Water Street, a Library Street and many other sinks of wickedness?'

(Edward Blackoe, proprietor of the George Hotel, Friargate, in a letter to the editor of the *Preston Herald* on 24 June 1865.)

CONTENTS

A former Preston handloom weaver's cottage from A. J. Berry's *Story of Preston* (1912). There were very few houses of this type in the town and it is possible that it stood in Blaylock Street before extensive demolitions.

FOREWORD

I CAME TO THE SANDHOLE, metaphorically speaking, by accident. At the end of February 2018, I had finished a chapter about my old school, The Catholic College, for the *Portrait of Winckley Square* book, and a biographical essay about the life of the Preston philanthropist and photographer, Robert Pateson. As a result I decided to return to researching even further details of my family's history by focusing on ancestors who lived part of their lives in two poor areas of Preston, namely the Canal Street district and the area at the northern end of Bow Lane, once known as the Irish Rookery. I decided to start with the latter.

The three principal streets in this neighbourhood were Buckingham Street, Poplar Street and Clarence Street with alleys and byways leading off all three, all demolished in the 1930s. As I began to research this area, I found evidence of a very lively population and a sturdy Irish presence. What I also came across were a few references to men being arrested 'in the Sandhole'. I had no idea what or where the Sandhole was and, it turned out, neither did anyone else. From this I gained the impression that not only was the place beyond living memory, not only undocumented, but also purposely forgotten.

The Sandhole was never shown on any town maps, being in use only as a colloquial, geographical expression.

Eventually, the *Preston Chronicle*, after a fashion, almost reluctantly, gave the answer.

This illustration of a group of cottages in Queen Street, Preston was published in 1844. These cottages were referred to in Reverend John Clay's report on the link between the poor housing in Preston and the high death rate within the city. Image: © Harris Museum and Art Gallery, Creative Commons BY-NC-SA

It was Preston's Victorian red light district. I thought carefully about how to proceed. Should I forget about it and go back to the Irish Rookery or pursue it further and find out what had been forgotten about this area? Eventually, after discussing it with friends and family, I decided to research what I could and see where it might lead.

I had never done research on anything similar before. As well as the Robert Pateson biography, I have written an outline history of St Walburge's church, researched all the names on the seven Catholic war memorials in Preston, produced a study of the origins of Preston's main War Memorial and had five illustrated local history books published, but this type of social history was all new for me and I had to go about learning more research skills.

Now, I have researched enough material to produce a worthwhile investigation of the area and its inhabitants. On the face of it, it is rather grim, but there is in it, I found, something of humanity, not just the unlawful and immoral, but the desperation of the permanently lost, some of whom never had much chance in life who, were regarded in the late Georgian period as 'barbarous' by 'civilised' society. There was also evidence of people, living at the base of society, and evidence, through a probable murder, of lives spinning out of control through the lack of any safety net.

Though many worthwhile books, papers and articles have been written about Preston through its Guilds, its buildings, its transport, its entertainments and its people I feel that this account has its place in the city's social history and it needs to be known.

A later copy of Preston householders in 1690 with west at the top, east at the bottom and Cocker Hole running south from Church Street.

1

Victorian Preston

The Sandhole was never shown on any town maps, being in use only as a colloquial, geographical expression. A map drawn about 1690 to indicate the householders of Preston, shows fields to the south of Church Street which ran down to the Syke and beyond. This map shows a lane running parallel with these fields known as the Cocker Hole which ran down to the River Ribble. This lane was the forerunner of Water Street and the area was, until 1812, swampy and there were five willow fields which gave Willow Street its name. Water Street took its name from the Syke (from 'sic' in Old English, meaning brook) which was rose from a spring near the corner of Queen Street before running down Leeming Street, along Shepherd Street, down across what is now Winckley Square, through Garden Street to Broadgate. It was latterly used as an open sewer and was culverted in 1812 and is still running in pipes below the streets. Other street names like Laurel Street, Oak Street and Vine Street gave this disappearing area of the Sandhole a connection to countryside long gone by 1822. The name 'Sandhole' itself, reminiscent of a more rural era, seems to have been dropped, at least by the Preston newspapers, by the mid-1860s. I have used it beyond that date for the sake of clarity.

In 1786, Leeming Street was laid out along the path of the old Cocker Hole and was a continuation of the new Water Street from the corner of Shepherd Street, running south.

By 1791 other streets in the area were developed, such as Queen Street, Charlotte Street, Paradise Street and Library Street which were on the close fringes of the Sandhole. In his history of Preston, published in 1900, Henry Fishwick talks about the 'rapid march of Preston' where arable lands close to Church Street which were formerly

> pasturages and for the production of vegetables are now entirely covered over by neat houses, occupied by the man of wealth and artisan. We have the whole of the vicinage of Avenham (which was originally green fields.)

A further comment on Preston, in 1900, gives the impression of the freedom of former days, especially in this area, when he advocates the creation of open spaces for the enjoyment of working people 'to join in those exercises of health which their fathers delighted ... which are now unhappily for ever supplanted by the dangerous soul-killing and enervating false pleasures of the tavern.'

He could have had the Sandhole in mind when he wrote that.

Running east to west from Stoneygate to the Water Street/ Leeming Street corner is Shepherd Street. Doctor Richard Shepherd (1694–1761) practised medicine in Preston and was Mayor twice. During his lifetime he acquired an extensive library which he left to the town on his death, bequeathing £1000 (£150,000 in modern money) for further additions and salary for a librarian to oversee it. By 1830 there were four thousand books and fifty years later it held ten thousand volumes. In his *Handbook and Guide to Preston* (1882), William Pollard describes the home of the Library in Shepherd Street as 'the upper part of a plain and unpretending building' on the corner of Rose Street. In 1851, the books had been removed because the library had to be put in

> a more eligible and convenient site ... not only from the expansion of the population (estimated in 1760 as 6000 to 69,542 in 1851), but owing to the circumstances of that locality in which the library was then situated was daily becoming one of the least attractive parts of the town and altogether unsuited as the depository of such priceless literary treasures.

The locality in question was the Sandhole and the lower part of the building was the notorious beerhouse, Liverpool

House. The books were removed to the Institute for the Diffusion of Useful Knowledge on Avenham Lane, before being moved to the Literary and Philosophical Society on Cross Street in 1867. In 1895 the books were removed again, this time to the Harris Library where they were accessible in the Reference Library. At present (2020), they are stored in the basement.

The houses which were part of the early development of the area, and would be 'occupied by artisans', were the type favoured by handloom weavers were built in Rose Street, Blelock Street and Vauxhall Road. They had a half-sunk cellar, that is, a cellar which had windows at footpath level and a front door which was reached by way of two or three steps. These cellars were damp, thereby maintaining the right conditions for keeping the fragile cotton pliable for weaving but having enough daylight to work by. The period about 1780 to about 1820 was a golden time for handloom weavers as the mechanisation of the spinning industry meant that there was plenty of yarn for the weavers to work with. In 1852, Reverend John Clay, the Anglican chaplain of Preston Prison, remembered when Penwortham handloom weavers used to arrive in Preston on Mondays 'to lay in a stock of rum for that and the following two days. Starting home laden with liquor they were known as the Jamaica Fleet.'

David Hunt quotes Colonel Laurence Rawstorne, recalling

> At the time that (hand)loom weaving was at its tip top price … all other conditions way to it. A good handloom weaver would make his thirty shillings (£1,225) a week or even more; he would work half the week and drink the remainder.

It was not to last. The advances in technology and the cotton mill owners' increasing use of steam-driven power looms in large machine shops in their factories brought an end to the prosperity of the handloom weavers and their families. A correspondent to the *Preston Guardian* on 24 December 1837 declared that, having read the pay ledger

"A good handloom weaver would make his thirty shillings [well over a thousand pounds today] a week or even more; he would work half the week and drink the remainder."

for twenty married Preston weavers, he found that their pay fluctuated from thirty eight shillings (£1500) in the first month to as low as eighteen shillings (£719) sixteen months later. Four thousand men signed a petition to Parliament for some assistance, stating that they were working sixteen to eighteen hours a day to make a bare living and that they were 'steeped to the lips in poverty'.

A meeting on Chadwick's Orchard (now the Market) was called on 31 May 1837 to agree a memorial (i.e. a memorandum) to the Mayor, asking him to use his influence to somehow relieve their distress. Little came of it. Donations came from out of town, but the situation was terminal. Some Preston handloom weavers left to work on farms, a reversal of the classic Industrial Revolution drift into towns for work. In 1840, handloom weavers from Wigan emigrated to Belgium to continue their trade.

The result of this depression among the handloom weavers who lived in the Sandhole is that increasing numbers left and their landlord found new tenants for their houses. A good impression of this change in population can be gained from the 1841 and 1851 Censuses. In 1841, when the pinch was definitely being felt, there were a hundred and twenty weavers living in Sandhole streets, including ten in Laurel Street, seven in Blelock Street, fifteen in Oak Street, twenty-two in William Street, sixteen in Rose Street, fifteen in Shepherd Street and fourteen in Leeming Street. By 1851 there were only twenty-four in the whole area and five of them were lodgers.

Once their houses were empty, the landlords could put them to different uses. The half-sunk cellars let in daylight and so bringing in families on all available levels was a good way of making money. These cellars were not the classic cellar dwellings found in other parts of Preston or in other towns, which had no access to natural light, and were therefore more acceptable to the authorities. Landlords could put tenants on all three floors. When asked by the magistrates in the 1870s why people continued to rent out this type of Sandhole property, Senior Inspector Oglethorpe declared

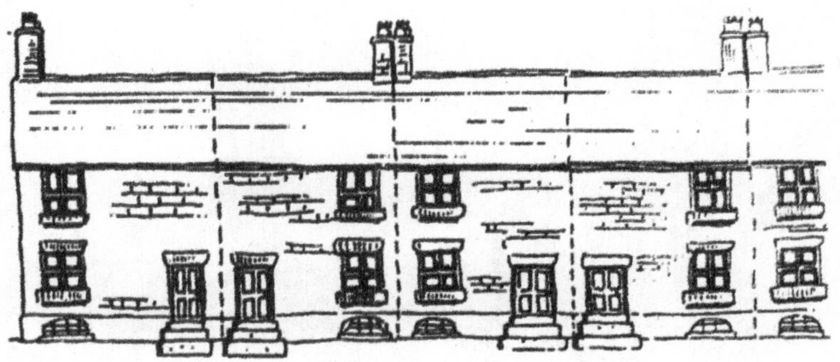

Handloom weavers' cottages with half sunk cellars.
From *Housing in Victorian Preston* by Nigel Morgan. Drawn by Angela Eccles

that the landlords were receiving four shillings a week (£159) for house only worth half a crown (£99). A Parliamentary Report in 1844 noted that 'Preston cellars were converted from weaving shops to residences as handloom weaving declined. While damp conditions were good for weaving, they were less appropriate for housing.'

Another use they were good for was as brothels and there were already a few in 1841.

If we could ask a Preston man or woman of the 1860s where the Sandhole was, more than likely the answer would be vague, not much more than 'behind the church'. The church in question is the Parish Church of St John the Divine (now Preston Minster) on Church Street. Because the boundaries of the area were notional and colloquial rather than definite, I have taken Queen Street in the south, Rose Street/William Street in the west, Church Street in the north and Water Street/Leeming Street in the east as the main extents. However, from time to time, other thoroughfares and their licensed premises will appear and receive mentions, such as Grimshaw Street, Turk's Head Court, Old Cock Yard and Library Street.

The public houses and beerhouses in the Sandhole, mainly in Shepherd Street, Water Street and Leeming Street, all had reasonable reputations to start with, but as the area

The old church of St John, demolished in 1853. The new church was built between 1853 and 1855.
Below: Preston Minster as it stands today

deteriorated, the police regarded the Rifleman, the Black Swan, Liverpool House, the Griffin Inn and Lodge Bank Tavern as bases for prostitutes, thieves and those who associated with them. Among these characters was a low type of man who was called a 'bully', who was either married to a prostitute or pretended to be, usually living on her earnings. Kellow Chesney quotes Henry Mayhew on the subject of bullies: 'They were often of a sporting turn, and ranged from the smart, hard faced loungers subsidised by women of the town, to louts who lived off the poorest street drabs.'

The police regarded the Rifleman, the Black Swan, Liverpool House, the Griffin Inn and Lodge Bank Tavern as bases for prostitutes, thieves and those who associated with them.

Mayhew's contributor and researcher, Bracebridge Hemyng thought of a bully as 'a brute ready to stick at nothing, who spent his day dozing and 'sucking a cutty' (a short tobacco pipe) and pottering round the corner to the pub or errands to the pawnshop.'

Although some Sandhole bullies proved elusive, most fitted into these categories.

As for the licensed premises themselves, they were not the only ones in the town with a similar clientele which were watched by the police. Others included the Shakespeare in the Strait Shambles, the Roast Beef in Friargate, the Highland Laddie in North Road, the Bear's Paw in Church Street and the Turk's Head in Turk's Head Court, among others. The 1830 Beer Act had promoted the growth of beerhouses, so much so, that in the 1860s there were over four hundred licensed premises in Preston. Changes came in the form of the 1872 Licensing Act which was intended as a social reform. It limited the number of hours that a beerhouse or public house could stay open. Before this they could be open for fifteen hours a day and some people sat there rather than spend time in their poor, damp dwellings. In fact, there are many stories of individuals falling asleep, usually drunk, during the day. On Sundays, the Act prevented licensees from opening until one o'clock and to close again from three

The Bear's Paw, Church Street, in recent years

o'clock until six o'clock. Incidentally this hit people in poor areas quite hard, as they, mostly women and children, would have to queue up with containers like jugs to take beer home, especially as some areas had unsatisfactory water supplies.

The municipal police force in Preston, if not in its infancy, was in its youth of operations. It was established in 1815 with seven officers in Turk's Head Court (known until about 1800 as Cockshutt's Backside). In 1850 there were only fifteen officers, three for day work and twelve for night duty, working, from 1832, at a new station in Avenham Street. The force expanded to forty-eight by 1856 and when the force left Avenham for its new station and police court in Lancaster Road in 1858, the number had more than doubled to ninety-eight. The nature of life in the Sandhole meant that it had to be under constant surveillance. Those in charge of the licensed premises and the disreputable parts of the population were often charged in the police and borough courts but were often dealt with lightly by the magistrates, which must have caused the police some frustration.

After being sworn in before the Mayor, each new constable was issued with a uniform which comprised of a blue frock coat, a cape, a stovepipe top hat, two pairs of trousers, a jacket and two pairs of blucher boots. The Watch Committee, which oversaw local law and order, frowned on police misbehaviour which was punished by warnings, fines, suspension and dismissal. The worst misdemeanour was drinking on duty, an offence which afflicted other town forces more than Preston's, the worst being that in Liverpool. Policing in this period was dangerous and difficult, so while it was reprehensible on many levels and not excusable it is not surprising that it happened. Despite this, there were those who prospered, like P.C. Kenny who started in 1863 and was an Inspector by 1870. P.C. Oglethorpe rose through the ranks to become Chief Inspector in 1872 after the sudden death of the sitting incumbent, James Dunn.

One regular presence in the town in general, and in the Sandhole in particular, was that of the military in the form of soldiers on short term leave from Fulwood Barracks, opened in 1848. The British Army maintained seventy battalions on home service and the same number abroad, moving regiments round every two years or so. In Britain, until the 1860s, soldiers were confined in crowded, noisy, barracks on a monotonous diet. In addition, the men were not allowed to marry. Only six wives per hundred men were tolerated by the military authorities and were put to official domestic duties and allowed only half rations. It is unsurprising, therefore, that soldiers in garrison towns sought warmth and comfort in licensed houses and connection with women of the town who were only too glad to take their money. A steady stream of soldiers eagerly joined people and visited places in the Sandhole for these purposes. Sometimes there was violence and minor riots broke out, occasionally resulting in serious consequences. However, the Corporation always wanted to stay on good terms with the Army, probably

Only six wives per hundred men were tolerated by the military authorities and were put to official domestic duties and allowed only half rations.

because of the money and trade it brought to the town. Often, the police would be caught in the middle and often saw military offenders treated leniently.

The position of women in Victorian society is more or less well known. Women of all classes were expected to be mothers and run the family household, though after marriage they owned nothing as all their possessions passed to their husbands. The Married Women's Property Acts of 1870 and 1882 changed all that. Women were expected to give birth to large numbers of children, while being in charge of domestic affairs, causing many to die of exhaustion, as my great, great grandmother, Ellen Garlington, did in 1884 aged fifty one.

> The Victorian woman was the angel in the house, the Griselda of her pompous day, the helpmeet who conceived children in submission and without desire, the eternal inferior. Her whole career lay in marriage, her security was founded in her husband's ability to provide for her, her ambition satisfied itself in helping him along his path through the world.[1]

Women were, in their youth, supposed to be untouched by men before their marriage. Any woman who went against this was thought to be tainted, and so was her family, a situation reflected in novels of the period.

There are any number of reasons why women became prostitutes, but some of them just made mistakes with men, with the result that some families shunned them and, in desperation, they turned to prostitution. Others were so badly paid that they needed to supplement their meagre income. In the clothing business, outwork allowed women to take on work sporadically and work at home. Much of it was backbreaking, tedious, exploitative and poorly paid. Susie Steinbach describes distressed needlewomen of the 1840s as 'icons of poverty'. Henry Mayhew interviewed a young woman who had been doing slop work, i.e. the manufacture of inexpensive clothing, for three years, who said, 'I struggled very hard to keep myself chaste, but I found that I couldn't get food and clothing for myself and mother …' Another claimed, 'I used to work at slop work … at the shirt work … working from five o'clock (am) until midnight … still it was impossible to live. I went to the street solely to get a living for myself and child …'

Laurence Stone states that

> At the bottom of the ladder of professionals were the common street whores who could be taken into a coach or a dark alley … others were lower class girls who had been seduced and abandoned and were therefore more or less unmarriageable.

Donald Thomas states that teenage prostitutes in Liverpool and Manchester interviewed by Edwin Chadwick's researchers in the 1840s showed themselves not to be victims of unfeeling families or poverty but were often runaways. 'Many had left to become thieves or prostitutes between the ages of twelve and fourteen, wanting drink and clothes.'

From the eighteenth century onwards the age of consent had been twelve. Judith Flanders states that in the nineteenth century, sexual intercourse with a girl under ten years of age was a felony, with a girl under twelve a misdemeanour. The age of consent was raised to thirteen in 1875 and to sixteen in 1885.

The age of consent was raised to thirteen in 1875 and to sixteen in 1885.

Flanders also quotes The Edinburgh surgeon, William Tait (1793–1864), as dividing prostitution into two groups. The first contained those with a 'licentious inclination; the second comprised of those who had 'poor social circumstances'. This latter group were badly affected by '… lack of skills, lack of education, abandonment by or death of parents, (while) others … having been seduced and abandoned.'

Bracebridge Hemyng states that 'some have been prostitutes from girlhood, their mothers having been prostitutes before them. Several have been in houses for a considerable number of years …' Recruitment was definitely a factor and it was not always done by family.

David Thomas asserts that most of the many brothels in Liverpool and Manchester were run by women. Judging by the Census returns for 1851, 1861, 1871, Preston House of Correction/Prison records and court records most of the brothels in the Sandhole were also organised by women, who lived independently of men, the direct opposites of the classic Victorian wife. A few individual women worked independently, sometimes 'associated' with a bully.

In addition, for most of the nineteenth century, women, especially uneducated women, were regarded as second-class citizens, domestically subjugated and viewed as substandard if they had made poor life choices as far as love or sex were concerned. For men or women who made life mistakes, or became ill, or became unemployed in the Victorian period, a swift fall to the bottom of society was a distinct possibility, often spiralling out of control because of a complete lack what we might call, in the twenty-first century, a safety net, unless we count the workhouse – and most Victorian people were determined not to go there.

Many aspects of life in most industrial towns and cities in the Victorian period would be an assault to the senses and sensitivities of twenty first century people. These days, the vast majority of people strive for almost perfect hygiene, having the means, like hot and cold running water and showers, to achieve it. Most Victorian people did not. The period 1840–1890 was a time of sanitary improvement, for example, of more effective ways of removing excrement with flush toilets and sewers, but in many areas the progress was slow. Most residential areas started the period with ashpits where the cold remnants of cold fires could be deposited for the use of covering excreta in earth closets until it could be collected at night by the soil men. One of the problems with these was what ended up in these pits: all types of rubbish, with the vermin it would attract, as well as ash. Added to this problem was the use of horses.

With the exception of canals in the early period and steam locomotives from the 1840s onwards, the main transport in urban and rural areas relied on horses. An average mature horse produces about thirty pounds (14kg) of manure a day and two gallons of urine (9 litres), which working horses deposited on the streets of Preston. Town scavengers and street sweepers fought daily battles against the resulting mess, which was particularly bad on rainy days. In 1877, there were four hundred and fifty businesses in the town which would have had at least one or two horses. Others who made and traded heavy goods would have had more. In addition, there were seventy firms of carriers who would have had fleets of horse-drawn vehicles. This means that, day to day, there may have been around two thousand horses on Preston's roads and streets, more on Wednesdays when around two hundred carriers' wagons would leave town on commercial business. Horse transport was also needed to convey goods to the market, which was held every day except Sunday, added to which there were smaller groups of stalls round the Corn Exchange and the Parish Church. Other animals were also in the town regularly: cattle until the cattle market in Brook Street was completed in 1867 and, once a week, a pig market was also held in Church Street 'under the church wall'.

Horse manure, and the hordes of flies it attracted, caused diseases such as diarrhoea and typhoid, especially in children. Another phenomenon which would attract flies was the corpses of dead horses. Horses, often worked to the limit by their owners, lasted only about three years and it was not uncommon for them to die in the street. Shifting the bodies was a problem and they were often left until they were soft enough to cut up to facilitate removal.

There were small slaughterhouses around the town where butchers killed their own meat. Two examples of the period were one in Ward's End (off Lancaster Road) and another in Rose Street, where a man also lived who skinned animals for a living. Until the early 1870s the Shambles (now Lancaster Road), demolished to make way for the Harris Museum and Art Gallery, and the Strait Shambles which ran into it from the market place, contained many butchers' shops where slaughtering took place. There was a sense of pride and competitiveness in this, as seen by this example:

> Our Shambles will this day present a fine show of fat beef, many fine cattle having been slaughtered this week. Mr George Shepherd has slain a fat ox weighing upwards of 1200 pounds and Mr John Turner and Mr Robert Frankland

> have also killed beasts of nearly the same weight. (*Preston Chronicle* 26 May 1842)

Three dozen butchers were regularly fined for slaughtering pigs, sheep and cattle and allowing the fat, blood, guts and body fluids to run down the steep pavements and into open gutters.

All this adds up to the fact that when a Victorian journalist or commentator writes that something stinks, it really did stink because they were used to fouler smells than we are accustomed to encountering a hundred and fifty years later. A good example of this was reported in the *Preston Herald* on 7 February 1871. Margaret Boylan, a lodging housekeeper of 57 Leeming Street (i.e. in the Sandhole), was charged with 'keeping swine in a filthy state'. Inspectors had found two pigs in the cellar and two more on the cellar steps. In their report they stated that '... the smell was very offensive and the rooms throughout the house were in a filthy condition'. Conditions are almost unimaginable to us in the present day, yet people, mostly poor, had to live in this sort of atmosphere and environment. It is little wonder that the prevailing medical theory of the time was that disease was spread by vapours or miasma. The author of the 1842 Report on Sanitary Conditions, Sir Edwin Chadwick (1800–90) believed this until his death, despite the work of Doctor John Snow and Louis Pasteur on the real cause of disease. One of the causes of this type of olfactory offensiveness was that people who had moved into towns in the classic drift from rural areas to look for work were unable, or unwilling, to leave some of their country ways of life behind.

During the nineteenth century, Preston had four main newspapers, which included the *Preston Chronicle* (1812–93) and the *Preston Herald* (1855–1918), (from here on referred to as the *Chronicle* and the *Herald*), the former being published weekly on Saturdays and the latter often published on Wednesdays and Saturdays. Reading them now, researchers find two newspapers of good quality, as were the other two, competing for a growing readership as the population of

Preston increased and as the standard of education improved from about 1850 onwards. When the 1870 Education Act was passed, bringing in compulsory education, the town did not have to build any extra schools unlike other towns because so many good ones had already been established. Preston never had a School Board.

The newspapers set out to be educational and informative, but with a political slant. The *Chronicle* was a Liberal publication while the *Herald* was Conservative. Both made a determined effort to cover items of international, national and local news in some detail, so reading them now, in this era of instant news, local history researchers have a rich, interesting source of information, not available in modern publications, while national and international issues are also covered in depth. The Preston of the mid- to late-nineteenth century had a growing population, many of whom lived in or near the town centre, yet the number of interesting stories of local interest is vaguely reminiscent of a village newspaper where the comings and goings of ordinary people were captured, almost in a parochial manner.

Seemingly insignificant events were reported to alert and be recorded for ordinary people. Examples abound, like parish celebrations, garden parties, meetings of friendly societies and small-time amusements. Most events were advertised, even those organised by Catholics, though Catholics were still looked on with suspicion as not entirely British or loyal. This feeling, fairly widespread at one time, has been forgotten, fortunately. The result of this assiduous local reporting is a vividly painted picture of life in Preston at the time and the characters who are described within it. Added to this are weekly sections which were set aside for readers' letters, some of which are tedious and wordy, while others are enlightening and erudite, mostly on local affairs. The editorials attempted to comment on the main news stories.

Advertisements, printed on the front pages, covered a wide range of announcements such as the sale of houses, notices of bankruptcies, declarations of legal affairs and the dates and details of forthcoming events. Some, however,

One of the diseases which afflicted Victorian society was syphilis and advertisements for cures appeared fairly regularly.

would cause some surprise today. Three of these are pertinent to this study. One of the diseases which afflicted Victorian society was syphilis and advertisements for cures appeared fairly regularly. For instance, the *Herald* of 12 September 1863 announced the work of 'Doctor Shaw and Co' who held daily consultations for 'Special Diseases of both sexes, including syphilis'. In the same paper the Dispensary published its medical report for 1865–6 on 27 October, showing that deaths from syphilis over the twelve months numbered sixty. The numbers were still similar in 1875 when the druggist, G. Hillidge of 140 Friargate, recommended in the *Herald* 'Hillidge's Alternative Medicine – for the cleansing and clearing the blood of all impurities, including syphilis'.

A second advertisement, featuring laudanum, ran for three years in the *Chronicle*, promoted by William E. Fell who declared himself to be a 'Dispensing and Manufacturing Chemist' and sold a number of what would now be considered dangerous drugs, including chloroform, from his premises at 15 Avenham Lane, a short walk from the Sandhole. The laudanum he sold was 'of extra strength and purity'. This drug, a dilute version of opium in liquid form, was popular with prostitutes who took it to relieve pain caused by the later stages of syphilis, in preference to alcohol.

A third preparation advertised in the *Chronicle* during 1865 and three times in 1869 was 'Kearsley's Original Widow Welch's Female Pills' which purported to 'create appetite, correct indigestion, remove giddiness and nervous headache … useful in windy disorders, shortness of breath and palpitation of the heart'. In addition, they were advertised as 'perfectly innocent'. This, however, was all a cover for their real purpose as abortifacient pills, which was subtly hinted at earlier in a long-winded delivery, just after recommendations by 'most gentlemen of the Medical Profession' as 'a safe and valuable medicine in effectually removing obstructions and relieving other inconveniences to which the female body is liable …'

An advertisement for Widow Welch's Female Pills

With the Sandhole being situated in the poorer part of town its inhabitants, who were not all involved in the sex trade, were affected by changes in the financial situation of the country. The economic conditions nationally, in the early to late Victorian period, went through a number of phases, some of which created hardship. Up to the end of the Napoleonic War in 1815, trade was good, and Britain was known as the Workshop of the World. After the war, until about 1840, trade became stagnant, caused by dislocation and the changes brought about by the Agricultural and Industrial Revolutions. The ten-year period after this was a time of prosperity brought about by new inventions and techniques, a streamlining of the factory system and improvements in transport. From this period until the early 1870s Britain regained its reputation as the Workshop of the World, as shipping lines extended across the globe and Britain was far better equipped industrially than any other nation. The standard of living rose, real wages rose by a fifth and all classes were more prosperous.

There were, however, local and national problems which would cause Preston people distress and, in some cases, ruin. This often took the form of strife in cotton manufacturing, where factory owners refused to pay a living wage. In 1808, a strike nearly involved military action when operatives struck for better pay. A month's strike in 1821 came to nothing after wages were cut by ten percent. A three month walk-out by six hundred and sixty spinners in 1842 over pay put a further 7,840 other operatives out of work. Further dissatisfaction over wage cuts caused strikes by cotton workers all over

Lancashire who were supported by Chartist sympathisers, and this resulted in riots in some towns. In Preston, a stone-throwing crowd at the bottom of Lune Street was fired on by a group of soldiers, causing four deaths.

Another ten percent wage reduction in 1848, intended to be a temporary measure to help factory owners over a financially tight spell, had not been restored by 1853 and the operatives came out on strike. The cotton masters warned the workforce that if they did not return by 13 October they would be locked out of the mills. The Great Preston Lock-Out lasted from October 1853 to May 1854 – thirty-eight weeks. The town was financially paralysed and trade was at an all-time low. Operatives in other towns in Lancashire, particularly Blackburn, raised money for the distressed workers who eventually accepted defeat and returned to work.

The Great Preston Lock-Out lasted from October 1853 to May 1854 – thirty-eight weeks.

A national slump which caused distress was the short but deep depression of 1857–8, caused by the United States not honouring its import costs because they had overspent on the drive to develop states in the west of that country. One example of the local people who suffered was the young Preston photographer, Robert Pateson (1827–1910), who was driven to the point of suicide, before being rescued by his cousin at the last second. Once he recovered, he went on to become a fine photographer and one of the town's most notable philanthropists.

The American Civil War caused the Lancashire Cotton Famine as, from 1861, the Union navy blockaded the Confederacy ports in the South from where the raw cotton was shipped. During this period to 1865, the Preston Poor Law Guardians came into conflict with the laid-off workers. At one point, the police station in Lancaster Road was attacked, but further trouble was averted when the Preston Relief Committee was set up and began its 'admirable work' as Hewitson describes it, in January 1862. It continued until

1865, distributing food and organising outdoor relief such as laying out Avenham and Miller Parks.

In the 1870s, two national downturns affected Preston people. The first, the Agricultural Depression, caused a rise in the price of food, especially cereals. The second began almost imperceptibly in 1874. Trade had boomed after the Franco Prussian War (1870–71). By that year, trade had worsened and thus began what has become known as the Great Depression. There were strikes by miners and metal workers against the reduction of wages. This spread to the cotton workers of Lancashire as the millowners attempted to impose a wage reduction of five percent extended to ten percent in April 1878. After a short strike and lock-out the Preston operatives grudgingly accepted the factory owners' terms. There was violence and factory burning in other towns, particularly Blackburn.

After a short strike and lock-out the Preston operatives grudgingly accepted the factory owners' terms.

On 16 May, Preston Borough magistrates called for calm and put the police and special constables on alert. They also put a troop of the 17th Lancers to patrol up and down Fishergate. The atmosphere built up to a climax on 19 May, but the storm blew over, though it unnerved many in business and commerce. The presence of the police and soldiers seems to have restored order. Distress caused to the people of Preston through financial hardship was long in abating. There was a charitable scheme set up for those temporarily out of work and by June two thirds of the workforce were back in the mills and, four weeks later the rest were back in work, on the owners' terms, having accepted the reduction. There had also been a decline in the value of money. The spending power of the pound (20 shillings) in 1830 had fallen to eighteen shillings by 1880.

Before moving on, it is worth reiterating that there were hardly any social or financial 'safety nets' for the poor who had fallen on hard times in Victorian Britain. One unfortunate event, an illness, either mental or physical, an accident or a simple mistake could send anyone and their family into a spiralling decline that many would never recover from, once they had fallen over the edge. For most, that edge was the workhouse. One particular, unfortunate event was the by-product of the system where the man was the sole earner of the family. Professor Emma Griffin states in an interview in June 2020.

> The simple issue was that men could die – particularly in this period when men's work was often dangerous and the death rate was high. It was a risk for any family that they might suddenly tumble to the bottom of the social pile because their breadwinner had died.[2]

The Report of the Poor Law Commission in 1834 neglected the causes of distress in towns in favour of saving money. Their recommendation was that outdoor work or 'relief' was to be stopped and in its place would be a 'workhouse test', rigorously applied. Those who received aid would have to enter a workhouse where conditions would be on a par with the most unattractive, lowest class existence in the outside world. Parishes were formed into Unions and its officials were to be known, ironically as it turned out, as the Guardians of the Poor. The Bill followed the Report and became law later that year. The workhouses, detested by the poor, were places where the young, the old, the respectable, the depraved, the deplored and the insane were all herded together, though the men and the women were segregated to prevent any more pauper children becoming burdens on the Union. Such was the official safety net that the poor had to consider or starve. It wasn't until 1929, nearly a hundred years later, that reforms were made to this system.

From 1840 gradually, then increasingly, outside agencies made attempts to change the situation in the Sandhole by daring to go in and try to make a difference. Both Anglican and Catholic clergy tried various ways to show Christian concern and charity, although, as can be imagined, some of their efforts were disdained by those in the area who were intent on carrying on the trade and business they felt was theirs to do. The Anglican parish of Saint Saviour and the Catholic parish of Saint Augustine, both situated on the Sandhole's doorstep, consistently provided the means to change attitudes and the atmosphere with institutions such as school, parish centres and activities to attract people from a desperate way of life. One Christian organisation moved away from the Sandhole altogether, namely the Baptists. Seven years after Doctor Shepherd's Library had been removed from Shepherd Street in 1851 because 'the locality was … daily becoming one of the least attractive parts of the town', they left their chapel in Leeming Street where they had been since 1783 to a more fashionable and salubrious spot on Fishergate. An improved and extended version of their chapel became St Saviour's church in 1859.

One organisation which came out less favourably in comparison with others was the town's Temperance Association, established in 1832 in response to the growing problem of alcohol consumption in the town and the increase in licensed premises as a result of the 1830 Beer Act. From the beginning there was always a difference of opinion in the group. One section wanted drinking alcohol in moderation, that is, total abstention from spirits but allowing beer: the other wanted total abstention from alcohol. This difference in policy was further defined when Joseph Livesey and his Teetotallers joined the crusade. He had taken the pledge in 1831, as had his followers, total abstinence being their abiding principle. For the next forty years or so, Livesey sent erudite, though long winded, letters to the newspapers, gave rousing speeches in Preston and other towns, and wrote pamphlets for the cause. As far as making inroads into the Sandhole or being a presence, apart from dropping leaflets into lodging houses at times, the temperance group seemed to just shout from the side lines.

One section of the Temperance Movement wanted drinking alcohol in moderation, that is, total abstention from spirits but allowing beer: the other wanted total abstention from alcohol.

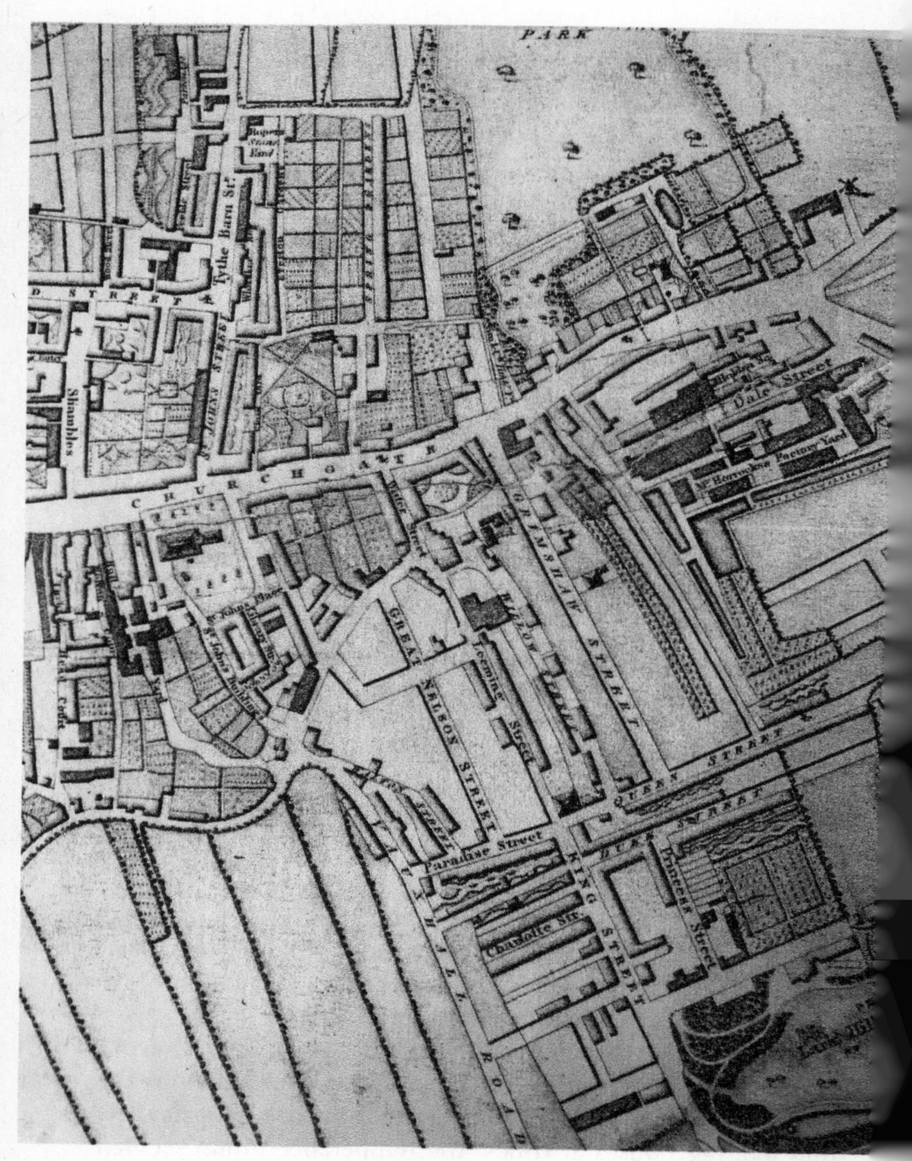

The Sandhole area in 1809 according to Shakeshaft's map.

2

INTO THE LOWEST DEEP

AT A POLICE COURT HEARING in the 1860s, a local councillor was heard to remark that when he was young there had only been one prostitute in Preston. Either his memory was deficient, or his knowledge was, because by the 1830s there were already a number of them working in the town. From the mid-1830s the *Chronicle* reported court cases involving prostitutes, naming them but not, at first, connecting them to a definite address. In addition, possibly to add a little more interest, the reporter often commented on the woman's appearance.

The charge was usually 'wandering around the town for the purpose of prostitution'. The punishments were often heavy, especially in comparison with that meted out to women committing similar offences thirty years later. In June 1836, Mary Ann Dawson and Mary Higgins received two months in the House of Correction (now the Prison). Ann Richardson, 'a debased character' and Betsy Hayley, 'a citizen of Dublin' were jailed for three months in two separate cases in 1837. Six months later, two curious cases took place where sentences were handed down on character alone. Mary Cowell, 'a woman of the town' was given fourteen days, while Ann Birren and Frances Halford were given seven days each for being 'disorderly characters'. This was probably a euphemism but, throughout the period, newspaper reports were surprisingly open and candid.

At certain times, the justices of the peace could be persuaded to show clemency. Mary Smith, charged with drunkenness and prostitution in March 1838, was described by the anonymous *Chronicle* reporter as 'a very interesting looking female' who appeared to possess 'superior attainments'. She begged for forgiveness and promised to leave town, for which she was discharged. The plan was successful in this case and was put into practice several times over the next forty years with varying success.

The following month, Hannah McTure, described by the *Chronicle* as 'about sixteen' and 'an interesting young woman' was charged with prostitution. The court heard that only a short time before she was 'in good work and was respectable and well behaved' before being 'led off by wicked companions'. She appeared in a 'distressing state of wretchedness and disease'. The Bench took pity on 'the poor creature (who) as a matter of charity was sent to the House of Correction for six weeks'. Whether she was given sympathetic treatment in the prison hospital is not recorded.

The standard punishment for soliciting in this period, at the very start of Victoria's reign, was a month in the House of Correction. Such was the punishment handed down to 'wretched creatures' Mary Kennedy and Rebecca Rian Clark, 'a well known bad character' Mary Ann Edwick and an unnamed 'decent looking woman'. Another, Bridget Barrett, was fined five shillings (£22 in 2018). Forty years later, offenders would only be fined twice as much for running a brothel. The policy at the time was to fine and punish single offenders rather than target a district or establishment. One interesting exception where a crime had not been committed was the imprisonment, for one week, of 'three girls of notorious character': Mary Ann Crabtree, Hannah Crabtree and Maria Armitage. The magistrates thought it best to 'take care' of the women during the 1839 Horse Fair which was held in Church Street, presumably to preserve some of the town's decorum and spare its blushes while safeguarding visitors from being accosted and robbed. As Emily Brand explains, 'Selling sex may not have been invented in the

Georgian era, but the permissive society which reigned in the "long eighteenth century" (1660–*c.*1840) allowed for new, exciting and public encounters.'

Without doubt, the after effects and attitudes of the Georgian era would persist in the Sandhole in its nocturnal way of life and business well into the 1860s.

Until the late 1840s the Borough magistrates continued to put most of the emphasis on arresting and charging individuals, whose addresses went unreported as a means of minimising the problem. The *Chronicle* continued to make comments about the female offenders such as, 'very low girl' Hannah McClare, and 'miserable and destitute creature' Sarah Gee, 'unfortunate woman of interesting character' Mary Tomlinson. Strangely, the last person named appeared in court in May 1840 and was described as 'a clean and interesting girl', but by the time she reappeared in July she was described as 'wretched'. For the first offence she received seven days in the House of Correction: for the second she received six weeks. The women were usually described as 'wretched', 'miserable' or 'deplorable' along with the usual Victorian euphemisms of 'unfortunate' or 'abandoned'. The usual punishment for prostitution being a month and two months for a further offence, in April 1840 Hannah Rigg, described as 'a young creature' in an 'advanced state of pregnancy', was sentenced to two months. She gave birth to a girl the following day in the House of Correction.

In March 1838, the *Chronicle* reported that in the previous nine months a hundred and fifty licences for beershops or beerhouses had been taken out, bringing the number in Preston to two hundred and thirty. In England and Wales at this time there were 27,554 beerhouses, many of them brewing their own ales, all because of the Beer House Act of 1830. This allowed any householder to open his or her house to sell beer on payment of two guineas (£250). They would be free from the jurisdiction of the magistrates, but they could only sell beer or cider. They were

In England and Wales at this time there were 27,554 beerhouses, many of them brewing their own ales

allowed to open from four o'clock in the morning until ten o'clock at night, although evidence shows that the beerhouses in the Sandhole adjusted their hours to allow late night closing. The Temperance Movement supported the Act before and just after it became law because beer was regarded as a healthy option to gin whose effects were found to be ruinous to people's health and family life. It very soon changed its collective mind. Beer was also cheaper. In 1830 a pint of beer cost about fourpence a pint (£1.50), whereas the equivalent value of gin was tenpence a pint (£3.69).

Writing in 1903, the social reformers Beatrice and Sydney Webb cite an early example of a situation that would became widespread after the 1830 Act and which should have acted as warning. They quote the *Leeds Intelligencer* of 25 April 1786 reporting that

> … nightly depredations in the town and neighbourhood (are due to) the immense multitude of the lower sort of alehouses within this borough … these little pothouses are the rendezvous of nocturnal villains where they plan their depredations and where, not infrequently, they divide their spoil.

The warning was there but no-one, it seems, took any notice. After the 1830 Act was passed, petitions soon came in from justices of the peace and clergymen. The Webbs went further, describing the situation as 'the tippling, late hours and disorder, the indiscriminate intercourse of young and old and both sexes, the music and dancing, the gambling, the receiving of stolen goods or the proceeds of poaching, the filling of prisons and the raising of the poor rate' and in that description covered just about every activity in the Sandhole over the following fifty years and just about every complaint made about it. James Harrison, the Honorary Surgeon at the Dispensary, stated in 1835 that

> the practice both of dram and beer drinking has materially increased of late years, since the passing of the beer bill. I attribute the increased consumption of spirits and beer, and the great increase of prostitution, which has resulted from these causes in this town to the beer bill and not to any influence of the Irish.[1]

John Burnett finds that the beerhouse was socially and sexually segregated as it was the working man's 'home from home' but not his wife's 'if she valued her respectability'. Respectable women would call in for a drink and stay for about quarter of an hour. In contrast, the women of the Sandhole cared little for respectability. Burnett asserts that beer consumption was affected by industrial depressions. Like Rev. John Clay wrote in 1842, Burnett states that crime caused by drink rises when times are good. The rapid rise of beer drinking in the 1860s and 1870s was a result of the improvement in workers' wages and there was 'little in the line of amusement or leisure but drinking.' He quotes T. R. Gurvish and R. G. Wilson's back projections (in The British Brewing Industry 1830–1880) that in 1844 male drinkers drank seventy-two gallons of beer a year. In the peak year of 1879 it rose to a hundred and three gallons, that is, sixteen pints a week, though some men would have cleared that in a couple of days.

In 1879 the average male drinker consumed 103 gallons of beer a year

In November 1839, licensees in Church Street and Water Street, i.e. the Bear's Paw, the Griffin Inn, the Rifleman Inn and the Black Swan were charged with harbouring prostitutes in their house which was held to be against the tenor of their licences. The Borough Solicitor, Mr Bannister complained that the situation was 'becoming all too common in the town'. The magistrate, who was the Mayor, said he would deal with such cases with 'all possible severity'. He then, surprisingly, proceeded to dismiss the charges, reprimand the defendants and simply make them pay the court costs. This roughly marks the time when the Corporation must have decided to contain prostitution and the resorts of thieves to the Sandhole and similar places to prevent immorality and lawlessness from spreading to other, more respectable areas of the town.

Once Parliament realised what a monster had been unleashed there was an attempt to repeal the Act. Lord Brougham proposed the Bill, stating that beerhouses had a negative effect on the morals of the people. He quoted the towns of Huddersfield and Halifax where 'beershops were the scenes of daily and nightly gambling, frequented promiscuously by girls for prostitution and boys for gambling and profligacy'. He also asserted that in Leeds, in an eighteen-month period, that drunkenness rose by over two hundred percent. He took the bold step of proposing a total abolition of beershops altogether. This met strong opposition from the Marquis of Westminster who said that if the Bill progressed unchanged it would ruin forty five thousand people and a further two hundred thousand others who depended on them.

A second reading was proposed by John Pakington M.P. (1799–1880) who declared that the Act was right 'in the sight of all ... was undermining the morals of all'. He was concerned that beerhouses were becoming a haven for poachers, drunkards, prostitutes and thieves. The new Bill proposed a property qualification to promote respectability. In places of over five thousand inhabitants the licence would cost fifteen pounds (£1500) and in places of over two thousand, eleven pounds (£1100). The whole proceeding was stopped by the Speaker because it had not been discussed in committee. When it finally passed into law, it emerged in a much-changed form. The main thrust of it was that the licensee should live on the premises so they could be more accountable. And so, for the next twenty-five years, the status quo continued and life in the Sandhole carried on. Many years later, David Lloyd George remarked, 'Every government that has ever touched alcohol has burnt its fingers in its lurid flames.'

The first recorded instance of a person being charged with running a 'disorderly' house in the Sandhole was reported by the *Chronicle* on 15 July 1837. Ellen Barnes was ordered by the magistrates to leave her house in Laurel Street because it was found to be a place of ill repute and that she had allowed 'disorderly conduct and drunkenness to be committed' there. The court heard of the 'outrageously disgraceful character of the brothel'. No house number was recorded. Barnes must have left town because no further record of her is to be found.

Four years later, the Census showed, for the meantime at least, that Laurel Street was occupied by families. Around the corner, however, two unnumbered houses show the tell-tale signs of being brothels. At one, three twenty-year-old women, Betsy Edmondson, Betsy Edwards and Sarah Woods, all professing to be female servants, were living together. While this could be innocent and above board, a house full of young women all professing to be 'female servants' was used as a cover story to tell the Census enumerator. A few doors away lived three other unrelated women, Grace Simpson (35), Nancy Duncroft (25) and Jane Penerith (30). The only one with an occupation was Simpson who professed to be a weaver, another cover-all cotton occupation for the Census, bearing in mind the growing reputation of the Sandhole. Other 'occupations' would be used in future Censuses. There were, of course, in more reputable parts of Preston, houses were women boarded and houses where men boarded, often because families were so large that the family home was overcrowded.

As the 1840s progressed, serious concern was being expressed about the sanitary condition of the streets in and around the Sandhole. 'A Report on The Sanitory (*sic*) Conditions Of Preston' (1843), written by the widely respected Reverend John Clay (1796–1858), the Chaplain of the House of Correction revealed some dreadful conditions. He states that 'There is, in the lowest deep, a lower deep, and in the districts of the worst kind there are certain street and courts, the worst of the district.'

The thrust of this section of the Report centres around Willow Street and Queen Street, both situated at the southern end of the Sandhole. Following the then held view that smell or miasma was the cause of illness, Clay come to the right conclusion for the wrong reason, knowing nothing of germs. He reports on a district 'where sickness and death prevail'.

> … defective ventilation, and cleaning and draining of streets … the same evils with regard to dwellings – the overcrowding of rooms and of beds – the filthiness of apartments, persons, clothing and bedding – a prevalence of damp, yet want of water – absence of proper and decent accommodation as to privies (earth closets at this time) – the keeping of pigs in, or too near to, dwellings and, pervading all, sickening smells.

One court in Back Willow Street was closed at both ends by privies. The approach to Back Queen Street was through several lobbies or ginnels and facing the end of each was a row of privies, the door of each being only six feet from the houses' front doors. Clay found that

> … the space between one privy and another is filled up with all the imaginable and unimaginable filth, so that each street consists of a passage little more than six feet wide, with dwelling houses on one side and a continuous range of necessaries, pigsties, middens and heaps of ashes etc on the other with a filthy, sluggish surface drain running along one side. The doors opening onto this street are the back doors of the Queen Street houses, but twelve houses have their only outlets, doors and windows upon this disgusting and pestiferous passage.

Only eighteen months earlier, thirty-six people died in Queen Street, Back Queen Street and Queen Street Court. This amounted to one death per fourteen people or seven and a half percent of all the inhabitants.

In 1841/2, thirty-six people died in Queen Street, Back Queen Street and Queen Street Court. This amounted to one death per fourteen people of all inhabitants

Just over a year later, the editorial in the *Chronicle* of 11 January 1845 stated opinions on Preston's health and sanitary conditions and what was to be done about them. Over a period of forty years, editorials of this type were unusual. The greater majority of them usually commented and made judgements on national and international issues and events. What makes this editorial unusual is that it comments on a phenomenon which has real resonance today but was exceedingly unusual in the Victorian period.

In this, the *Chronicle*'s editor pressed for legislation on drainage, lighting, supplying water to, and generally provided for, the health and recreation of towns. He declares that the public health had been a concern for many years as it affected 'people of all classes, their safety and welfare, a topic which affects the *mental health* (my italics) of the population as well as physical health and well being'. This comment is extremely surprising. While many people thought that disease was spread by miasma or poisoned atmosphere, the writer of this article has considered a phenomenon which would only be considered for the first time in the 1860s by the American scientist, William Sweetser (1797–1875), and then in the early twentieth century by others. Sweetser called mental health 'mental hygiene'.

The editor continues by conceding that some good had been done by Local Acts, but asserts that after a great deal of talk in the council chamber and numerous meetings finds that efforts to remedy the situation with 'inestimable gains in improving health, ameliorating manners and habits, and the prolongation of human life … have been desultory and all could have been done if money had been released for the purpose'. He says that some good had been done but it had been limited to 'specially favoured spots'. Needless to say, the Sandhole was not one of these. In fact, shortly after this time, the authorities seemed to embark on a policy of containment and gradual neglect. He continues:

> There are many who live in cellars, some of them damp and dark, yet still unsupplied with water, which serve as living and sleeping rooms for the whole family, in which cooking, washing and all the necessary domestic operation of the occupiers are, perforce, performed. There are still five thousand houses, some containing more than one family, which have no water supply. This demands remedy.

On the subject of this type of deprived and impoverished living, Beatrice Webb, the social reformer who lived in

In 1846, at 36 deaths per thousand of the population, Preston's death rate was the second worst in England

disguise among the poor in London in the 1880s, recorded in her autobiography in 1926, 'To put it bluntly, sexual promiscuity, and even sexual perversion, are almost unavoidable among men and women of average character and intelligence crowded into the one-room tenements of slum areas ...'

Returning to the editorial, the writer goes on to discuss the results of the poor approach to public health in Preston. The town's death rate was the worst in England except for Liverpool, being 28 deaths per thousand of the population in 1845 (rising to 36 in 1846) with the health of the poorest being the worst. In 1846, a hundred and six people died of cholera and diarrhoea and ten from typhus.

> Hence arise other concomitant evils; a high poor rate, a want of cleanliness and lax morals. An improved sanitary system ... would reduce the amount and duration of sickness about a third, and due care and precaution would alone be the means of cutting nearly five hundred deaths [1,635 in 1845, 2,189 in 1846] which now come from remedial causes. The money saving therefrom would supply a motive for the work required. In relief for the poor, it has been calculated that £500 a year [£48,000] would be spared through diminution of disease, of widowhood and orphanage, while in wages the cost of medical attendance, the annual sum saved would be a little less than £20,000 a year [£1,900,000].

The editor's reasoning is that if the health argument is not persuasive enough then the financial saving argument might push the Corporation into some effective action.

In the writer's urgent opinion, the money saved should be used for the 'health, convenience, comfort and safety' of all and the 'enterprise' being 'controlled by the public themselves at their own expense', that is, using public money rather than private finance. The editorial ends with '... the health and lives of the community are constantly jeopardised, needlessly, by the state of things which has been too long suffered to exist.' Although this unusual, groundbreaking editorial applies to the whole town, most people still lived in or near the town centre, many of them in St John's Ward in which the Sandhole stood, where sanitary conditions were dire up to the 1850s. In the 1840s the only streets in that area which had proper sewers were Leeming Street (115 yards) and Shepherd Street (155 yards). The latter was lit by eight gas lamps but Leeming Street had only three. Queen Street had four; Water Street had two; Blelock Street, Laurel Street and Rose Street had one each, while Grimshaw Street and Greaves Street remained unlit.

Edwin Chadwick, mentioned earlier, pressed Parliament to pass a Public Health Act which would have national relevance. He published his report in 1842, with later additions, to which Rev. John Clay contributed. The real reason behind Chadwick's interest in health was not health based at all but financial. If the health of the poor were to be improved, he believed, there would be less expenditure on illness and poverty. Fewer people would apply for relief, less would have to be spent on families where the husband had died and less would have to be spent on the sick.

The Act was eventually passed in 1848. It promoted improved drainage and the provision of sewers; the removal of all refuse from houses, roads and streets; the provision of clean drinking water and the appointment of a medical officer for every town. The government had been finally forced to act after a terrible outbreak of cholera, but this Act had no compulsion about it as it had limited powers and no money. Preston, however, had to set up its own Board of Health because of the high death rate. The paving and sewering of the streets began in 1852 and was completed in 1857.

The Act set up a national committee called the Central Board of Health which reported on the sanitary conditions in Preston a year later in 1849. It found that

> The first and fiercest attacks of fever arise in blind courts, the miserable cellars and overcrowded cottages and back streets of the Town. In those places where life and health are most precarious … sound and systematic regulations, vigorously enforced and perseveringly maintained, would reverse the causes of so lamentable waste of life and

> happiness. It is time that those regulations were brought into permanent operation. (*Chronicle* 2 June 1849)

Three months later the Preston Guardians reluctantly appointed assistants to the five overworked doctors employed by the Preston Union to work in areas most affected by cholera. The same reluctance would be evident in the next decade when the town's Board of Health would drag its feet in appointing assistants to help the overwhelmed Medical Officer of Health, Doctor Broughton.

One of the regulations of the 1848 Act concerned cellar dwellings.

> No cellars are to be let separately (except as warehouses or storerooms) or as dwellings, unless seven feet in height from floor to ceiling – one third of that is to be above the level of the street adjoining the same … nor unless the same be effectively drained, ventilated and provided with a fireplace and a chimney …

All of which neatly excluded the houses formerly occupied by the handloom weavers in Blelock Street, Rose Street, Laurel Street, Shepherd Street and Leeming Street.

In the later 1840s the magistrates, the Watch Committee and, therefore, the police, shifted their angle of attack from targeting women who 'wandered through the town for the purpose of prostitution' to the places where thieves and prostitutes congregated – the beerhouses and public houses. This may have been influenced by Rev. John Clay's report on the House of Correction in 1847. During the previous year he had become

> '… acquainted with practices, resorted to in some beerhouses, which must be mentioned, in order to show what demoralising agencies are added to those already existing in them, viz the keeping of prostitutes. From three entirely different sources, and at different times, I received statements fully confirming each other, which leave no doubt of the extent to which this profligate system is carried on. Sixteen houses in one town, harbouring, or rather maintaining, fifty prostitutes have been named to me. But this is not the full amount of the evil. Women, married women, occupied to

> all appearances with their own proper avocations at home, hold themselves at the call of the beerhouse, for the immoral purposes to which I have referred.

The first detail to note here is that Clay knows that married women are working as prostitutes, which is almost undetectable in the Censuses unless the woman has been convicted of the crime. Some of these women may not have been married at all, but were attached in some way to a live-in bully, that is, a kind of pimp or a man who pretended to be married to a prostitute. Other women were married but often lived in unhappy situations and with violent consequences.

Some of these women may not have been married at all, but were attached in some way to a live-in bully, that is, a kind of pimp or a man who pretended to be married to a prostitute

Among the sixteen houses were the seven in the Sandhole, namely the Rifleman Inn, the Griffin Inn and the Black Swan in Water Street, Liverpool House in Shepherd Street and the Lodge Bank Tavern and Foundry Arms in Leeming Street. While Liverpool House always had a bad reputation, the Rifleman Inn and the Black Swan began the 1840s in a fairly respectable manner. The former, at Whit Monday in 1840 and 1841, was the venue for an end of day celebration for the Most Ancient and Honourable Order of Free Gardeners, their associates and families. Whit Monday every year was a day of processions round the town after services at St Paul's C.E. church and St Wilfrid's for Catholics. The *Chronicle* calls it a day of 'gaiety, bustle, and merrymaking. A holiday for factory folk from their toil.' The Black Swan was a venue well known for its food. Every Christmas a Mr Penny, a coachbuilder, used to throw parties there for his employees. The *Chronicle*'s comment on the 1852 event was 'an excellent meal was provided by Mrs Hind and the evening was spent in an agreeable manner.' A month earlier, Mrs Hind had also provided an 'excellent dinner' for some employees of Swainson, Birley and Co. and their overlooker. It is a good indication of the deterioration of the area that this sort of celebration ceased at both of these establishments after this time.

In the 1840s, the refocusing of police activity brought more varied Sandhole crime to the attention of the *Chronicle*, the types of which were replicated in different degrees in the following three decades. Sarah Gee was sentenced to three months in the House of Correction in December 1841. Described by the *Chronicle* as 'an incorrigible, disorderly pauper, a deplorable looking creature', she was charged with three offences. Firstly, she had 'absconded' from the workhouse which once stood near the corner of Burrow Road and Deepdale Road. This would normally be dealt with by the workhouse staff, under the direction of the Guardians. Secondly, she had taken workhouse clothing with her, presumably to pawn. Clothes, bedding, boots and shoes were prized items in the Victorian period and there was always a ready market for them. In Stave Four of *A Christmas Carol*, Charles Dickens describes how the dead Scrooge's staff steal bed linen, curtains and even the shirt his corpse is lying in and take them to a low pawnbroker to raise cash. As there were seven pawnbrokers close to the Sandhole, this is what Gee intended. Thirdly, and most importantly, she had taken some young girls with her from the workhouse with the intention training them to be prostitutes. This would not be an isolated example.

Francis Nelson, who had assaulted Margaret Bond, a brothel keeper in Blelock Street, had his case dismissed with Bond being warned 'as to the type of character of persons she admitted to her house'! George Pomfret and Henry Coar were fined five pounds each (£493 in 2018) for assaulting the police. Police officers were called to The Garden Gate beerhouse in Queen Street to remove Pomfret who was drunk and disorderly and, as P.C.s Atherton and Stirzaker took him away, Coar rushed out of the Weavers' Arms beerhouse and attacked them. At the time of the court case, Stirzaker could hardly walk and Atherton was too ill to attend. This is not surprising as Doctor Booth had bled him five times and applied leeches to him!

In Queen Street at this time there was a thriving trade in the production of illegal whisky, but after police raids in March and June 1851, stills were found at the houses of Margaret Cross and Mrs Bradshaw. Both found guilty, they were fined the enormous sum of thirty pounds (£3,220) after which illegal distilling seems to have ceased. At this southern end of the Sandhole there was plenty of lively, if not desirable, activity about this time. In July 1852, Catherine Sergeant was 'drunk and riotously behaved' and entertained a large crowd who were 'hissing and hooting at her'. At this, her seventh court appearance of the year, she was imprisoned for a month.

Around the corner in King Street, at the Weavers' Arms, the police were summoned to an incident caused by William Nixon, described by the *Chronicle* as a 'Hibernian'. He had attacked a number of people with a knife and cut them round the head. He hit Samuel Astley, whom he did not know, with a poker, and when P.C. Steanson (see later chapter) arrived, after forcing his way in, he found Nixon about to run away but he detained him. The police constable also found several people bleeding. Esther McCann, who was not present, spoke up for Nixon at trial and was given one month of imprisonment for perjury. Nixon was committed for trial at Quarter Sessions in Lancaster.

A year after the 1848 Public Health Act became law, a report was sent to the General Board of Health on the state of the town. Some streets in and near the Sandhole were mentioned specifically. Turk's Head Yard, a short walk distant, was described as paved but without drains. It had several filthy corners and what was said to be the largest cesspit in the town. Nearby was a large slaughterhouse in a dirty condition and producing 'a most offensive smell'. Also here was Mahommed's lodging house which was over-crowded and dirty.

In nearby Bolton's Court, there was a range of piggeries and open dung heaps with a large trough for holding manure. At the end, close to the National School which had 700–800 pupils, there were eight public slaughterhouses 'in a very discreditable state, stocked with pigs and producing a very bad smell.' Behind the Parish Church, between Stoneygate and Library Street ran 'a filthy and narrow passage with an open gutter between two rows of cesspools clogged with accumulations of night soil' [excreta]. The report states that there had been a plan to build two rows of cottages there with an alley between them. 'Such an alley in Preston,' asserted the inspector, 'is sure to be a receptacle for filth.'

On the western side of the Sandhole, round the corner from Library Street, there stood in Rose Street a 'dirty and offensive slaughterhouse ... much complained of by the neighbours'. It was 'badly pitched [paved], ill supplied with water' and was 'much complained of by the neighbours.'

At the centre of the Sandhole, Laurel Street, 'which stands in a quarter of bad repute,' had cellar dwellings and unpaved road. Close by, William Street was 'unsewered, dirty and the seat of fever.' The road was unmade and all its cellars were occupied, 'though they are deep, damp and blocked up behind.' People paid only sixpence (£2.50) a week rent to live in them.

Queen Street was reported to be well supplied with privies, 'though with cesspools under occupied rooms.' The inspector found neither water supply nor drainage and he stated that 'as in most courts and in side streets the filth is collected and heaped by the wayside'.

Not only did the Sandhole and the streets surrounding it have a bad reputation, by 1850, it was populated by the poor, the desperate and the criminal

Slightly further to the south and nearer to St Augustine's Catholic Church stood Great Avenham Street which was paved and the houses were reported as well built 'though there is no drain and is therefore very unhealthy.' The back premises were crowded and 'the cesspools are in a bad state. An adjacent street, Pleasant Street, had inferior housing and the landlord 'refuses to provide a water supply, preferring the householder to use a pump at the end of the street which is situated in a mature manure depot and ... gives out tainted water.'

Not only did the Sandhole and the streets surrounding it have a bad reputation, by 1850, it was populated by the poor, the desperate and the criminal, some of which lived the kind of life they wanted to lead while others were, for different reasons, trapped in this way of living.

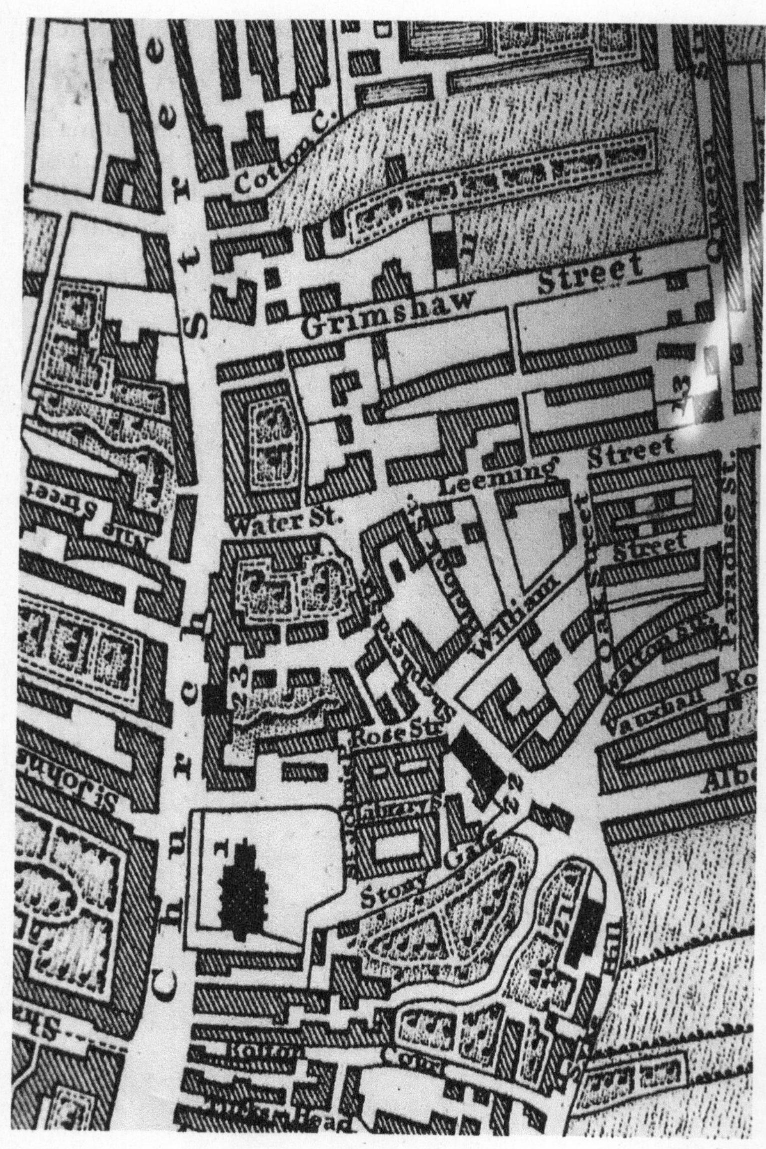

The Sandhole according to Baines's map of 1824

3

'Wretchedness and Crime'

The 1850s and 1860s were a time of development. On the one hand, the Sandhole grew into a more established red light district: on the other was the growth of agencies and forces, both spiritual and secular, which were determined to undermine and counteract it.

The 1851 Census shows the development of the area quite plainly. The head of the household at 4 Greaves Street was 38-year-old Martha Taylor who had been imprisoned for 'a murderous assault on Joseph Dudson at a brothel in Blelock Street in 1841 with Thomas Etherington. Ten years later she is shown as running a brothel with three young women, none of them related, and a man, J. C. Wearden, who stopped over on the night of Sunday 30 March. Also in the house was a known prostitute, Elizabeth Fazackerley (20) who was arrested with another prostitute, Mary Ann Hodgson (19) for their part in a theft at Liverpool House during an orgy. Hodgson lived next door in Greaves Street, which gives the impression that immoral activities were participated in not exclusively to the place where they resided. It also shows that women were prepared to work together when the opportunity arose.

At 4 Blelock Street, the Leeming family who lived in the main house had the classic nuclear structure of two parents, both in their thirties, and five children. In the cellar lived the Greenwoods, both in their twenties and their four children aged one to seven. The mother, Joan, was a well-known prostitute who would be convicted of theft, that stock-in-trade of most Victorian street women, in February and May 1854. This was during the Lock-Out when her husband, John, was unable to work.

The threat of violence was never far away, despite the best efforts of the police. The Watch Committee, usually chaired by the Mayor, organised the town into beats or patrols. Beat Number 2 was undertaken by two or three police officers who patrolled Grimshaw Street, Queen Street and all the streets in the Sandhole, completing a tour of the area within an hour. This showed how important this part of time was because the other patrols had only to be completed every 75 or 90 minutes. One night, in September 1851, Francis Nelson, 'a youth well known to the police', assaulted P.C. Stirzaker while he was trying to 'quell a riot ... in which Nelson was involved ...' when Nelson violently attacked him. He was later apprehended in a public house three months later in January 1852 and sent for trial. He must have gone to earth for some time because he usually lived at 1 Willow Street with his mother and younger brother.

Around the corner lived another violent man, Richard Miller, at 2 Laurel Street. Having been convicted of assault in a brothel in 1842, he was charged along with Abraham Seward of violence towards some soldiers at the house of a Mr Bamford. A piquet of Lancers had been sent to search for a member of their regiment who was missing. Bamford said that the soldiers caused trouble while searching his premises and, while this was happening, Miller knocked one of the Lancers over with a pair of fire tongs and split his head open. The trouble spilled over into the street where large crowd appeared, armed with weapons and missiles. Seward was one of them. The soldiers drew their swords just as the police arrived to put an end to the uproar, at which point Miller threw down the tongs. Seward ran off, but they were both apprehended. The court did not hand down custodial sentences in this instance, but ordered Miller and Seward to compensate the soldier, which they did on 23 January and the matter was, surprisingly, dropped. At the time, Miller was

34 and living with his 31-year-old wife and six children aged twelve years to twelve months. Also living in the house, as lodgers, were a couple, Joseph and Caroline Jackson, and two unmarried women. These two, both unrelated and from out of town, declared their professions to the enumerator as 'silk weaver' and 'dressmaker' which were classic covers used in the Censuses by prostitutes.

The two unmarried women declared their professions as 'silk weaver' and 'dressmaker' which were classic covers used in the Censuses by prostitutes.

Three months later, the *Chronicle* recorded the first and only reference to a gang in connection to the Sandhole, James Alston (25), John Gregson (30) and John Newsham (24) were arrested and charged with fighting on 13 March in the Sandhole, assaulting a police officer and attacking a soldier. Alston, who was fined five shillings (£27) was a boot and shoemaker who lived with his twenty-one-year-old wife and two-year-old twins. The other two were reported as belonging to 'a gang of scoundrels which infests the Sandhole'. They were sent for trial at the Quarter Sessions at Lancaster. Gregson lived with his older parents and sisters at 21 William Street. Newsham lived with his wife, Alice (27), and eighteen-month-old daughter, Ada, at 26 Paradise Street. It is surprising that organised gangs, specialising in 'protection' and blackmail did not play a large part in the Sandhole's history. Instead, the theft, the violence and other criminal activities showed little more than very basic planning and were often the spontaneous actions of individuals or, occasionally, small groups.

An example of this occurred a few months later in September when William and Jane Shenty (possibly prostitute and bully), 'both denizens of the Sandhole', were charged by Eliza Woods, 'an unfortunate woman', with assault, possibly because of encroachment of territory or taking customers. On the night of Thursday 9 September 1852, the Shentys beat Woods 'in a ferocious manner.' She appears to have fought back because all three turned up at court with 'black eyes, scars, scratches etc in profusion'. The male Shenty had kicked Woods in the face, but he complained that Woods had grabbed him 'by the forelock and split his head with a poker'. They were all ordered to find surety or bail in lieu of imprisonment, which is highly unlikely. There is no further mention of these individuals in Preston after this date, which give an indication of the nomadic nature of this type of character. An indication of the growing violence in the Sandhole at this time may be seen from a statement by Mrs Brown of the Foundry Arms in Leeming Street. When she and her husband were charged with keeping a disorderly house, she said they had tried their best, 'but if (we) did not allow people to come in and do as they please (we) would get our brains knocked out.'

Another thread which runs through the story of the Sandhole is that of theft in all its forms, some examples being humorous and others just plain stupid. It was also the stock-in-trade of many prostitutes who saw it as a means of making money with little or no sexual contact, which may have been avoided by the use of tricks and ruses. Stephen Knight, in his research on the Whitechapel Murders, *The Final Solution*, states that he interviewed a London prostitute who claimed that she had only made a full sexual connection twice in twenty years.

A London prostitute claimed that she had only made a full sexual connection twice in twenty years

Mary Ann Edwards, described as a 'coloured' woman by the *Chronicle*, picked a man's pocket in December 1851 in an unnamed Sandhole beerhouse, by seizing him by the coat and taking his purse containing £5 (£533) in silver. Some money was recovered but she was also suspected of other robberies in the area. Edwards, aged 20, lived as a lodger at 15 Shepherd Street, the home of Mrs Ann Swanly, a widow of 37 and her six children aged 19 to three months. Also lodging there were Mary Ann Kendle 44, Mary Ann Henderson 26 and Margaret Bell 27, all unmarried and all professing to have cotton-based professions. In the cellar lived Elizabeth Marsden, her two young sons and another lodger called Rose Hodgkinson 25, who said she was a handloom weaver. Twenty months later, Edwards was charged with stealing a pocket watch from Thomas Ward while he was walking along Shepherd Street. She and two other unnamed women accosted him and asked him to treat them, so he bought them all a gin in the White Lion in Syke Hill, a short walk from the Sandhole. Afterwards they followed him, and Edwards locked him in an embrace while the others ran off with the watch. Ward reported the theft to P.C. Whittaker who arrested Edwards. At the police court she was committed for trial at the Sessions in Lancaster.

The 1851 Census shows two brothels next door to each other, namely at number 2 and 4 Greaves Street, the former run by Lucy Mulholland aged 23 and the latter by Martha Taylor (see above). Both houses are shown as full of young women, the oldest being twenty-four. Mary Ann Hodgson and Elizabeth Fazackerley (see above) lived at numbers 2 and 4 respectively. These were the ones who went to Liverpool House in March 1853 with the intention to steal while people were 'revelling in an orgy'. Working together, which was fairly unusual, Hodgson and Fazackerley stole two sovereigns (£198) from a man who was availing himself of the pleasures of the evening. The theft was reported, and the women were apprehended by P.C. Walmsley, but no money was found in their possession. The unnamed man did not pursue it, probably because he was too embarrassed.

The 1851 Census indicated at the corner of Queen Street and Leeming Street the site where St Saviour's Church would soon be established. It is simply marked by the phrase 'Baptist Chapel'. About two hundred yards away in St Austin's Place, stood the Catholic church of St Augustine of Canterbury in whose parish the Sandhole was firmly situated. Fifteen years earlier, in 1836, the need had been recognised for a new Catholic parish to be established for the developing area of Frenchwood and the east side of Avenham. The only Catholic priests in Preston were members of the Society of Jesus

(Jesuits) who ran three parishes already, namely St Mary's in Friargate (1762), St Wilfrid's (1792) and St Ignatius's in Causeway Meadow (1833) (now Meadow Street). As such, they felt that they could not commit themselves to a fourth parish so soon. As a result, Catholic businessmen invited secular priests (those who had not taken a vow of poverty) to establish a mission. At the time, the Catholic population numbered about 15,000 of which only a quarter could be accommodated at Mass on Sundays, so a new church and staff were needed to minister to a largely poor district that was already there, and its growing population. The first rector was Father Thomas Cookson. On 30 July 1840, at the opening of the church, which was built at the top of a hillside which falls away steeply into Frenchwood, Father Cookson spoke about 'the advantages to be derived by … the immediate neighbourhood.' He was obviously fully aware of the challenges in front of him.

One of the first problems he faced was the education of the young of this working-class parish, many of them working half days in the cotton mills. The new school, which stood

Shepherd Street School in Preston in 1902 showing a classroom full of children sitting in rows at their desks Image: © Harris Museum and Art Gallery

next to the church, was finished in 1841 at a cost of £2,000 (£178,600). He also established the guilds. In this era, and well into the twentieth century, most Anglican and Catholic parishes had guilds which were, at their base, mutual benefit groups long before any system of national, social assistance was set up, rather similar to secular groups such as the Oddfellows. As mentioned earlier, Whit Monday was the day used for processions and festivities celebrating these groups. In addition to this, the guilds provided opportunities for communal worship, a sense of belonging and entertainment. Father Cookson must have seen the establishment of these groups as an important part of the cohesion of the new parish and a bulwark against the influence of the Sandhole. This is probably why the Men's and Boys' Guilds were established a year before the church was completed. The Young Women's and Girls' Guilds were instituted in May 1840, two months before the church was opened. These social groups were seen as a priority and were well subscribed. The 1851 Census shows that Father Cookson is still in place at the age of 47, assisted by a young curate, Edward Swarbrick, aged 27. Incidentally, both were local men; the former was born in Poulton and the latter in Garstang.

The development of St Augustine's parochial structures moved at a furious pace. By February 1844, the schools were up and running with 220 pupils in the Boys' School (120 in the evening) and 160 pupils in the Girls' School (80 in the evening). The Sunday School was attended by 200 girls and 200 boys. In March 1844, education inspectors found the schools as 'efficient and satisfactory' after only two years. The following month, a parish library was set up with over 400 books. At this time and for some decades to come, libraries and reading rooms were seen as essential for self-education and improvement, so much so that many towns and villages wanted them. Education, it was generally thought, would free people from ignorance, poverty and immorality, so everything possible should be done to promote it.

On 11 November 1848, the *Chronicle* reported on a meeting held at Fox Street School (St Wilfrid's) to promote 'the extension of education to the poorer portion of the Catholic community, 5000 of which are Irish'. Father Cookson was asked to propose a resolution 'that this meeting, deeply sensible of the paramount importance of education, pledges itself to use every effort to extend its benefits among the labouring classes of the Catholic community'. Mr Charles Townley, a Catholic businessman, seconded this and, in his speech, quoted the Anglican chaplain at Preston Prison, Rev. John Clay. His figures showing the lack of education are relevant because many inhabitants of the Sandhole ended up there.

During his time as chaplain, Rev. Clay promoted the improvement of education for all, especially the working class, because it would help solve some of society's ills, the main one being the creation of an underclass out of which it was almost impossible to escape. As far as he was concerned, being literate and numerate did not make a person educated. He deplored the fact that some prisoners felt they were not welcome in church and therefore their children had no religious feeling or spirituality. He detected that 'poverty and wretchedness are usually attended by a neglect of religious duties and absence of religious feeling' (1839). In 1846 he condemned teachers who 'desecrated' the New Testament by making it a 'lesson book', making it 'wearisome' and 'reinforced by blows'.

On the subject of education, Rev. Clay routinely asked prisoners sixty questions which constituted his 'Prisoners' Character Book' every year. In 1843 he asked these questions of twenty-five prisoners and found:

> Four had never been to school and the rest had only attended for a month or similar.
>
> None could read and only two knew the alphabet.
>
> Eleven could not say the Our Father and none could recite it properly.
>
> Only one man and none of the women knew who Jesus Christ was.
>
> Five of them had never been in a church.

All of them only had a sketchy idea of what right and wrong were.

Five of them had a vague idea of what repentance was.

Thirteen had never heard of the Duke of Wellington. A few more knew about Lord Nelson.

Seventeen did not know about Queen Victoria.

All the men were adequate in arithmetic, being able to calculate money.

Six men and all the women could count to a hundred.

None of them knew the months of the year in the correct order.

None of them knew the months where Christmas Day and New Year's Day occurs.

By 1853 he had extended his sample and interviewed 1,636 prisoners and found:

674 were unable to read anything.

646 did not know Jesus Christ's name or any sort of prayer.

977 could not name the reigning queen.

957 did not know the meaning of 'virtue' or 'vice'.

1,111 could not name the months of the year in the correct order.

479 were unable to count to a hundred.

It is unsurprising, therefore, that the Catholic educators in Preston fully agreed with Rev. Clay's findings and his views on what was needed.

> I have ventured to be urgent on this topic, because observations will be submitted by gentlemen who must have it frequently brought under their consideration and to whom it must be evident that education – practical as far as possible – based essentially on religion and promoted with judgement, energy and perseverance – and nothing else will do – will obviate and prevent a thousand more evils than the best plans of prison discipline – deterring or reformatory – can ever do to remedy.

He had come to the conclusion that rehabilitation in prison was needed more than just punishment. He was also certain, as were others, that the roots of many problems were beerhouses and licensed premises, especially those which offered rooms for dancing and singing. In 1853, Rev. Clay wrote to C. P. Villiers M.P. explaining the problem of drink in Preston and quoted facts and figures. In 1848, 177 licences for beerhouses were granted and 64 men were committed for trial or were imprisoned. Over the following five years the numbers grew, culminating in 1853 when 235 licences were granted and 192 men were under the law. Using the 1851 Census statistics he extracted from the total population of 69,542 men who were over twenty years of age, those known to be temperance members, gentry and upper class, and was left with 12,000 men. There were 424 licensed premises, which meant that, proportionally there were 28 men to each, which he thought ridiculous. Others felt the same, but for the next twenty years or so, the vast bulk of licences were renewed despite objections. In the letter he continued, 'To attract more customers, occupiers of beerhouses and low grade public houses resort to worse practices than mere drinking, such as women, dancing, singing, gaming and brutal sports such as dog fighting and cock fighting.'

To illustrate this further, he interviewed eighty-four prisoners who were about to be transported for life to Australia and asked them what they had seen and experienced in beerhouses and low-grade public houses. Presumably these people, by this stage, had nothing to lose or hide.

56 had participated in gaming

41 had been to places which harboured prostitutes

30 had been where there had been Sunday drinking

23 had been where stolen goods had been received

22 had come across robberies being planned

17 had been in places which took clothing in exchange for drink

15 had been in places where dog fighting or cock fighting had been promoted

14 had been where violent deaths or deaths from excess had been witnessed

13 had been in places which harboured thieves and pickpockets

10 had been in places which had dancing rooms

6 had been in places where forgers of coin congregated

In further conversations with Preston convicts in 1852, Rev. Clay found that out of 189 only 20 were unaffected by alcohol. The others were damaged by 'demoralising company in alehouses'. He again emphasised that 'education was the key, but education could do little for the labouring class so long as they were seduced from its effects by public houses and gin shops'.

In a further blast against 'singing rooms' and 'dancing rooms' he stated, 'At a singing room in Preston (possibly the Albion at 23 Church Street) ... seven hundred boys and girls collected together to have their bodies poisoned with smoke and drink and their minds poisoned with ribaldry and obscenity.'

All this is relevant to the places, customs and pastimes pursued in the Sandhole and its satellite streets. It is little wonder that the Catholic community in general, and St Augustine's in particular, felt the need to act after examining Rev. Clay's findings, despite the religious intolerance of the time. Shortly, the Anglican community would also take positive action.

With all the above 'attractions' on offer in certain parts of the town and, in particular, the Sandhole, it was inevitable that some elements of the military would be drawn in. The prospect of soldiers, out of barracks with money and looking for somewhere to spend it made the Army attractive to some and a target for others. Their visits sometimes ended in theft or violence. In 1851, Charles Halford of the 46th (South Devonshire) Regiment was brave enough to steal clothes from Liverpool House, owned by James Proctor. A year later, Henry Buller of the 94th (Scotch Brigade) was sent for trial for assaulting Ann Curtis, who lived in the Sandhole. He hit her so hard with a jug that she could not attend court.

In May 1855, Bridget Maxwell was accused by John Dunlevy, a militia man, of robbing him of a shilling (£5). As Dunlevy was leaving the Black Swan, Maxwell approached him, looking like she wanted to talk to him and took hold of him. He felt her hand in his waistcoat and missed the money, whereupon he began to assault her in the street in front of witnesses. Another woman called Jane Greenwood swore in court that Dunlevy had given Maxwell the money and he was sent for trial for assault. Maxwell was a young girl. The *Chronicle* had reported two months earlier that she had admitted to being a prostitute and under the age of sixteen. At the time, according to police estimates, she was one of twelve girls working as prostitutes in Preston of the same age. She continued in her way of life and was arrested in December 1856 for theft. She was with Samuel Heaton, a private of the 66th (Berkshire) Regiment, in a brothel on a Saturday night where she stole his pocket watch and thirteen shillings (£60), probably when he was drunk. At her trial, Maxwell pleaded guilty and was sentenced to six months' imprisonment with hard labour.

Bridget Maxwell admitted to being a prostitute and under the age of sixteen. She was one of twelve girls working as prostitutes in Preston of the same age.

Sometimes the Preston police had problems with the sheer number of soldiers coming into town. Prior to embarkation to Malta on the way to the Crimea, some men from the 28th (North Gloucestershire) Regiment came into Preston and caused trouble on Monday 23 and Tuesday 24 February 1856. The reason was that some of their number had been arrested on the Saturday and Sunday for disorderly conduct on the streets. During the Monday night set-to, the Superintendent, Mr Gibbons, was wounded and Inspector Ringland received a cut on the head. On the Tuesday night, there was trouble outside the Malt Shovel in Patten Street (behind Friargate), when soldiers attacked and kicked a woman who was helping a drunk man back to his home. Hurrying to the scene, P.C. Steanson (see later chapter) arrested the main culprit and, in the process, was attacked by another soldier who was attempting a rescue until P.C. Hillside arrived. The policemen proceeded to take their prisoners to the police station, then situated in Avenham Street. As they arrived, twenty soldiers appeared, having run out of the Sandhole, swinging their belts and swearing they would do 'the b—y police'. Steanson and Hillside got to the safety of the station with their prisoners just in time. On the other side of the town centre, P.C. Dunderdale was not quite so fortunate. On Fishergate he was fallen on by 'a whole posse of redcoats'. He fought hard but was knocked down and his head cut in a number of places before a large number of police arrived. The town surgeon, Mr Spencer and his assistant spent two hours dressing the wounded who included a civilian who had helped the police. All those arrested were detained overnight and put before the magistrates the following morning at the Town Hall. There it was decided that no action would be taken as long as all military personnel were confined to barracks during the next night. On the Thursday night, the regiment passed through the town en route for Liverpool, where they embarked on the steamer *Nigeria* for Malta.

The Army was not beyond occupying a place and defending it if need be. In March 1855 an argument, which quickly escalated into a riot, broke out at Thomas Conlon's beerhouse in Pottery Hill, close to where the top of Corporation Street now stands. Locals and ten soldiers from the 34th (Cumberland) Regiment started fighting and the locals were driven out. Most of these were tough canal boatmen who refused to be put off and proceeded to throw stones and large missiles into the beerhouse, destroying the windows and much of the fittings.

The *Chronicle* of Saturday 15 May 1858 reported what it described as 'a brutal assault on P.C. Stirzaker in the Sandhole by two soldiers, Thomas Bates and William McNaren the previous evening. The police officer stated that he had found Bates on the ground, drunk, and when he helped him to his feet, he was attacked by four other soldiers who took off their belts and struck him round the head and shoulders with the buckles. They nearly tore his trousers off, but he was saved by a special constable and another officer who took the defendants into custody. The magistrate, Mr Ainsworth, said Bates was guilty of 'a cowardly, brutal and unsoldierly attack upon a man who had done him a kindness'. Bates was fined £5 (£494) and costs or three months' imprisonment. McNaren was fined two pounds (£197) or four weeks' imprisonment.

On some occasions, just the appearance of the police brought out the worst in some military men. Three men of the 55th (Westmorland) Regiment John Donough, Thomas Havallan and John South were charged with assaulting several police officers. On the night of 2 July 1861 P.C. Goulding was called to a disturbance at the Roast Beef Inn on Friargate. When he arrived, he found the accused arguing with others of the same regiment. On seeing him, they pulled off their belts and struck him and he was severely injured. After this, they broke windows and caused damage amounting to £3 (£275). South then turned and made 'a further furious attack' on Goulding, forcing him to 'draw his staff and strenuously fight back'. However, he was unable to 'quell the disturbance'. When P.C.s Dawson, Morley and Aughton arrived, the soldiers had moved into Vickers Street (near where the Market now stands) where they attacked the police with their belts 'most ferociously' Both sides were badly injured. South did not appear in court at first because of his wounds. As a result, the prosecuting solicitor decided not to press charges as the soldiers had suffered punishment at the hands of the police. However, the Mayor, Robert Townley Parker, disagreed and sent them for trial at the sessions in Lancaster because he could not have the peace of the town broken 'by military men or any other party' and the accused had been guilty of a 'most wanton and unprovoked attack' on the police.

The marauding nature of this type of soldier on leave in a strange town was further illustrated by a 'brutal outrage' reported by the *Chronicle* on 29 January 1862. Thomas Johnson, John Mullins and Robert Leat of the 55th Regiment were charged with violent assault of Superintendent Gibbons and Lawrence Almond, the licensee of the Haymarket Tavern in Clayton's Court (where the Miller Arcade now stands). On the night of the 28 January the accused entered the tavern and, after fifteen minutes' drinking, Mullins spotted three women in the back room. He grabbed hold of one of them and 'knocked her about the room while the other two did the same to the other women'. When Almond tried to intervene, the prisoners took hold of him, hit him round the face and 'dashed his head against the wall before striking him with their belts'. One witness stated that 'he fought like a brick'. Gibbons said that he went into the tavern because he heard people shouting for the police. He also stated that he was certain that he was assaulted by Mullins and Johnson but not Leat. Mrs Almond testified that the same had happened to her husband, so Leat was discharged. The other two were committed for trial at the sessions in Lancaster.

A week later, William Patterson, a private of the 29th (Worcestershire) Regiment was charged by Mary Talent, a prostitute who lived in the Sandhole, with assault. About half past midnight on 3 February, Patterson was walking down Water Street with his belt in his hand when he spotted Talent standing on the corner of Shepherd Street and, for no reason, struck her on her neck with the buckle. For this and other attacks (see below) he was sent to prison for three months.

On the same evening, around the same time, Patterson and three other privates of the same regiment – Robert Fearon, Thomas Heywood and John Perry – were charged with being drunk and behaving riotously in Church Street. Witnesses stated that the prisoner were 'singing, shouting and swinging their belts round their heads and crying out, 'Let's kill every —— one of them', whereupon they commenced to strike any person who came near'. P.C.s

Moorby and Swift testified that the prisoners were very disorderly and one of them 'struck Moorby a severe blow on his head with his belt.' After a set-to the soldiers were overpowered: their belts and collars were seen to be 'saturated with blood'. They were sent to sessions for trial.

Some soldiers struck up misguided relationships with women from the Sandhole. Charles Swift, the licensee of the Black Swan in Water Street in 1854, charged Richard Hothersall of the 66th (Berkshire) Regiment and a prostitute called Catherine Ward with causing damage. He had tried hard to prevent Ward from entering his premises on 24 November because she was drunk. Hothersall thought Ward was hard done by, so he took it into his head to take her side and kicked panels out of the front door and broke several windows before pulling down part of the gas fittings. Both were apprehended by P.C. Peters. Ward was fined five shillings (£26) and Hothersall was made to pay compensation.

Some soldiers struck up misguided relationships with women from the Sandhole.

Occasionally, trouble broke out when soldiers from different regiments came into contact with each other as they did in February 1856 in the Black Swan. The *Chronicle* headlined the article as 'Another Military Riot'. Six or seven men of the 34th (Cumberland) Regiment were in the house drinking when about twenty men from the 18th (Royal Irish) Regiment entered and began lashing out with their belts, causing the men from the 34th to vacate the premises. Decanters and other glassware were smashed, and a door was broken open to gain access to those who were hiding but they had escaped. A great crowd gathered outside to watch and the police had to intervene. Members of the Swift family had been injured during the fighting before the attackers moved onto Church Street. Here they were confronted by the police. They hesitated, then proceeded to attack the police who defended themselves with their staffs and the public who used 'staves'. In the aftermath, injured soldiers and police officers were treated by Mr Spencer at his surgery. Those soldiers who had been detained by the police were picked up later by a piquet sent out from the Barracks.

Occasionally, soldiers were the victims of crime themselves. In March 1865, George Brown, a private from the 66th (Berkshire) Regiment, fell asleep while drunk in the Bear's Paw in Church Street which, by all accounts, was not an uncommon occurrence. Licensed premises, open for fifteen hours a day, offered a place to rest and escape. As Robert Roberts comments in his social history of Salford before the Great War, *The Classic Slum*, the pub was 'the shortest way out of Manchester'. While Brown was asleep, Richard Shaw removed his shoes and pawned them at Elizabeth and James Dickinson's pawnbrokers in Water Street. Later, there was a loud argument between the two men in Blelock Street, which witnessed by Sarah Armstrong who lived nearby and caught the attention of P.C. Kenny who arrested Shaw after finding the pawn ticket on his person. The shoes were retrieved and returned to Brown.

On Monday 15 July 1850, Thomas Shepherd, a deserter from the 85th (Buckinghamshire) Regiment, attacked P.C. Atherton in the Liverpool House beerhouse in Shepherd Street, thinking he was part of a piquet which was out looking for him. He was arrested, found guilty and sentenced to two months' hard labour. Deserters were not uncommon in the town at this time. Perhaps this was because they thought they would have a better life here, and a warm welcome in the Sandhole, especially if they had money on them. This prompted the Colonel of the 66th Regiment to state to the magistrates that there was too close a bond between soldiers and licensed house keepers. He revealed that Samuel Leighton had allowed Shepherd to change his clothes. This prompted a new case at the magistrates' court where Leighton was charged with allowing Shepherd to change clothes with a civilian. P.C.s Hoole and Leach testified that Leighton had come to them to inform them and that he had tried to prevent it. Through lack of evidence he was discharged.

Liverpool House ... was full of soldiers and prostitutes, most of them 'in a beastly state of intoxication and conducting themselves in a riotous and disorderly manner'

Liverpool House (latterly known as the Dog and Rat) had always had a bad reputation. About sixteen months earlier, Leighton had been charged with permitting drunkenness in his house one Sunday night. Police reports stated that the place was full of soldiers and prostitutes, most of them 'in a beastly state of intoxication and conducting themselves in a riotous and disorderly manner'. The Mayor stated that it 'was the determination of the Bench to put down these disorderly houses' and yet the situation persisted for the next twenty years or so when there seemed to be a policy of containment rather than eradication. Leighton was told that if another complaint were made against him, he would lose his licence. He was fined forty shillings (£210) and costs.

A change of licensee later in 1850 did not bring a sudden change in the atmosphere or tone of the establishment. Not long after John Proctor had taken over the licence, the police were called after a nasty incident where Thomas Harrison (a probable bully) had committed an aggravated assault on Ellen Nichols, whom the *Chronicle* described as 'an unfortunate woman who has no more sense than to cohabit with him'. P.C. Dyson was called 'to the notorious Liverpool House where he found the complainant insensible and bleeding on the floor and her paramour standing over her'. When she was examined, she was found to have several broken ribs and was 'in a precarious state in the House of Recovery'. Harrison was remanded for trial at Lancaster.

Proctor also took in lodgers and one simple trick that lodgers used to perform was not just to abscond, but to walk off with bed linen and clothes which could easily be disposed of or pawned. A woman called Ann Thompson tried this in 1852 and Proctor called the police. P.C. Breakell arrested her and a girl called Balshaw who had pawned the items. Both were sent for trial. Among the immoral or illegal activities which took place was pickpocketing. The *Chronicle* reported that Mary Ann Milner and William Webster (a probable bully) were arrested by Inspector Rigby in a brothel in Blelock Street. The previous evening, they had stolen a sovereign (£106) from Robert Hamer from Bolton in 'that charnel house known by the sign of Liverpool House in the Sandhole'. Milner was remanded for performing the robbery but Webster, like many bullies, was a shady, elusive character and had made himself scarce.

In 1856, Proctor lost his licence and tried twice to secure the licence for the Lodge Bank Tavern in Leeming Street, thereby extending his influence. Inspector Ringland strongly objected because Proctor had been summoned once for keeping a disorderly house and for 'having company in prohibited hours'. His application was refused. Ten days previously, he had been bound over to keep the peace after assaulting an unnamed woman, which is some sort of guide as to his attitude towards women. His first wife, Mary, was named in the 1851 Census, but was not present at 37 Shepherd Street on the night it was taken. Unusually, an explanation was entered by the enumerator as: 'Mary Proctor 38 Wife at 108 Hudson Street, visiting her sister and brother-in-law'.

Number 108 Hudson Street, nearby, was occupied by the Woodhouses and their five children, the youngest of which was nine months old. In their entry, Mary was classified as a visitor with her four-year-old son, Simmonds. This evidence strongly suggests marital estrangement and taking refuge. She died the following summer.

Proctor remarried in June 1857, aged 45, at the Parish Church, to Elizabeth Hardiker, aged 38. She gave her profession as 'dressmaker' which could have been true, but it could also have been a cover for prostitution. Unfortunately, his violence and misogyny ran forward into his second marriage. In September 1857 the *Chronicle* ran an article with the headline 'An Irredeemable Scoundrel' in which Proctor was charged with aggravated assault on his wife. He had attacked her 'violently and inhumanely' by kicking her, cutting her nose, blacking her eyes and 'causing so much bleeding that she was in a weak condition'. He then locked the door and repeated the crime. P.C. Topping arrived at the house and arrested Proctor.

Mr Dunderdale, the prosecuting solicitor, described her injuries as 'of a very severe character'. She was bruised all over her body and there were remains of old wounds. Superintendent Gibbons testified 'I know nothing good of this man. He is an utterly worthless being – always in the company of prostitutes and such like characters.' Proctor begged for mercy and promised to leave town, but the magistrates found him guilty and committed him to the House of Correction for six months with hard labour.

Three months later, Proctor was back at Liverpool House, breaking the law yet again in a case which showed how he attempted to dominate those around him. There may not have been any gangs as such exerting their influence, but there were some individuals, both male and female, who had local power. The first charges of having his beerhouse open at an unlawful hour and refusing to admit the police were heard during the week ending 19 December 1857. A young prostitute called Mary Jane Lawe (sometimes known as Lowe) was seen by P.C.s Cross and Carter leaving the back door of Liverpool House at half past one in the morning with a half-gallon jug of beer. The policemen had seen a light in Proctor's cellar and had watched a man in shirtsleeves drawing beer from a barrel. When they took the jug away from Lawe she turned and shouted, 'John, come and help! There's two chaps going to take the ale from me!'

At this, the door slammed shut and Proctor refused to open it to the police. At this point in the court case, where the prosecuting solicitor had finished going through the evidence, the defending solicitor, Mr Blackhurst, refrained from asking any questions or making any observations, but Proctor was fined forty shillings (£187) anyway. The reason for this unusual break with procedure was that he had had to caution Lawe not to tell lies in court. As a result, she had refused to be sworn and therefore he could not use her as a witness. The magistrate, Mr Ascroft, said he wanted to clamp down on perjury, so he had Lawe arrested. The factor which swayed this was that it became known that she lived and worked in a house nearby which was owned by Proctor.

The following day, Mary Jane Lawe was charged with perjury because she had told the police that she had not obtained the ale at Proctor's house when she had been first remanded. When questioned, Lawe stated that she had been induced by Proctor to make the statement she gave to the police but was unwilling to repeat it in court because Mr Blackhurst had warned her that she would be in serious trouble. She was remanded for a further day and the magistrate, Mr Ascroft, made it clear he would be going after Proctor. The evidence from the previous case was re-presented on the Wednesday, including the statements of P.C.s Cross and Carter, after which Ascroft discharged Mary Jane Lawe. He then proceeded to charge Proctor with suborning a witness.

Lawe had stated at first that she had bought beer at the Imperial Hotel (formerly the Albion, later the Royal Hotel) at 23 Church Street, but later refused to say it on oath. On this particular day she made another statement that Proctor had taken her to the Imperial and 'persuaded' the landlady, Mrs Carter, that she had served Lawe with four pints of beer. She also testified that she lived in a small house in Shepherd Street adjoining Proctor's beerhouse for which she paid eight shillings a week (£39). Considering that twenty years later tenants were paying half that amount for houses on Laurel Street and Blelock Street, Lawe's rent to Proctor was steep in comparison. In addition, she had to buy any ale she needed, i.e. for entertaining, from him. He had further power over her because he knew she was a prostitute and she owed him money. With all this in mind, Proctor asked her to lie for him, saying it would 'do her no harm and him a service'.

It became perfectly obvious to all in court that he had put undue pressure on Lawe, who was described by the *Chronicle* as 'a bad character' and was thought to be untrustworthy, but Mr Ascroft committed Proctor to the Assizes for perjury. When bail was applied for the Bench refused. When it was stated, by the defending solicitor, that Proctor had a large family, which was a slight exaggeration, Mr Pilkington answered that he 'cares very little about his family, leading this course of life'. Although Proctor was back for the 1861 Census, the beerhouse lost its licence and was sold not long after.

Mary Jane Lawe died of consumption in the prison at Lancaster Castle where she was serving a twelve-month sentence for robbery,

Two years later, in early June, Mary Jane Lawe (recorded in the *Lancaster Guardian* as Lowe) died of consumption, now known as tuberculosis, in the prison at Lancaster Castle where she was serving a twelve-month sentence for robbery, sentenced in October 1859. On 9 August 1859 she, together with Alice Parker and Mary Marsden, both prostitutes, had stolen £16 (£1,574) from John Barton of Ribchester in the Sandhole but were arrested by P.C. Steanson (see next chapter). When they were searched at the police station only £12 12*s.* 11*d.* (£1,244) was found. Ten months later, knowing she was going to die of consumption, Lawe asked the matron to look inside a secret pocket in her clothes to retrieve her share, £4 10*s.* (£442.80), which was hidden there and give it back to Barton. The matron passed it to the Governor, Captain Hansbrow, who gave it to Superintendent Gibbons and Inspector Ringland who had just escorted a woman prisoner to the Castle. They restored the money to Barton and Lawe died the next day aged twenty-one.

Life was short in Victorian Britain but was more so in Victorian Preston. In *An Atlas of Victorian Mortality*, Robert Woods and Nicola Shelton quote life expectancy at birth at the start of the 1860s as 25 to 39.9 years, and life expectancy at twenty in the same period as 33 to 39.9. In his research study *Mitres and Missions in Lancashire – The Roman Catholic Diocese of Liverpool 1850–2000*, Peter Doyle states that

> Liverpool was not unique in the conditions endured by its poorer inhabitants. Preston suffered from great poverty with a large number of insanitary cellar dwellings and a terrible cholera outbreak in 1849. As late as the 1880s it had a

> general death rate higher than Liverpool's and both its fever death rate and its infant mortality were higher that its more notorious neighbours.

Sometimes death came more quickly and possibly even more cruelly than by disease. In certain brothels in the Sandhole, in a space of little over a year, there were three horrific, fatal accidents caused by alcohol, fatigue and the fashion for wide, crinoline dresses. The *Chronicle*, in its issue of 19 December 1857, ran a paragraph giving the bare bones of a story. The previous evening, Mary Gaffer,[1] or Gaffery, aged 18 or 19, was severely burned when her clothes set on fire. In a more detailed account in the same issue, the girl is described as running out of the house in Laurel Street, where she lived, with her clothes on fire. She was first seen by John Whiteside, an assistant bill poster, trying to put out the flames by rolling herself on the ground. He and some others tried to help, and she was 'carried upstairs of a miserable hovel to bed'. She was attended by Mr Haldane, the surgeon, and a Catholic priest from St Augustine's, 'to which persuasion she professed to belong', the *Chronicle* added, tartly. Her dress had set alight while she was asleep in front of the fire, 'intoxicated'. From the start there seems to have been no hope of recovery from the terrible wounds she had sustained: 'her breast, back and face having been literally roasted'. She was taken to the House of Recovery where she 'lingered on in unspeakable agony until she died on Sunday night' (20 December).

In a space of little over a year, there were three horrific, fatal accidents caused by alcohol, fatigue and the fashion for wide, flammable crinoline dresses.

A little over a year later, the *Chronicle* published a report, on 15 January 1859, under the headline 'Woman Burned To Death', of an inquest which had taken place three days earlier. Mary Ann Balshaw had died as a result of her clothes setting on fire. Described as 'a woman of loose character', she lived with Alice Cross in a Sandhole house. On the evening of 1 January, between seven and eight o'clock, Cross went out and when she returned, she found Balshaw 'in flames in the middle of the floor'. There had been no candle in the house, the only heat coming from a small fire in the grate. She had been drunk at the time. Some people had considered her to be 'of weak intellect and had often wished herself dead.' She had been 'a denizen of the Sandhole' i.e. a prostitute since her mother had died in 1852 when Balshaw was seventeen. The verdict of the inquest was 'mortally burned during intoxication'.

Less than two weeks later, on Thursday 27 January, Catherine Riley, known as 'Cockney Kate', died at a brothel at 4 Blelock Street where she and two other women had been drinking there all night. At half past eight in the morning, neighbours heard screams and Riley was found with her clothes on fire while her companions were both still fast asleep. With assistance the flames were extinguished but, as the *Chronicle* article says, 'the burns will undoubtedly cause her death'. She was taken to the House of Recovery where she '(lay) in the greatest agony' and died the following day.

In July 1857, Preston Corporation set in motion the sewering and levelling of some streets in the older parts of Preston including Willow Street, Oak Street, William Street, Leeming Street and Blelock Street. Four years later, sewers were constructed in Library Street, School Street and Queen Street between Grimshaw Street and King Street. In addition, the Local board of Health had paid £135,235 (£12,670,000) to the Waterworks Company to provide water for the town with a fuller supply and at greater pressure. The reservoir at Fulwood was abandoned as too low in height at eight feet in favour of another at Grimsargh at fifty-six feet. Water supply was then increased where it had been inadequate, including parts of the Sandhole, namely Leeming Street. Water Street and Queen Street.

In March 1858, the *Chronicle* declared that Blackburn, 'pre-eminently notorious for its immorality and debauchery', had 106 known prostitutes out of a population of 63,100. Eight months later it quoted Preston police statistics which said that Preston (population 82,985) had 205 known prostitutes, twelve of whom were under the age of sixteen. Around the same time, the *Chronicle* stated that Liverpool (population 443,900) had 2065 prostitutes and Manchester (population 338,300) had 1500. In Preston there were thirteen resorts of thieves and prostitutes, including one public house and ten beerhouses, and there were thirty-four brothels.

In Preston there were thirteen resorts of thieves and prostitutes, including one public house and ten beerhouses. There were thirty-four brothels

A year later, the newspaper quoted the judicial statistics for England and Wales, among which were:

Criminal classes at large 134,922

Police Force 20,256

Brothels 7915

Cases of drunkenness 51,861

Prostitutes 'at large' 28760

Proceedings against prostitutes 2,436

The *Chronicle* ends the article with a final statement where there are some compassionate remarks which express a desperate truth about women caught in a vicious circle of lack of education and poverty then falling into the bottom of society and forming an underclass from which there was little chance of escape.

> 'Something must be radically wrong for such a state of things to exist. Means must exist to recover these poor creatures from the depths of misery and sin into which they are plunged.'

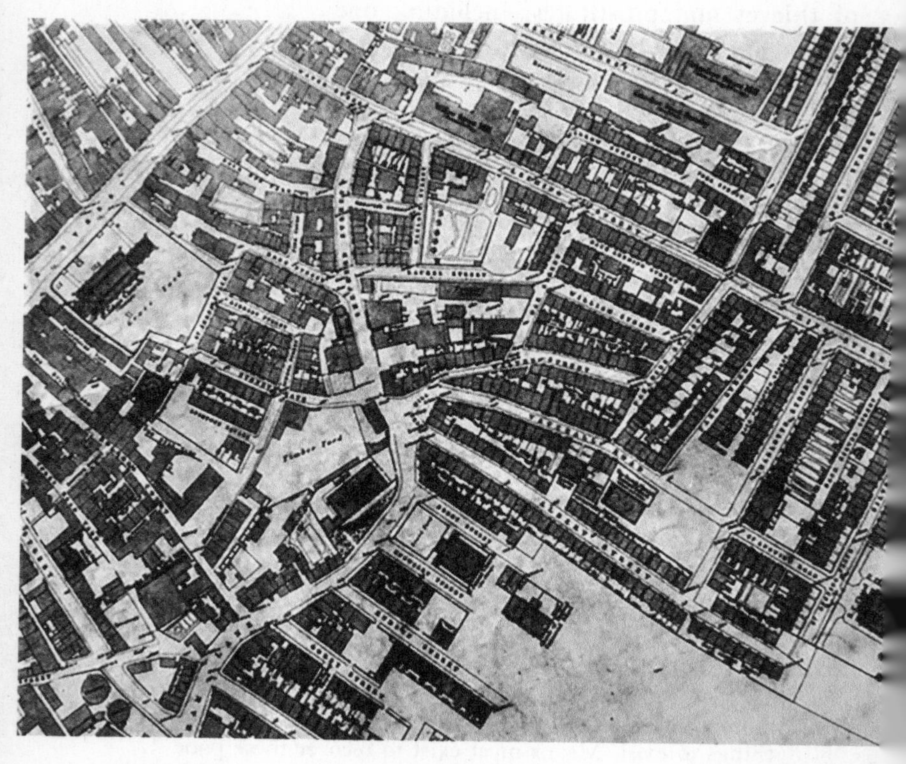

The Sandhole area 1849 showing the Parish Church (left) and St Augustine's Church (right).
(Ordnance Survey 60' to the mile)

4

'The Sharpest Officer'

On Saturday 2 December 1865, the *Chronicle* published a short report in their 'Local Intelligence' column headlined, rather bluntly, 'The End of an Ex-Policeman'. The basic information it imparted was that James Steanson[1] the deceased, 44, had broken his six-month alcoholic fast by drinking in the Albion vaults and the Griffin before going to a brothel in Blelock Street. According to a woman who lived there Steanson fell down some steps when leaving. 'She did not trouble herself to ascertain whether he was hurt or not by the fall.' Between four and five o'clock next morning he was found insensible by the door with his skull fractured and there were other bruises on parts of his body. Doctor Moore stated that the injuries may have been caused by the fall and the verdict was 'Accidental Death'.

And that would have been that if other newspapers like the *Preston Guardian*, the *Herald* and the *Sheffield Daily Telegraph* had not also carried their own reports. It would also have meant that the memory of a once-respected police officer, who had later become mentally ill, would have been forgotten and so would a story where all the dangers, cruelties and vagaries of Victorian life were played out. It would also have obliterated a probable murder.

As with most people of this period, Steanson left no letters, no diary and certainly no photographs, but from police and army records it is possible to gain some mental image of the man. He had grey eyes, brown hair and had a scar on his right cheek. He was five feet seven and three quarter inches tall, which made him almost three inches taller than the average man of the time and almost six inches taller than most women. He was born in July 1821 at Loughgall, Markethill, Armagh and joined the 39th (Dorsetshire) Regiment, then stationed in Ireland, on 1 January 1841 and served with them in India at Kamptee near Nagpur. In 1843 he fought with the 39th at the Battle of Maharajpore on 29 December in the campaign to regain the area of Gwalior from a force known as the Marathas. The British were victorious and the East India Company awarded a medal called the Gwalior Star to all the British soldiers who took part in the battle. It is in the shape of a six-pointed star, made from guns captured in the campaign, with a silver disc at the centre with the date of the battle inscribed on it. This medal will have some significance later in Steanson's story.

The regiment arrived at Fulwood Barracks on 24 June 1848 for its two-year stay in the town. Sometime during the first year, Steanson met a young widow called Isabella Dawson, formerly Beswick. She was a carder in a cotton mill near 18 Hopwood Street where she lived with her parents and siblings. On 10 November 1844, at the age of 22, she had married James Dawson at the Parish Church in Church Street. Aged 21, he was a bookkeeper from Water Street. During the next year they had a son, John, but James died the following winter.

The circumstances of Isabella Dawson and James Steanson meeting each other are unknown, but they married at the Parish Church on 25 November 1849. Steanson entered his name as 'Stevenson' and when Isabella died in 1888 her name was inscribed on the gravestone as 'Stephenson'. The entry in the marriage register has two anomalies – his address and occupation. He gave his address as 18 Hopwood Street, that of his new in-laws and his occupation as 'labourer', which he had been before he joined the Army. This

Queen's Regulations forbade the marriage of soldiers without permission

was because Queen's Regulations forbade the marriage of soldiers without permission, so this marriage was illicit as far as the Army was concerned. Steanson is not recorded in the 1851 Census for 18 Hopwood Street, though his wife is, because he had left with the 39th on 27 April to go to their new posting in Belfast. He resigned from the Army on 17 July, returned to Preston and took up residence at 68 Hopwood Street with his wife. They had three children: Rachel (born 1852), Margaret Ann (1854) and Charles James (1857).

Steanson finished his police training in April 1852 and was sworn in with James Monks in front of the Mayor, Thomas Monk on 20 May. From that day until the day he resigned in August 1859, he proved himself to be a most assiduous, hardworking, observant and courageous police officer which was amplified by the *Sheffield Daily Telegraph* after his death by describing him as 'the sharpest officer in the service'. People in Preston would know about his work through the local newspapers which were published weekly, sometimes twice weekly, and made a serious effort to broadcast the fullest possible spectrum of the news ranging from the very serious to the ephemeral, from national interest to local topics. On the last point, the columns covering local news and interest read like a well-considered and intelligently written parish magazine. Some of the detail they contain may surprise but also interest modern readers as people's names loom large and enrich the articles with human interest. As a result, it would not be a surprise to find out that police officers' names are mentioned regularly in court, crime and incident reports. In the seven years and four months he served in the Preston police, Steanson's name appeared in a hundred and fourteen newspaper reports. These give a measure of the man's standing and calibre. The following selection will give a flavour of this.

On the night of 21 May 1853, Steanson was called to the Weaver's Arms in King Street where violent incidents were taking place. When he finally forced his way in, he found 'many people cut about the head'. William Nixon had gone berserk and had attacked a number of customers with a knife and a poker. As a result, he found 'several people bleeding'. He arrested Nixon who was sent for trial at Lancaster. Similarly, he charged a 'rough customer' called Edward Bamber for assault. Steanson had gone to his lodgings to calm him down but it turned into a 'scuffle' and Steanson's coat was 'much torn'. The *Chronicle* reported in November 1853 a situation where Hugh Cross, described as a 'brute', was drunk and exposing himself to anyone who passed the Grey Horse in Church Street. Steanson had to use force when arresting him. Similar force had to be used when he arrested 'a rough looking Irishman' called Francis Macdonald who was part of a gang of 'six or seven men' who had robbed John Charnley in December 1855. The following year, he and Sergeant Hilton were called to a beer shop called Uncle Tom's Cabin where there was a riot in progress caused by Thomas Kelly, John Welsh and Michael Scannel. When he and other police officers moved in to arrest the men, they were attacked by two women, Mary Kelly and Mary Ann Allen and, during the ensuing fracas, a witness was badly injured and lost the sight of one eye. Kelly was fined £4 10*s*. and costs (£413) and Welsh £2 (£183). Scannel was discharged.

One of the attributes of a good police officer is having good powers of observation. In September 1852, while on patrol in Walton Street at one o'clock in the morning, Steanson went to 'investigate a peculiar sound' coming from Miss Ellen Greenwood's house in Vauxhall Road. He stood and watched for a while and eventually he saw a shoeless man drop from the back wall and disappear into a cellar across the road. He gained entry to it and arrested Richard Whittingham, a member of a notorious gang of thieves from the Sandhole. The sound he had heard was Whittingham trying, unsuccessfully, to prise open a downstairs window with a blunt instrument. In 1854, Steanson spotted two men walking up the street where he lived, carrying a heavy bag. He followed them into a yard where he saw them weighing it – forty pounds of stolen brass. When he questioned them, they refused to answer so he arrested them.

This skill in observation stood him in good stead when spotting deserters. In 1856 he arrested James Dickinson who had just joined the local militia. In fact, he had deserted form the Royal Marines at Plymouth where he was returned. Steanson had recognised him from a description in the *Police Gazette*. In 1858, Steanson was called to the Shelley Arms because a man was being abusive to Mrs Parker, the landlady. As he arrested John Develin for being drunk and disorderly, he noticed that the man's boots were military issue and charged him with desertion. Develin was absent without leave from the 88th (Connaught Rangers) Regiment. Later that year he tracked down two deserters from the 22nd (Cheshire) Regiment. He arrested them and the two married couples who had sheltered them.

Steanson encountered fire at least twice while on his beat. One night in November 1856, a fire broke out in the corn mill belonging to Richard Porter in Lune Street. Though good work by the fire brigade saved the building from being gutted, the contents and the furniture store at the front were all on fire because the floors were all made of wood. The firemen were beaten back a number of times and it took two hours to contain the blaze. Steanson showed great courage as the *Chronicle* reported that '(he) rendered himself particularly conspicuous by his courage in rescuing property which would have been destroyed'. The actual damage to stock amounted to around £200 (£18,360). In 1858, at midnight on 1 December, Steanson noticed a fire in the boiler house of Kay Street Mill near Marsh Lane, the property of Robert Gardner. With some assistance he was able to put the fire out before the fire brigade arrived.

On 3 December 1856, the Steansons' second child, Margaret Ann, died at home in Hopwood Street, aged two, of hydrocephalus (swelling of the brain through excess fluid) for 19 days. Steanson was present when she died and reported the death to the registrar. From then on, he seemed to throw himself into his work. A few days after his daughter died,

He found a man drunk in a passage in Water Street at half past two in the morning and decided to take him to the police station where the man said he was called John Smith. Steanson realised he was wearing soldier's underclothes and charged him. It turned out that he was a deserter from the Royal Artillery.

In February 1858, he arrested two men in a house in Heatley Street for robbery and uncovered 'an inordinate amount of money'. He found on one of the men three cards. 'He practises the three card trick' explained Steanson in court. Later that year he arrested Ellen Lawler, who was a swindler and a slippery character. Posing as a servant of Mrs Goodair, she obtained goods at various shops to the value of £8 19*s*. (£884). Eventually she was followed by a Mr Wardley who took her to Mrs Goodair's house, but Lawler dashed into a shop, ran into the back and escaped by the back yard door. Steanson eventually tracked her down to Wood Top near Burnley. When he arrested her, she tried the same trick on him, but he eventually recaptured her.

Three months later he arrested James Forrest of the 15th (East Yorkshire) Regiment for stealing a purse containing £11 (£1,087) from a sleeping sailor. Steanson thought the sailor was a deserter but, it turned out, that he was at the end of a long leave between ships. In March 1859, he had to call for assistance while trying to break up a fight between two prostitutes at half past two in the morning. The instigator of the violence was so enraged that it took three policemen to arrest her, and she had to be taken to the station in a truck.

The following September, Steanson arrested Thomas Hayes for desertion from the 5th (Royal Irish) Lancers before being put, with other officers, to raiding lodging houses under the Common Lodging Houses Act which covered the public health of poor and migratory people. At 53 Leeming Street he found three married couples, two single women and a child in one room. In another raid he entered a house in Lady Street at seven o'clock in the morning to find five women, three of whom were prostitutes, a married couple and two children all in bed. The owner, William Sumner, was fined five shillings (£25). Presumably these last duties were performed during a month's notice as Steanson had resigned in August 1859 before taking up his new post in the West Yorkshire Police on 27 September 1859.

The death of their second child, Margaret Ann, in 1856 must have devastated the Steansons, as it would any couple. In more recent times, some people casually think that in Victorian Britain the death of a child had less impact, was less upsetting and less painful because death was more common then. The literature of the period is full of death, sometimes of it affecting young people and young children, and its consequences are described and discussed. An example of this is that of Anthony Hewitson, the well-known journalist and respected local historian, commissioned the photographer, Robert Pateson, to photograph his three-year-old daughter, Ada, on the day of her death on 20 November 1873. Mrs Hewitson wanted the image set into a brooch. For the Steansons, however, the situation became rapidly worse.

In June 1858, their other two children died within the space of three weeks. Charles James died on 3 June after suffering from pneumonia for nine days, aged seventeen months. Rachel died on 24 June aged six, of anasarca (two weeks) and hydrothorax (one day). These deaths are three complications caused by measles, all of which are easily curable nowadays. Measles was a virulent killer of children in the nineteenth century. Between January and June 1860, for instance, 124 children in Preston succumbed directly to the disease. Isabella Steanson was present at both the later deaths and their certificates bear her mark (x). The loss of all their children must have seriously disrupted the Steansons' lives on every level, physically, emotionally and mentally. It is more than likely that there was a marital breakdown because when Steanson went to Yorkshire, his wife stayed at 68 Hopwood Street.

Judging by Steanson's later behaviour, it is possible that, in suppressing his grief at the children's deaths, a form of post-traumatic stress disorder set in

Judging by his later behaviour, it is possible that, in suppressing his grief at the children's deaths, a form of post-traumatic stress disorder set in, caused by the way men were, until recently, expected to behave. In an article called 'How To Raise A Boy' (*The Tablet* 12 January 2019) the historical novelist and feminist, Clare Clark, dismisses the theory put forward by Simon Baron-Cohen (now discredited) that male and female brains are different. She says that girls learn what is expected of them early and boys are told that they are not expected to have gentleness and empathy as qualities. This was a developmental problem confronting Victorian men in general and Steanson in particular. She concludes that

> Men who repress their emotions are still disproportionally more vulnerable to depression, alcoholism, drug abuse and suicide. They are more likely to be violent to their partners. As long as our ideals of masculinity prize physical strength above emotional resilience, assertiveness above vulnerability and self-assurance above understanding, our sons will suffer and our daughters with them.

She could easily have been writing about James Steanson a hundred and sixty years ago.

A research[2] conducted from 2008 to 2010 on the long ignored topic of grief over a dead child in middle age was undertaken for the University of Wisconsin and contains findings which relate to this form of grief and the effects it has on middle-aged parents. It shows that the traumatic event of the death of a child can have long term effects. It found that an average of just over eighteen years after the event, parents reported depressive symptoms, poorer wellbeing, more health problems and were more likely to have a depressive episode and marital disruption than other parents. The study also showed that recovery from grief was associated with having a sense of purpose. It goes on to say that, traditionally, it is generally thought that parental grief, after an intense response over a few weeks, tails off over the months and recovery happens in two years. However, the study quotes earlier research done in 1995 and 2003 which show that this period is too short and that bereaved parents have reported thinking about their child daily for up to four years and as long as nine years. Bereaved men seem to have been hit the hardest, the research suggests. It shows that the highest level of depressive symptoms occurred in bereaved parents, particularly fathers, who returned relatively low scores for having a purpose in life.

The reason for Steanson resigning from the Preston force is not recorded in the Watch Committee minutes but he did attempt to maintain a purpose in life, at least for just over a year. Finding a meaning in life is held to be important for long term functioning in fatherhood and a lack of it causes depression.

From 27 September 1859, Steanson worked in Under Agbrigg near Wakefield until 25 October when he was transferred to East Morley, Leeds. He was dismissed on 18 October 1860 because he had given way 'to habits of intemperance'. (*Sheffield Daily Telegraph* 4 December 1865). He returned to the family home immediately. He was obviously self-medicating his grief with alcohol which meant that trouble lay ahead for him and his wife.

In her research study 'Grief and Substance Abuse – Coping After Loss'[3] Laura Nott comments

> It is common to experience a range of emotions from denial and anger to sadness and despair. Some will turn to alcohol or drugs in a desperate attempt to numb the pain and grief. Unfortunately, this can lead to addiction ... Grief can trigger clinical depression which increases the risk of suicide.

She adds that if this happens, the addict will need support and detoxification. Neither these nor counselling nor rehabilitation were available to anyone in this period, so Steanson became a public nuisance, a drunkard and an example of failure for everyone.

In her study, published on her website, 'A Cure for Melancholy: Victorian Medical Advice on Treating Depression' (2017), Mimi Matthews lists signs of melancholy classified by Dr G. Fielding Blandford in 1871, five years after Steanson's death. Steanson suffered from two afflictions on this list.

> Mischievous Melancholy: marked by sullenness, moroseness, spite and occasionally terminating in suicide or the injury of others.
>
> Self Complacent Melancholy: where the person is self satisfied and affable, occasionally rejoicing in a visionary superiority of rank station or wealth.

The only cures available involved cold baths, long walks and travelling and certainly not antidepressant drugs. If the patient was rich, he or she could be attended upon day and night; if the patient was not rich then Blandford asserts that there was 'nothing left for it but to send him (or her) to the asylum'. The asylum and the workhouse were two places, for all his desperate behaviour, that Steanson was successful in avoiding.

The 1861 Census, taken on Sunday 7 April, shows Steanson back at home at 68 Hopwood Street with his wife and stepson, John Dawson. He declared his occupation as a railway porter and his wife as a dressmaker, rather than the factory operative she had been earlier. He had been back in Preston for sixteen months, but the marital situation must have been poor and this became obvious on 5 June 1861 when Isabella summoned him to court for abusing her. She testified that he regularly ill-used her, the last time being on Tuesday 4 June when he had kicked her and put her out of doors despite not giving him any provocation. He denied striking her, but she said it was the third time he had kicked her and the third time she had summoned him to court. Also, she stated that he had 'sold up the goods since Christmas'. Steanson's defence was long and incoherent and no-one in court could understand it. Inspector Gibbons said that one day he had seen Steanson drunk and drawing a large crowd in the street while arguing with his wife. Steanson found money for the bail, but Isabella declared to the Bench that she dared not live with her husband any longer.

In the *Chronicle* of 27 September 1862, Steanson was reported as being fined for being drunk and breaking his brother-in-law's windows and assaulting the police. He was then living at his sister-in-law and brother-in-law's house in Everton Gardens (where the north end of the bus station now stands). Just less than a year later, in September 1863, he was back in court for assaulting his wife and harassing her. She testified that they had not lived together 'for some time'. The previous Wednesday he had turned up at her lodgings and broken two windows and some shutters. The following afternoon he made a disturbance in the street and, at eleven o'clock at night, he returned, knocking at the door. When she tried to get him to go away, he knocked her down and assaulted her. She had not troubled him and wanted to be left in peace.

Just less than a year later, in September 1863, he was back in court for assaulting his wife and harassing her. She testified that they had not lived together 'for some time'

Steanson said that he had called for his star. Presumably this was the Gwalior Star which had been awarded to him in India in 1844. He said his wife wanted two shillings for it (£9.40), so he went 'to a certain party in town' obtained the money and 'gave it to her son (my emphasis) for the star'. When he went to work for the West Yorkshire Police, he declared on the official form that he had one child: now John is her child, which is an indication of the estrangement between the two. Steanson went on to say that his wife 'came out of the house, up with her foot and knocked me down the street'. Isabella's sister corroborated her statement then 'a squabble took place' which was cut short by the magistrate. Steanson was told to find bail, which he must have done because he never went to prison. What could easily have put him in prison would have been when he attempted to pawn the Gwalior Star. Under Section 92 of the 1797 Mutiny Act the pawning of medals was illegal.

On Saturday 3 January 1863, the *Chronicle* reported that Steanson had attempted suicide by cutting his throat. The previous Sunday morning, 27 December, he had returned to his lodgings in Everton Gardens but 'was refused because of intoxication'. He managed to get through a cellar window and while there made a four-inch incision on his neck, narrowly missing the jugular vein. Someone from upstairs called a doctor and Steanson recovered during the week. During the week beginning 5 January he wrote to the *Herald* to say that the cut had been accidental. Whether any credence can be attached to this is doubtful because attempted suicide was a criminal offence which carried a prison sentence or even execution.

In 1864, Steanson was cautioned for being drunk and disorderly in July, pestering a woman in September and in October creating a disturbance outside his in-laws' house and breaking a window. During the inquest into Steanson's death, however, his brother-in-law, Charles Beckett, testified that he had stopped drinking, having signed the pledge at Whitsuntide (June), only to restart on the night of his death, and that he was in employment as a labourer at Mr Robinson's tool making firm in Snow Hill.

So, to sum up, James Steanson, after an exemplary time in the Army, including an experience of battle, and time in the police during which he showed himself to be 'the sharpest officer in the force', he had become a nuisance and an embarrassment to his family and to the town in general. Much of his behaviour after returning from Leeds shows symptoms of subdued, deep grief, as discussed earlier. It is reasonable to assume he had become an alcoholic and something which worked against him and other heavy drinkers was that alcoholism was not seen as a disease – though some medical experts were beginning to lean that way rather than the prevalent attitude that persistent heavy drinking was a vice or a loss of control, and therefore controllable by the individual. Unfortunately, Steanson must not have been an isolated case. There must have been many others who had become detached from and lost to society caused by a disease and a mental state not recognised as such until the next century.

On the night before Steanson's death, John Woodhead had been drinking with him and two other men at the Albion vaults and later in the Griffin Inn in Water Street. There had been no fighting, but Woodhead testified that William East had hit Steanson after they had left the Griffin Inn.

Under oath, East denied this, saying he did not hit Steanson and no-one else did. East, who was twenty-four at the time, was already well known to the police for theft, assault and drunkenness, but his evidence has the ring of truth because he did not take the opportunity to claim any false glory which fighting might have given him.

The *Preston Guardian* describes the circumstances of Steanson's death as 'shocking and mysterious'. There is no doubt that he suffered a horrible, possibly agonising death on a pavement in winter. It probably all began because he was ashamed that he was drunk after having taken the pledge and was hesitant about going back to his lodgings. The evidence which was taken shows that Steanson was not doing much more than hanging around after midnight. About one o'clock he spotted Ann Collett and Barbara Marchant leaving the Griffin Inn. They had been in the Black Swan in Leeming Street until midnight before they moved on to the Griffin Inn.

At this point it is worth looking at these two women on more detail. Ann Collett was a known prostitute and drunkard who ran brothels, firstly in Laurel Street then, sometime after 1861, 5 Blelock Street. In February 1860, for reasons unknown, the landlord of the Rifleman Inn in Water Street, David Mellor, assaulted her when she was leaving his premises with a friend whom Mellor had attacked first. When Collett tried to intervene, he kicked her 'very violently'. He was found guilty in court and sentenced to three weeks in prison for what the magistrates described as 'disgraceful and cowardly conduct'. At the 1861 Census she was 'Head' of the household at 5 Laurel Street, round the corner from Blelock Street, where four unmarried, young women lived who were from various out of town locations. She gave her profession as 'power loom weaver' but this can be discounted as a lie. She died on Thursday 13 January 1870 at her home in Shepherd Street 'very suddenly' at the age of 31. She is described in the *Chronicle*'s report on her inquest, conducted by Myles

Ann Collett was a known prostitute and drunkard who ran brothels

Myers, as 'of light fame … known to have irregular habits … went on drinking sprees … sometimes had delirium tremens'. She had fallen ill after drinking heavily and, because she lived by herself and had no relatives, she was looked after by a woman called Margaret Whiteside[4] for two days before she was found dead in bed. The verdict at the inquest was 'death brought on by habits of intoxication'.

Barbara Marchant, at the 1861 Census, while she was living at 3 Blelock Street, gave her place of birth as 'England', thereby denying connection to any location. It is possible that she ended up in Preston because of the prison system where released prisoners were freed in the town where they had been incarcerated without any means or resources to return to their own locality. She may also have followed a soldier on his travels and ended up being disappointed. In the 1841 Census she appears as a four-year-old, the fourth child of George and Elizabeth Marchant of Thomas Street in the St Leonard's district of Shoreditch, Tower Hamlets. Ten years later, the Census shows that the family had moved to 27 Old Nichol Street, Bethnal Green, Tower Hamlets. Her age is recorded as fourteen and Shoreditch is confirmed as her birthplace.

Prostitutes suffering with the latter stages of syphilis preferred laudanum to alcohol because of its superior analgesic properties

On 14 May 1866, Marchant died in the old workhouse on Deepdale Road, in the last stage of syphilis. She had been plagued by a painful syphilitic ulcer on her leg for three years. She was twenty-eight. These last facts about her venereal disease explain a great deal. On the night Steanson died, Marchant had not been drinking alcohol. The reason for this is that prostitutes suffering with the latter stages of syphilis preferred laudanum to alcohol because of its superior analgesic properties. Her bad-tempered attitude towards Steanson may have been caused by the pain she was in or the dysphoria caused by the laudanum. Hallie Rubenhold states that in tertiary syphilis 'behaviour becomes erratic, if not irrational, inappropriate or violent'.[5] He might, in his drunken state have made a comment about her appearance. Emily Brand asserts that 'sometimes a painted face could barely disguise the rotting frame beneath'. The fate of sick and old prostitutes was shocking. Often, they were kept out of sight and put to household chores. Coincidentally, Marchant gave her occupation in the 1861 Census as a servant, which may not have been far from the truth. Eventually, Emily Brand states, '(they) would be cast out entirely to pine out a diseased existence in some garret or cellar', which was a similar fate as Marchant's at the workhouse.

Myles Myers (1809–1873) presided at Steanson's inquest and was both the coroner and a solicitor. He lived in the select part of Avenham, at 14 Ribblesdale Place, with his sister, Bridget. Both were unmarried. For thirty-five years he was the superintendent of the Parish Church Boys' Sunday School and Mayor of Preston three times (1867–8, 1871–2 and 1872–3). He was also the company chairman of the *Preston Herald*, which might explain two things. Firstly, the *Herald*, which had only been established the year before, printed a detailed report of the inquest and secondly it omitted certain small but interesting details which may have reflected adversely on their chairman. The reports carried by the *Preston Guardian* and the *Sheffield Daily Telegraph* contain these details and ask some probing questions.

According to the evidence heard at the inquest on Friday 1 December 1865, Steanson latched onto Collett, whom he must have known for some time, probably with the intention of sleeping off his intoxication at her house at 5 Blelock Street. Her evidence was useless in the context of the inquest and she summed it up with 'I do not remember anything of what took place during the night. Barbara Marchant took me home'.

Marchant's evidence, therefore, was crucial to the inquest and to our understanding. She said that Collett went to bed after a short time and Steanson got up to go (the *Herald*). The *Preston Guardian* account has some extra detail – Steanson sat in a rocking chair and Marchant testified that she said to him, 'It's getting late, will you go?' To which, Steanson replied, 'In a bit'. Suddenly, Steanson stood up, 'fell sideways into the street down the steps[6] or on his back.' She added, 'No-one pushed him … I went to bed.'

The *Sheffield Daily Telegraph* reports that Steanson opened the door and a woman in the house (Marchant) '… saw him tumble and then shut the door and went to bed'. It continues, '… no-one knows how he received his injuries (see Dr Moore's testimony below) and the supposition entertained by some (is) that they were produced by falling in the street.' Clearly, the reporter for the *Telegraph* doubts that the injuries came from a fall but from something else.

At the inquest, Police Constable Thomas Earnshaw stated that about half past four or twenty-five to five on Thursday morning he found Steanson on his back outside 5 Blelock Street and moved him next door but one. He saw that Steanson's head was 'very much bruised' and 'he was entirely helpless and speechless'. The police had been called to 'quell disturbances' between eleven thirty and midnight in Water Street but Earnshaw could not remember seeing Steanson there, even though Blelock Street was part of his beat. The fact is that patrols were strictly timed on this beat to pass a given point every seventy five minutes. Steanson had been lying in the street, paralysed, for three hours when he should have been passed, not just seen, at least twice. There was a gas lamp at the centre of Blelock Street, near to where the modern streetlight is now which illuminates the street adequately. A short passage in the *Sheffield Daily Telegraph*, but not in the Preston newspapers, possibly not to cause trouble, ran thus:

Steanson had been lying in the street, paralysed, for three hours

> Some of the jury men animadverted (i.e. criticised) on the fact that the deceased should have been allowed remain in

> the streets, helpless and insensible for three hours, and to say the least of it, it does seem strange that the police should have been so long in noticing a dying man in one of those disreputable thoroughfares of the town, where the greatest vigilance and watchfulness should always be exercised.

Perhaps the police did see Steanson and presumed he was drunk. Perhaps, also, they decided that because he had been a nuisance and an embarrassment to all and sundry, and them in particular, they would leave him there to sober up as the weather was dry and fine.

Edwin Moore (1831–1909), the police surgeon, stated that he had first seen Steanson at 8.45am on Thursday 30 November and described his state as 'perfectly helpless and insensible'. He was convinced that Steanson had a fractured skull and was dying. He eventually passed away at 11.45am. Performing the post mortem, Moore found '<u>several marks of violence … recently done</u>' (my underlining).
He found:

> There was a graze on the forehead over the left eye and a graze on the windpipe.
>
> There was a graze on both his knees.
>
> There was a bad bruise on the left leg on the inner part of the shin.
>
> There was a bad wound, a round bruise at the back of the skull and the cut into it was about half an inch into the fleshy part.

When Moore opened his head he found that the skull was fractured about four inches in length. Some of the blood vessels were ruptured and had bled onto the brain which was the cause of death. He seemed uncertain about how the main injury had occurred, but declared that 'if the deceased fell backwards with great weight, the injury might have been done. <u>It might have been caused by a violent blow</u>' (my underlining).

The *Herald* reported that the coroner said the evidence did not show anyone had inflicted the fatal blow. If they

His skull was terribly fractured and he had one or two serious bruises on his knees.

believed the evidence of Barbara Marchant, who seemed to be the only sober witness that knew anything about the matter, the jury's verdict would be that the deceased met his death accidentally. If, on the contrary, they thought that there was a great degree of doubt upon her statement, they might return an open verdict. After a brief consultation, the jury returned a verdict of 'Accidental Death'.

However, the *Sheffield Daily Telegraph* had its doubts.

> His skull was terribly fractured and he had one or two serious bruises on his knees. No-one knows how he received these injuries and the supposition entertained by some that they were produced by falling in the street is only borne out by the testimony of one of the women living in the house where he called who saw him tumble, and then shut the door and went to bed.

The fact is that the verdict of 'Accidental Death' was the best outcome for the authorities, as an 'Open Verdict' would have involved further investigation, which would have been expensive in time and money and would involve, as a result, a more intensive investigation into the activity, or lack of it, by the police in the early hours of Thursday morning. As it was, Steanson was a fallen character, an embarrassment and an unpredictable nuisance. Why should time and money be expended on him? However, the incidents leading up to his death are worth a re-examination.

Witnesses stated that Steanson was drunk, having been drinking in the Sir Walter Scott in North Road, near its junction with Church Street, the Albion vaults and the Griffin Inn. Here, at one o'clock, he met up with Ann Collett. At this point, not only did he know he had drunk too much, but also that he had broken the pledge he had taken in June to avoid alcoholic drink. In Victorian parlance he had 'fallen off the wagon', and as such, was too ashamed to return to his in-laws' house in Everton Garden in his inebriated state. As a result he attached himself to Collett and went back with her to 5 Blelock Street where he hoped to park himself to 'sleep it off'. While they walked the short distance from the Griffin Inn, Marchant walked off ahead on her own. She may have been annoyed because she had been with Collett all evening, only to see Steanson step in at the last minute. It must be remembered that Marchant was a woman with a face disfigured by lesions and pustules, and in pain in her bones from syphilis, which was terminal, and may have been seeking sympathy and friendly reassurance from Collett whom she had known and lived with for some time.

Marchant was a woman with a face disfigured by lesions and pustules, and in pain in her bones from terminal syphilis

On arrival at the house, Collett, who was drunk, said she was tired and went upstairs to bed. As a witness, she was useless because, as an alcoholic, she would, at this stage be suffering from Wernicke-Korsakoff Syndrome[7] which is a deficiency of Vitamin B1 in the brain and a cause of blackout. This may have happened to her in the Griffin Inn when some witnesses said they had seen her asleep, which Marchant had denied. After Collett went upstairs there was no-one downstairs except Steanson and Marchant. Upstairs there were two other women and two other men, as testified by John Roberts who was one of them.

Carl Wernicke discovered Wernicke Encephalopathy in 1881 which is brought on by alcohol abuse and causes paralysed eye movements and mental confusion. About the same time, Sergei Korsakoff discovered Korsakoff Syndrome which is a loss of memory caused by alcohol misuse

From this point, the only testimony available is Marchant's. She stated that Steanson had sat in a rocking chair, presumably to try and recover from his intoxicated state before he went home. Obviously annoyed, she said, 'It's getting late, will you go?' His answer 'In a bit' must have annoyed her further, so she attacked him, causing the graze over his left eye and on his windpipe. He must have got up to go, possibly opening the door. At this point, Steanson suddenly fell down the steps. Marchant is reported as saying 'he went sideways or on his back' (*Preston Guardian*) and he 'fell sideways, not on his face ... No-one pushed him' (*Herald*).

If Steanson had fallen sideways or on his back, his injuries would have been different. Falling down three small steps would not take a person backwards as the momentum is forward. That is why his knees were recently grazed. As a former soldier and policeman, even with his dissipated habits, he would have had enough strength and balance to fall or stumble down the steps, not to lie insensible and in agony in the street. If he had fallen backwards, he would have fallen backwards into the threshold and the bruise would have been linear in nature and appearance. Dr Moore found a deep bruise about four inches in diameter and a cut which penetrated half an inch into the fleshy part of the head where blood vessels were ruptured causing bleeding into the brain. He strongly suggested that the injury 'might have been caused by a violent blow'. The evidence points to the fact that Marchant had hit him, very hard and in anger, possibly with a doorstop. This would make him stumble forward, possibly knocking partially insensible, causing him to tread heavily on the inside of his left ankle with his right foot before falling onto his knees in the street before collapsing. Marchant then closed the door without looking, which is unusual, but she was angry, in pain and possibly afraid to look at what she had done.

Steanson died of an edema caused by a cranial contusion. Trauma brain injury, stated by the Mayo Foundation,[8] can result in prolonged or permanent changes in a person's state of consciousness, awareness or responsiveness. In a vegetative state, the person may be aware of surroundings, open their eyes and respond to reflexes. In a minimally conscious state, a person would suffer severely altered consciousness with some signs of awareness, which is similar to Steanson's condition after the impact. As it was, he all but died on the pavement in Blelock Street, being 'helpless and speechless' for three hours. This was a dreadful way to die and a terrible indictment of the worst aspects of Victorian life, such as utilitarianism, lack of compassion and the prevailing *laissez faire* attitude. This period was a disastrous time to be poor, and poverty took many forms: mental, spiritual and material, any one of which could tip people like Steanson, Collett and Marchant into that awful, downward spiral from which there was little chance of escape.

James Steanson is buried in the Church of England section of Preston Cemetery. With him are his children, Charles and Rachel, and his estranged wife, Isabella who died in 1888. Margaret is buried in a public grave in another part of the Cemetery.

Shepherd Street and Water Street
(O.S. 1849 60in to 1 mile)

5

'THE BLACK PARTS OF PRESTON'

THE WORD 'BLACK' HERE WOULD have a fairly wide interpretation in Preston in the 1860s. During the autumn of 1861 there were proposals being put forward to bring back horse racing to Preston. Racing on the Moor had discontinued in 1833 and on Penwortham Holme in 1846. A local person, not particularly against the idea, wrote to the editor of the *Chronicle* under the unimaginative pseudonym of 'A Prestonian'. How far his/her views are exaggerated is difficult to judge but the remarks expressed give an insight into Preston at the time, especially when read with other contemporary remarks. The correspondent starts by making the point that bringing racing back to the town would not encourage more immorality than existing events or festivals, as others have suggested, and continues, 'there is more drunkenness and debauchery carried on at our annual fair on Whit Monday.' Further on, he/she cites the circus held regularly on the Orchard,

> ... which is in reality a disgrace to the town ... Night after night this place is attended by the very young of both sexes, and the disgusting language and immodest behaviour of those boys and girls is horrid. I don't know that the proprietors are aware of it, but I mean to say, that there have been scores of young girls, through attending this

> cursed place, thrown on the streets of the town as common prostitutes.

The letter ends with the writer calling for everyone to cast aside social and religious divisions and bring philanthropy through donating money.

Other 'black' places were shown up in a weekly journal. In 1843, Joseph Hansom, the architect of St Walburge's church in Preston, Birmingham Town Hall and other buildings and the designer of the hansom cab, launched a building trade magazine called *The Builder* which ran until 1966 under that name. During the editorship of George Godwin, the magazine sent writers out to explore and examine the roads and buildings of Britain, town by town, in a detailed and authentic manner. In December 1861 it was Preston's turn. *The Builder*'s findings covered seven columns on 7 December and six columns on 14 December. The first instalment is entitled 'A Cotton Factory Town: Preston' and the second, 'The Black Parts of Preston'.

The first section opens with a favourable description of Fishergate, written as if a person were going out for a walk. The impression given is commendable with a few deficiencies pointed out, such as the Coroner's Court building in Winckley Street being 'shabby, dirty and old', the Grammar School in Cross Street where 'the four corners (of the playground are) converted into urinals by the boys and 'Lune Street is 'scandalously in want of scavenage (street cleaning)', 'a neighbourhood of bonded warehouses … and all the doorposts are made use of as urinals'.

The writer forms a good impression of the Market Place as 'a handsome, roomy, parallelogram surrounded on two sides by shops, inns and a hotel'. He recommends the rebuilding of the 1782 Town Hall (which was already in hand) and all the east side with its narrow courts and shambles (butcher's shops) being demolished to improve the area. This all happened, eventually. On this eastern side where many licensed premises were such as the Blue Anchor, the Swan With Two Necks and the Shakespeare, came in for some criticism.

> The gutters in the market place run with slops thrown out of the houses in the courts around; channels cross the pavement in Clayton-court – channels from urinals in a passage to the Blue Anchor – channels in a passage to Strait Shambles – all furnish tributaries to the stream down the market kennel (an open drain or sewer). Wilcockson's-court does the same: Ginbow-entry, leading to the Wheatsheaf and the White Hart, brings down the swimmings from exposed urinals and stable muck; and washings from the shambles are flowing down the livelong day.

When the writer reached the Shambles on Lancaster Row, where the Miller Arcade now stands on Lancaster Road, almost in view of the Sandhole, he was not impressed, stating that 'the whole place has an uncouth and unclean appearance.'

The whole place has an uncouth and unclean appearance.

The second instalment was published in full on 18 December 1861 by the *Chronicle* using the original heading of 'The Black Parts of Preston'. In this section, the writer starts his promenade in Maudlands and moves over to St Peter's district where a graveyard is discovered full to overflowing and insanitary conditions almost everywhere. Back at Fishergate the writer passes the

> fine rebuilt parish church … which is surrounded by miserable dwellings … and at the end of an adjacent site called Graystocks-yard and St John's-place there are a series of ruinous privies (toilets) and a pit of huge dimensions which appears to serve the whole of the churchyard district.

After making some encouraging remarks about the Bull Inn and the Royal Hotel, the writer moves further west: 'Church Street resolves itself into a poorer district, in which the three golden balls of the pawnbrokers are pretty frequent signs. As the roads and pavements are badly kept and swept, we are surprised to pass the office of the Board of Health here.'

The office had obviously been set up there as the place where it was most needed.

The writer's progress is steady but just when the reader expects him to turn right into Water Street and examine the Sandhole, he moves further on and turns up Grimshaw Street instead. This is highly suspicious. Perhaps he was being chaperoned and was shepherded into less dangerous territory. At the end of Grimshaw Street he visits Queen Street and sees the courts running out of it. 'There is a sprinkling of rag and bone stores, old brass and copper stores, a small shop where "herb, ginger, bitter and nettle-beer" are sold: then there are more rag shops and we are out upon London-road.'

Before finishing his report, he makes two comments which are pertinent to the condition of Preston and its people.

> Facing Preston, on our return (i.e. from Ribbleton), the town presents a most curious aspect – not a house, tower, or spire is visible; but in their places there are countless jets of dense smoke darting up into the sky, rocket fashion, and these diffusing into heavy clouds cast a threatening aspect over the landscape as of a coming storm.
>
> The enlisting sergeant will tell you that there are more recruits to be had in Preston than in any other town: but they are so weak from their tea and bread diet that it takes two years to feed them up … the men of Preston are done at forty; at forty five they are old and done.

Despite these conditions and being in the grip of the Cotton Famine and with 11,420 people claiming poor relief tickets that week, the 1862 Guild Merchant celebrations from Monday 1 September to Saturday 6 September went very well and were a great success. Although one in seven of the town population of 82,985 was out of work, the town was flooded by visitors. Six hundred thousand people visited on the Thursday for the Catholic and Trades Processions. The Trades Procession had 2,400 men 120 horses and 35 carriages and coaches in it. The Catholic Guilds were eleven in number and 4,500 members walked through the streets with bands and banners. The day before, the Friendly Societies had walked in procession. Needless to say, the nearest the week's walks came to the Sandhole and its environs was Church Street.

Robert Pateson's image of Preston railway station

Just before the 1862 Guild, the Preston photographer, Robert Pateson, produced an image of Preston Railway Station. Considering that he was producing a portfolio of masterly topographical and landscape photographs, many of which were shown at the 1861 Great Exhibition, this is a very odd choice. The station was only remarkable for its decrepit and dilapidated appearance. The roof, for instance, looks to be in the early stages of collapse. The reason for this decay was that two railway companies ran operations from the station and each regarded the other as responsible for is upkeep. The image shows a ground level wooden walkway across the tracks because there were no bridges or subways for passengers to use to leave and enter the station. As a result, all the visitors who came to by train Preston for the Guild had to use this walkway.

It is possible that the person who promoted the photograph being taken was the journalist, Anthony Hewitson, who was a friend of Pateson's. On 23 May 1863, Hewitson published a rant, a column of criticism in the *Chronicle* under his professional nom-de-plume of 'Atticus', under the heading of 'Everyday Gossip', which it turned out to be much more. The first part was taken up with a string of complaints about the railway station, together with some stinging comments. The second part was concerned with prostitutes.

He opens by recalling the recent publication of the town's bye laws and wondered if anyone had read them.

At the bottom of page 27 there is one which relates to prostitution.

> *'That if any common prostitute, or night walker shall, within the said borough, loiter or be in any street for the purpose of prostitution, or for the purpose of solicitation, to the annoyance of any inhabitant, or passenger ... shall, for every offence, forfeit and pay a fine of ten shillings* (£46).'

He continues,

> How often during the last twelve months have the lackered [*sic*], brass faced hussies of Preston paid the fine for impudent profligacy and shameless indecency?
>
> For a long period our thoroughfares have almost swarmed at nights with lewd, debauched females – with old, filthy hags who have used their years in badness and with young girls, just reaching the blush of adolescence, whose future can be nothing better than an incardinated purgatory of sin. How long is this to last?

Our thoroughfares have almost swarmed at nights with lewd, debauched females – with old, filthy hags who have used their years in badness and with young girls, just reaching the blush of adolescence

> [No-one is] safe while walking on the streets. The good are taken for the bad; the vile for the innocent.
>
> In Fishergate – in the very best street in the town – this abominable vice of hireling appeal and lascivious banter seems to undergo a deification every night. Let anyone disputing this just walk down our main thoroughfare any night in the week between nine and eleven, and, if double distilled proof ...
>
> How is it that such a scandalous piece of business is tolerated?

From here, Hewitson alters his tack slightly, by attacking the reluctance of the Corporation to act and the consequent inaction of the police. He does not hold back, and it might be from this point that the magistrates gradually, with the emphasis on 'gradually', begin to change the situation. This article could be seen as a spur or catalyst for others to join in by writing similar articles or letters in attempts to prompt action, or just to take direct action themselves.

He continues,

> The police and Corporation make a big enough noise about some things: they are infinitesimally punctilious about silly, little, pettifogging street obstacles; they grow lurid and armnipotent [i.e. omnipotent] with rage if a few egg boxes or butter mugs, or bales of calico are exposed on the parapets [i.e. kerbs] for an hour or two: and they have sworn by nine tenths of the church that no-one shall "roll, draw, drive, drag or carry on any footpath any hogshead, cask, barrel, tub, ladder, sack or fadge [i.e. a loose bale of wool]" without being liable to a fine of £5 [£469 in 2018], and yet they allow, in the teeth of a condemnatory bye law, a bigger nuisance, a more flagrant obstacle to the true welfare of the town than all of the grievances in their municipal statute book put together, to revel the whole night through, all year round, without ever instituting one practical step for its removal.

Hewitson does not pull his punches and places responsibility at the door of the Corporation. The last paragraph could hardly be described as 'everyday gossip'!

> The Council daren't for the sake of their own reputation, abrogate it [i.e. the bye law] and therefore they must – they are bound – to give it effect. Idiots only make regulations which are never put into operation. Put the law into force; it has an honest ring to it and it means decency and virtue ... stir up the police for they are sleepy as December hedgehogs about the whole affair and lots of them may be seen any dark night hobnobbing and conversing blandly with filthy, flirting women and dirty

Stir up the police for they are sleepy as December hedgehogs ... and may be seen any dark night hobnobbing and conversing blandly with filthy, flirting women and dirty back-alley jades.

> back-alley jades. Let that 'fine of ten shillings' be exacted in all cases – let none off. Bring all the dead-beating syrens 'to the scratch' [i.e. bring them to book]

As a precursor to other written exhortations in the form of letters or newspaper articles, Hewitson's rant is important and is a wake-up call for many to take up the same struggle against immorality on the streets. Some sympathy must be felt for the police who were working with magistrates who were obviously reluctant to act and perhaps community policing was too far in the future for Hewitson to appreciate. However, he came to the conclusion, as others did, that better and compulsory education was the answer, thus concurring with Rev. John Clay thirty years before. In a different sense then, even Fishergate could be regarded, at this stage at least, as a black place.

By the 1860s, the interest in reading about the world at large and events nearer their doorstep prompted more and more Preston people to buy newspapers like the *Chronicle*, the *Herald*, the *Preston Guardian* and the *Preston Pilot*. Competition between them was fierce. As a result of interest provoked by Hewitson it seemed inevitable that one of the periodicals would undertake some social investigations. These usually took the form of a journey into places usually avoided by the majority of townsfolk and gave a brief insight into lives being led there. In London in the early 1850s, Charles Dickens had made forays into Saffron Hill, Field Lane, Whitechapel and the St Giles slum area, published as 'On Duty With Inspector Field'.

Heather Shore,[1] in the *BBC History Magazine* of March 2019, states that 'Uninspiringly these were areas often associated with manufacturing and industrial development, high levels of population mobility, overcrowding, sub-standard housing a proliferation of lodging houses.'

This was mainly true of the Sandhole area and, in general, in other areas such as the courts running off Friargate and its satellite streets and the area immediately behind or to the north of the Adelphi public house.

The *Chronicle* sent one of their correspondents, named only as 'B', to investigate locations of interest in the town which may be anathema to most but would satisfy the curiosity of the many. The first article, published on 28 January 1865, under the general title '"Life" in Preston' and subtitled 'No I Gay[2] Life and Concert Halls'. B opens by stating that a stranger in Preston might get the idea that, despite its staple trade (cotton) and its large population, that the town was one of the 'quietest and best behaved places in Lancashire', but, he continues, 'the surface is very fair, but below the surface there is much which shock and appal'.

He announces to the reader his intention to tell the truth, to show things as they really are in places where people were prepared 'to go to extremes … Sensitive people will find much that is coarse … such people will find in these papers much that is far from pleasing, but the realities exist … If we offend any we shall be sorry, for we shall speak the truth.'

The next phase is a blast against prostitutes who cause young men to have 'a devotion worthy of a better cause' – as if these men did not have a choice! B does not say that Preston is any worse at night than any other town of a similar size – 'the police regulations are too admirable for that'. He does ask, however, 'is it not possible for a man to walk the distance from the Parish Church and the Theatre (which once stood on the corner of Theatre Street J.G.) without being accosted and stopped by numbers of girls, many of whom are of an age which a girl is considered a child?' He adds that the Orchard and Friargate are 'infested by "bonnetless girls"' and invites a 'thoughtful man' to walk the town at night to prove him wrong that there are 'scores of children' on the streets of Preston.

Orchard and Friargate are infested by 'bonnetless girls'

B invites the reader to consider 'the horrible life of these children and of the still more horrible future awaiting them'. He affirms that we would not allow this sort of existence in foreign places, so why should we allow it here? He expresses the hope that this article and the two which follow will be the start of the removal of this evil. He talks about the souls of these children not being laid to 'our account' (i.e. the *Chronicle*'s) if nothing is done about it.

He emphasises that he has no intention of being hard on 'unfortunates'. 'Heaven knows their life is sad and horrible enough, bearing with it its own terrible punishment in a loveless lot, an early death, a workhouse's hell and an unhonoured grave upon which rank weeds are allowed to grow.'

When his path crosses with them in the articles he says he shall 'speak of her gently' but go no further because 'it is the duty of a journalist to watch.'[3]

Removing one set of 'children' would cause others to fill the vacancies

The bye laws are strict enough, the writer says, but a policeman's command to 'move on' is not enough and that these children should be removed altogether. 'Their miserable lives are not necessary to the well being, so something must be done.' he realises that removing one set of 'children' would cause others to fill the vacancies, 'yet we argue that something might be done.'

He feels strongly that something could be done for the 120 women and girls who are known to the police as being 'on the streets'. As a result he proposes that Preston money should be spent here, in the town, rather than 'teaching savages to consume English spirits and the British way of decimating a population.'

In the rest of the article, B sets out to sample some of the entertainment provided by concert halls of the time. He begins by visiting a 'place of amusement within a hundred miles of Water Street', thus laying out his consistent method, used throughout all three articles of avoiding being specific about people and places. After scanning the advertising hoardings outside the place with a sceptical eye, he enters and finds that the claims made were 'bunkum' and the whole night's entertainment was 'as wearisome a thing as anyone could imagine'. One observation he did make, however, was a situation which the Chief Inspectors of police of this decade and later, Mr Dunn and Mr Oglethorpe, deplored. 'The rough seats were occupied by about seventy or eighty 'lads and lasses of the cotton operative class'. The girls were 'gaudily dressed ... [and] supping the porter they had received on paying their entry.' After some scathing remarks about the acts on show, B felt that one objection that should be made against concert halls like this is 'the youth of its patrons. 'What good can a lad, what good is a girl likely to receive in such haunts?' He makes his opinion very clear. 'It is probable that neither lad nor girl can frequent such a place without suffering in character or morals.' His judgement on the situation is that 'proprietors of public places of amusement of the character of the above have no business to admit children.'

On a visit to a concert hall in Back Lane (now Market Street West), he is equally sarcastic about the quality of the acts. He uses the type of audience he encounters here as a comparison to the first as a means of emphasising his argument.

> the audience, quiet and well behaved, consisted of respectable grown up people, not children, and apparently not a single fille publique [prostitute] was present. We have nothing to say against such an audience ... whereas an audience of children ... is only too willing to take lessons in pollution.

The *Chronicle* published 'Life in Preston; No II – Twopenny Hops'[4] on 11 February 1865. B opens, in a roundabout way, by describing how dancing is a wholesome activity. His opinion is that the recreations that the working class can indulge in are 'but few in number'. He then lists the main ones; 'the public house, the singing room with its well puffed attractions, the dancing room and you have enumerated almost all the places they are welcome.'

As an alternative he suggests 'Penny Readings' of which he cannot speak too highly, but they are like 'angels' visits, very few and far between and fill up only the odd evening.' There are Temperance Halls which he finds difficult to recommend. Taking the one in Preston as an example, he discovers that '... a dirtier or more unattractive place ... it would be difficult to find.' He also finds little about the activities there to entice an audience or attract people away from the evils of drink, saying that anyone 'must have superhuman patience … to attend … for a couple of hours listening to illogical twaddle'.

On the other hand, he praises the new working men's clubs which were doing their best to provide healthy and pure recreation. If only the 'old advocates of teetotalism had … offered the working man pure amusement in exchange for impure, their cause would offer greater power and influence and win more respect.'. In the future, those authorities which offered 'amusements and entertainments in opposition to the life and moral sapping activities offered in the Sandhole' would win people, men especially, over. These would include the Shepherd Street Mission and the work done by the Anglican parishes of St Saviour and St James and the Catholic parish of St Augustine. B continues by suggesting 'there should be evenings of music, dancing parties, dinner parties and scores of other things.' This kind of entertainment encouraging a sense of belonging would soon be promoted by the parishes. B further warns: 'if they don't find cheap and pure amusements for him [i.e. the working man], others will provide him with cheap and nasty ones. If they had not left a gap in the fence, the pig would not have got to the flowerbed.'

B turns his attention to hops or dances which were attended by young people. He, and an unnamed companion, set out to visit a few of these 'cheap hops', his first comment being that 'there are too many'. Their tour begins on a Saturday night, while the market is in its last hour of trading, searching out the less than salubrious area near the Parish Church (i.e. the outer reach of the Sandhole). He asks why the environs of the older, sacred buildings of northern towns should be populated by what he describes as 'a nest of sins'. The answer to this may be that the buildings are older and more decrepit than outlying areas of the town, and many people with money had already left to live a carriage ride away from the centre.

At the chosen venue, a few steps from the Church, he comments that the room is 'very dirty' and needs 'a little whitewash'. An old union flag hangs 'miserably' on the wall in 'disconsolate uncleanliness'. A long seat is occupied by boys wearing white comforters while the girls were 'permitted to stand or lean against the wall'. The air is 'impregnated by oil and perspiration' as the room became more crowded, which he suggests why the band sounded 'asthmatic' and playing 'instrumental shrieks and groans'. Girls were dancing together in an enthusiastic way, while some boys danced together, 'one being the teacher and the other the pupil.'

The whole place was very crowded, so that each pair of dancers had only 'three square feet of ground in which to go through quadrilles and the lancers.' Thirty years earlier, Rev. John Clay had criticised dancing for its closeness between dancers, especially when formation dances, which involved moving in lines and circles became overshadowed by the outlandish and scandalous waltz. B makes a similar judgement with a sideswipe at fashion. Because of the fashion which was popular with women at the time for wide crinoline skirts, the dancers were 'jostling each other ... such a thing is not compatible with decency, as we were compelled to witness'. As far as he is concerned, 'the whole affair was coarse; the talk was vile slang, the atmosphere was impure, and yet there were Sunday School scholars [B's emphasis]' recognised by his companion. Therefore, B declares that this sort of activity is no preparation for the Sabbath.

He returns to the theme of his first article by again asking the question,

> What becomes of the girls who frequent it? Do they grow up into fair young English women and become mothers of happy children or do they change into those miserable beings who reside in houses close by? Mothers of happy families? One hundred and twenty girls obtained affiliation summonses[5] at the Preston police office during the year ending 28 September 1864. If anyone can convince us that dancing rooms had nothing to do with the fall of these girls we shall be glad; as it is, the inference to anyone who has visited these hops is obvious and irresistible.

Later, he visits another hop, not far from the Market, which is of an even lower class than the first and this only reinforces his convictions.

In conclusion, he feels that it is against English liberty to suppress such places, so he suggests instituting similar venues where 'profanity, coarseness and vice would not be allowed entrance'. He claims that this would reduce the number of girls who would be thrown on the streets. He makes his reasoning clear.

It is not the dancing. We do not object to that, it is the company and the terrible licence allowed

> It is not the dancing. We do not object to that, it is the company and the terrible licence allowed. Little by little, the girl loses her modesty and the end is sure and certain ... after her life of vice with its daily battlings with hunger, and her wretched death in the workhouse infirmary.

B maintains that that is all below the surface. Above the surface for all to see is 'simply a place licensed according to some Georgian Act [of Parliament] for music and dancing ... here at home it is so hard to create any interest in the temptations of our own ... when there are [natives] at a distance of thousands of miles still remaining uninitiated in the British arts of destroying themselves. Above all the cant of society will one day be heard that terrible question, "Where is Abel, thy brother?"'

Some readers may find B pessimistic and prudish, but what does come through is a definite, almost desperate blast against the laissez-faire and therefore uncaring attitude of this era where one mistake, could become a complete downfall, especially for young women. For the modern reader it is a revelation because it gives a truthful insight into the popular amusement frequented by young working-class people. It is also a valuable, almost invaluable, insight into the lives of ordinary Prestonians living three generations beyond living memory. For his third and final journey, B ventured into the Sandhole itself.

'Life in Preston No III – Haunts of Vice and Crime' was published in the *Chronicle* on 25 February 1865 and is the most extensive and comprehensive description of the Sandhole in print. B's method here is to use a documentary form of investigation which became the staple of television programmes well over a hundred years later. His descriptions need little comment but, despite what he said in the first article about journalists just watching, he often comments as he reports.

In the introduction, B invites us to go for a walk or a 'ramble' with him. He has a companion who remains anonymous, though he appears to have some authority or gravitas, which becomes apparent at one point. He warns us that 'such things that we will see in the course of this ramble cannot exist without, in some way or other, working a terrible question upon those who have the power to remove or prevent them without festering throughout society.'

'We have not left the Parish Church a very few yards behind before we see we are in a "low" neighbourhood'. As in the first two articles, B is vague about specific places and people remain anonymous. However, if he walked down Stoneygate he would come to Shepherd Street and, turning left, he would be able to see Library Street, then Rose Street to his left, the Black Swan in the distance right ahead of him and Laurel Street to his right, which leads to Blelock Street, Oak Street and Greaves Street.

> The very houses have a drunken, unshaven look; their dirty steps and doorways are hardly to be distinguished from the roadway, both being equally unclean; the walls crumbling, the doors full of marks, suspiciously like the result of kicks and the windows patched with cheap and nasty material ... it is only the headquarters of dirt, vice and sin; the court of the Fever King, Devil-dom, or to give it its Christian name, 'Behind the Church'.

It is ... the headquarters of dirt, vice and sin; the court of the Fever King, Devil-dom, or to give it its Christian name, 'Behind the Church'

In the next section, B leans heavily on the use of the senses.

> It is a very bitter night, but in spite of the frost, the atmosphere is very sickly and hang dog smells lurk about, pouncing upon you unawares at corners and as you pass wretched doorways. Women and men pass us, poverty

> shining out of their glaring eyes and the mark of Cain[6] upon their dirt-begrimed brows.

Here B returns to his theme of inevitability.

> The children look emaciated and sickly, with old heads upon young and already weary shoulders, and little faces upon which Hunger has drawn deep lines of care, appearing exactly what they are, young fruit ripening for the jail, the convict ship and the hangman's fine touch. A neighbourhood like this brings forth such fruit as naturally as a plant sends forth its flowers.

Earlier in this project it was suggested that when a Victorian person said something stank, it really did stink because they were used to fouler smells than people are nowadays. B continues with this idea and some outrage.

> This horrible lack of pure air, these vile smells, these dirty homes: what man or woman can bear them without the aid of gin? We are very strong on moderation etc, Mr Magistrate, but if we were doomed to exist in such a locality we should sell ourselves, body and soul for a drink; and no wonder, we should end as people do in such places, by dying drunk, by dying drunk over, and fought over and in being carried away to a grassy cemetery where a white robed minister would bury us in consecrated ground, and as his 'dear departed brother', expressing his 'sure and certain hope of joyful resurrection' although he never came to see us when we were battling and struggling with the devil upon ground anything but consecrated.

As far as the writer is concerned, there is a clear indication of neglect and lack of care on the part of the authorities here and the suspicion that there was an unspoken policy of containment being put into practice so that the activities in the Sandhole did not spread. On his night venture into this area, B would not have seen 'ministers' there, but a number of poor parishioners of St Augustine's lived cheek by jowl with this situation and were cared for.

From this point in his account, B describes the types of people that he and his companion encountered.

> When we get a little further we find women – if we may apply the word to such beings. They assail us with a storm of 'maquerellage'[7] but catching a glance of our friend they assume a somewhat more decent speech. Their clothing is not of a very expensive nature, chiefly coloured prints, and in some cases dresses are dispensed with – perhaps under the pressure – but they group themselves in somewhat scanty attire, conversing in slang of an intense nature.

B and his companion move on and enter some houses to speak to people and form an impression of their living conditions.

> In one or two houses men are seated by the fire and their close cropped hair and general hangdog appearance say that they have just come out of jail and it will not be long until they return to it. It is evident that they are ready for anything from pitch and toss [which was illegal] to manslaughter. They are, to use poor Otway's[8] marvellous sentence, 'rascals who undervalue damnation'. What kind of mothers had them we wonder? Anything like these women here, who hover about them in a coarse, yet for them a loving sort of way.
>
> After a few sullen replies to some rather personal queries made by my friend, they fall into the old, listless attitude, gazing into the fire blankly and taking no notice of the women who occupy themselves in warming their feet in that manner which is peculiar to ladies.

Bracebridge Hemyng's description of a bully, quoted earlier, certainly holds good here in the dazed shiftlessness portrayed in these men. The women, for all their coarseness, seem to be more actively in charge and involved in the 'business'. From here, B and his companion move on to 'a low beerhouse', which is unnamed.

> There are three persons in the kitchen, two females and one

> man. One of the women of the genus tramp, is seated at a small table, shuffling a dirty pack of cards, telling her own fortune. The man, a fine specimen of humanity, so far as muscular development goes but whose body is surmounted by the head of the battered bulldog class, is smoking a long pipe in front of the fire.

The third person is rather a surprise and a shock at the same time; an enigma. What brought a person like that to a place like this? Perhaps she is an unwilling participant trapped in the downward spiral.

> The other girl sits in a rocking chair at one side of the hearth, and it at once strikes me that she is a 'being of a different order' to those whom she consorts. There is something in her appearance which, for the want of a better name, is generally termed 'ladylike', a gentleness of face and figure according but ill with the fierce aspect of the fortune teller and the brutal look of the man. She seems ashamed to be seen in such a place, as well she might be for parents are sorrowing for her night and day and she has known what a home of luxury was.

From here the 'ramble' continues because dancing has finished, and B wants to experience that activity in full swing. He moves on, 'trusting our guide's knowledge of this place, we go down steps, and up steps, into cellars and rooms, in almost every one of which vice and crime are strongly represented.' He is led to a place where some dancing is taking place.

> In one, lowly, dirty room of a beerhouse, crowded with young men and low prostitutes, a fiddler is scraping away industriously and perspiringly at an old fiddle and a girl is step dancing in the centre of the dirty floor. In another beerhouse, fiddling and singing are the order of the night; in every one it is vice with the paint off for most, if not all, of the men are thieves or worse, and the women, without exception, are prostitutes of the lowest and most depraved class, rejoicing in such pet names (all known to our official friend) as, 'White-Faced Bet', 'One Armed Sal', 'Heart o'Christ' etc. Here they are plying their horrid vocation, drinking almost fiercely and vomiting forth slang and blasphemy in licensed premises [B's emphasis].

As he and his companion move about the house, B is more than surprised by what they see. He does not hesitate to comment, despite his earlier declaration 'the duty of a journalist is to watch'.

> In a front room a man, a woman and their family are grouped round the fire. A nice place for children is it not? These girls grow up only into prostitutes. 'Broad is the way'[9] before them and they cannot miss it. They need no wicked young lords, no gay [in the 1860s sense] seducers or any of the novel writer's stock in trade to secure their fall: they must live and if they do not take to the horrible life by instinct and through example, their mothers will send them out for it.

Despite his condemnatory comments, he does show compassion here for those trapped in a circle of vice. He is sad that this way of life is perpetuated through families and how the girls are set on this predetermined path of prostitution, illustrated by the statement 'they must live', presumably without much education and certainly no other prospects.

He is sad that this way of life is perpetuated through families and how the girls are set on this predetermined path of prostitution

There were a number of lodging houses in the Sandhole, of various sizes. Three of them were owned by an Irishman called James Traynor. Two of them were in Leeming Street and one in Shepherd Street. There were others, but Traynor was the only one who dared to advertise occasionally in the Preston commercial directories of the 1860s. On the night of the 1871 Census, his lodging house at 20 Shepherd Street had eight members of his family in it and thirty lodgers. B decides to look at some examples of this type of establishment.

> We enter several 'lodging houses', but we are too early. There is nothing going on but frying and frizzling of all sorts of dainty titbits. Congregations of all sorts of men, women and children are gathered in the 'thieves'' kitchen.
>
> In all of these are scales [with] which the proprietor weighs the bread etc, begged by the tramps during the day, before he purchases it. Heaps of 'broken victuals' show that the beggars have been tolerably successful, and the fact that the

> tramps in most cases will not eat what is given to them is, we should think, a good argument in favour of systematic benefice [a benefit system].

If the sitting and eating conditions are not bad enough, B goes on to investigate the sleeping arrangements.

> In these places, lads, women, men, girls, beggars, thieves, tramps, vagabonds and prostitutes sleep together, without respect to age or any distinction of sex, huddling in imperfectly ventilated rooms and taking off their clothes before retiring to rest, on account of the vermin.

Which concurs with Kellow Chesney's remarks on the subject:[10]

> Often several couples slept in the same room and might vary their entertainment by changing partners during the night. In hot weather the parasites in their clothes and bedding, and the stifling atmosphere, made lodgers of both sexes lie on top of the beds – entirely naked – a powerful indication of how far they had abandoned all standards if one considers contemporary notions about nakedness, which were common to every class.

What sort of damaging effect did this way of sleeping have on the children? James Walvin has no doubts:

> For the poor, the sexual realities of adult life for, living with brothers, sisters and parents in overcrowded and squalid conditions, the sexual activities of parents and siblings could be seen, heard and even felt. And for children spared such experiences, the streets of urban Britain presented similarly unavoidable evidence of human sexuality.[11]

The assault on B's senses, through sights sounds and smells encountered by his ramble obviously have a debilitating effect on him.

> We begin to be sick at heart. We have seen enough and emerge into Church Street [presumably from Water Street], feeling sadly out of sorts, and depressed, for we cannot forget the horrible things we have seen, and yet, reader, <u>we have seen them at their best</u> [B's emphasis]. Picture the worst for

> yourself, if you please; we could not do so in the columns of this journal.

From here he ventures on a train of thought, searching for a set of remedies and thereby perceives the dichotomy of Victorian secular and religious life. The secular being the attitude that work and position were the mainstay of life and that poverty was almost a crime, as Judith Flanders says, 'prisons and slums were equated in people's minds: the prisons housed the criminally poor; the slums merely the poor.'[12] And David Gange, 'Removed from the view of the wealthy, who knew as little of the slums as the South Sea Islands, this degradation was nonetheless necessary to support their leisured existence.'[13] Those who were officially there for the welfare of the poor, the Guardians, used the 1834 Poor Law Act to the letter. Gone was the chance of outdoor relief as a means of earning some money during a time of temporary unemployment, only the hated workhouse was allowed to give any assistance in conditions worse than the poorest house outside.

As far as the religious life was concerned, it was the strict following of strict rules and blindly adhering to dogma, rather than following Christ's message of befriending the poorest and the despised. B blasts the situation where the Parish Church is half filled by the well-to-do, though no-one from its staff seems to have anything to do with the Sandhole. Anthony Hewitson, under his pseudonym Atticus, comments about the curates of the times as 'one has a better position and is going to it and the other one would like one if he could get it.' Unlike Methodist ministers or Catholic priests, Anglican ministers could almost pick and choose where they worked. The Vicar, John Owen Parr is described by Atticus as having a 'certain amount of narrowness' and was 'exacting towards Dissenters' and 'violent in his hatred of Catholics'.[14] In fact, in the *Chronicle* and the *Herald* of the weeks B was walking round

> *Rather than following Christ's message of befriending the poorest and the despised … the Parish Church is half filled by the well-to-do … no-one from its staff seems to have anything to do with the Sandhole*

the town, Canon Parr was reported as having strenuous arguments with Methodists in various Bible discussions, but not making an appearance in the poor area less than two minutes' walk from his church. In 1869, the annual stipend of the Vicar of Preston was £850 (£77,120) and there was a free residence on East Cliff, built in 1841. Parr was the Vicar from 1840–77. B continues:

> We believe that one of the most impossible tasks in the world is of rousing the religious public to a due sense of the importance of anything at home. Get up a society for sending the 'glad tidings of the Gospel of Salvation' to Kamschatka [*sic*] and friends will be rapidly forthcoming. The dear foreigners are so interesting, and so far off and so benighted, and our English lower orders so horribly near, and so well taught! Are they? Would to God that they had the 'means of grace' showered so unwisely upon the inhabitants of the South Sea Islands. We need missionaries in our own streets, – not cowardly men who are afraid and refuse to visit such places as through which we have taken our readers, but men who have the good of their fellows at heart.

Having provided his 1865 readers, and us, with hard evidence, he looks for remedies. 'The evil requires to be put down with a strong hand, and we shall venture to suggest one or two means to be employed.' He shows sympathy with the 'poor man and his family' with 'no other place to go than lodging houses. There are too many forced to go to such places for shelter' and they would not go there 'if they could go to a respectable place for the same outlay.' He reveals the number of people who were 'lodged and entertained' in registered lodging houses in Preston in the year ending on 29 September 1864 as 80,300.

He deplores the houses of vice in the town 'of which there are 182, including twenty-seven houses of receivers of stolen goods, thirty one public houses, twenty five beerhouses, two coffee shops and six "suspect houses" <u>all of which are known resorts of thieves and prostitutes</u> [my emphasis] and sixty one brothels'. He wonders why the law is not applied against them. He seems to think that churchwardens would put a stop to it all by starting proceedings against keepers of houses of ill fame.

> Are not the brothels and worst holes through which we have escorted our readers sufficiently near to the parish church? We venture to say that everyone of them is within a stone's throw from the sacred edifice.

It is uncertain here whether B is being entirely serious. It is difficult to see how volunteers who looked after the church could have had much of an impact. Churchwardens aside, perhaps this is another criticism of the Vicar, his staff and their complete lack of presence in this place.

He turns on the magistrates and asks why the keepers of licensed premises mentioned above, all known to the police, are allowed to keep their licences. He says that in other places, cafes are under threat of constant prosecution because they allow 'a few gay women [in the 1860s sense]' in and asks why Preston should be any different 'and why upon earth should the exception be in favour of the lowest of the class? Of what are the magistrates nervous?'

B also returns to his earlier question about why no clergymen are 'seen in the locality through which we have waded? Here are lost sheep sufficient to fill many a fold, "lambs" waiting to be fed, brothers and sisters of ours going devilward as fast as vice, crime and gin can carry them!'

Ironically, yet pertinently, ten years before this article was written, the church was rebuilt and rich benefactors came forward in numbers to pay for its rebuilding and renovation. Many worthies in the town, for instance, had their names attached to the new stained-glass windows they donated. One of them, donated by the Gorst family, represents 'Faith, Hope and Charity, inseparable from the principles of Christianity'. Another Gorst window is inscribed with 'The righteous shall be in everlasting remembrance'. On the south aisle represents Christ blessing little children – 'beautifully treated' says Hewitson. B seems to be suggesting that all this is hollow when it is only 'a stone's throw' from the Sandhole where the Christian compassion was missing from the staff of the 'sacred edifice'.

B's sympathy with the people of the Sandhole is both immediate and commendable. His necessarily veiled criticism is levelled at the Vicar of Preston, Canon Parr, and his staff, as the parish of St Saviour's was in its infancy and its church not even started. As for the staff of St Augustine's, Catholics merit very little mention in the Preston newspapers of the period, except for a few bigoted articles and attacks aimed at them. The daily routine of parish work would not be the subject for any report. St Augustine's parish was established with this part of the town as its prescribed area and there is evidence that pastoral work was being done. (See later chapter.)

In conclusion, B draws together his main complaints and criticisms together from his 'rambles'.

> Every stone in the locality we have visited cries aloud to Heaven against those clergymen in whose sight men and women's souls are but dross as weighed against their own comfort and sickly delicacy, against those magistrates who refrain from bringing the laws to bear upon those property owners who belong to the dens of infamy, the gentlemen whose incomes are part of the proceeds of crime and vice and who have commission upon even Disease and Death. B

Any modern reader might be excused for thinking that there would be a wave of support or a backlash of criticism in the wake of these revealing and hard-hitting articles. It might surprise that reader to find out that there was none. Forensic examination of the columns of the *Chronicle* and the *Herald*, especially the letters section, reveal nothing at all. The aftermath was completely and suspiciously silent. No writing of that type or intensity was published until nearly two years later.

Any modern reader might be excused for thinking that there would be a wave of support or a backlash of criticism in the wake of these revealing and hard-hitting articles

On 22 December 1866, the *Chronicle* published an article with the headline 'Thievery, Knavery and Harlotry', written by 'Phillipus'. The first part is concerned with the advance of political reform, leading to the 1867 Reform Act which enfranchised part of the urban male working class; the second part concerned the deterioration of morals in the town. This latter section is opened by the comment

> Crime is a gigantic stalking horse, always present in our midst, not easily removed, and an object by which all are more or less affected. A festering sore; the more it is tampered with, the worse it becomes and, when neglected, the further it spreads.

Phillipus takes a different tack to B in his appeal to put a stop to the vice he sees. He calls on everyone to pay less attention to divisions in politics and religion and pay more attention to the prevalence of crime. He advocates greater education for the young, a phenomenon which will become compulsory four years later in 1870. In the meantime, he asserts that ninety percent of boys arrested by the police know nothing about God – 'in a country bursting with Christianity and who send out missionaries to other countries.' He makes a few specific complaints, one of which is about the sort of people who populate Preston streets.

> One cannot walk many yards in the streets but he meets mere children the worse for liquor, or strutting about with short, black pipes in their mouths and giving utterance to the most foul and horrible imprecations … [or] with any articles of value about him by way of outward decoration but thievish eyes are upon them.

Phillipus blames whole families for teaching their children immoral ways, never attending school while thousands of others have. He feels that compulsory education would improve the situation: '… better to be shackled with a measure calculated, in the long run, to bring comfort and happiness to themselves and their children than to be slaves of drunkenness, theft and debauchery.'

Eventually, he turns to his last complaint – prostitution. 'In Preston, like most other large towns, [this] evil has made extensive strides.' The reason for this may have been

The Builder's black parts comprised of just streets and buildings, but other aspects of the town were worthy of that description – some of its people, their behaviour and the desperation that caused it and the depression that accompanied it.

poverty caused by the Cotton Famine in Lancashire (1861–5). He criticises the Borough authorities for not acting on their bye laws in a similar way that B did before him. He rails against importuning, assembly in licensed premises and a lack of a proper system of fines.

> Seldom do we hear of them [the bye-laws] being put into practice and yet we have numerous, notorious brothels existing in the very heart of the town; we have harlots prowling round our streets daily and nightly and committing breaches of the laws ... At night our streets resound with their tramping and brawling ... Our principal thoroughfares are made parades for these nightwalkers and it is no uncommon thing to meet with two or three of these wretched beings at almost every corner you turn after nightfall. Most of them have a besotted, stupid, filthy, disgusting and sickening appearance, and seem as if they would be greatly benefited if they had been through a course of ablutions under the direction of Daddy at the Lambeth Workhouse.[15]

Phillipus does have sympathy for many of the girls, regarding them as being trapped by circumstances, their family members and the women who ran Preston bawdy houses.

> Many of them are mere girls, just entered their teens, no doubt trapped into their debauched life by mistresses of brothels holding out to them great promises of reward. It is fearful to contemplate that these unfortunate beings have set apart their lives to the gaining of an existence by propagating sin and disease.

He surmises that there is a deep unhappiness in all of them, which may have had some foundation.

> their lives of debauchery are those of extreme misery, that they are constantly seeking to drown their consciences with drink and their houses can be no homes but perfect hells. Who is there left that is not aware of the characters of the

> houses in Turk's Head Yard, Old Cock Yard, Blelock Street, Shepherd Street etc?

He wonders how people who live in these areas make a living. He ponders on how vast amounts of drinks can be afforded or 'flashy and expensive clothing' and concludes 'that if patronage was withheld, this cursed and crying evil would not exist a day; and it is equally true that if there were no temptations there would be no sin.'

The punishments in the 1830s were fairly heavy for prostitution – usually a calendar month in prison.

Again, he criticises 'our local legislators' who create laws and then do not act on them. There is some substance in this. The punishments in the 1830s were fairly heavy for prostitution – usually a calendar month in prison. Between 1860 and 1870 there were no such cases reported on; prostitutes were mostly arrested for theft. In September 1839, Julia Lloyd received four weeks' imprisonment in the House of Correction for 'wandering the town for improper purposes as a common prostitute'. Thirty-two years later, in February 1871, Jane Pinder was ordered to pay a fine of ten shillings (£45) or spend one week in prison for keeping a brothel in Shepherd Street. In this situation the police must have wondered if it was worth arresting women for prostitution at all. The courts seemed to be more open to punishing prostitutes for theft, which appears to be their other stock-in-trade crime. However, Phillipus sees the police's approach to containment as casual at best and encouraging vice at worst: '… the police can be found at almost every hour of the night in public thoroughfares chatting and laughing with these incorrigible females.'

The police who patrolled the town centre had a forensic knowledge of the people who operated there, but had to be more concerned with other crimes such as larceny or violence

Obviously, the concept of community policing was far beyond Phillipus's imagination. Working within perceived confines, almost with their hands were tied, the best the police could do was contain as best they could. He continues, 'They cannot fail to be cognisant of the existence of houses kept for prostitution, forbidden by the laws; nor can they fail to see nightwalkers wandering round the streets soliciting parties to visit their dens of iniquity.'

By all accounts, the police who patrolled the town centre had a forensic knowledge of the people who operated there, knowing people by name and the areas they circulated in, but had to be more concerned with other crimes such as larceny or violence.

He continues by repeating his charge of encouragement and of their superiors looking on 'with too much indifference' so that 'it is almost unsafe for a female to go through the streets at night'. In his final paragraphs he shows he has the same mindset as B had, but with a greater depth of sarcasm.

> Need we longer speak of our civilised and Christian condition when brothels are permitted to be kept in almost every other street and harlots are allowed to turn our streets into places of profligacy and when encouragement is given to this foul and licentious traffic instead of its being suppressed.

This would be a good point at which to see how many brothels there were at this time, working from newspaper reports, court records (after 1869) and the 1861 and 1871 Censuses. In the 1860s there were six in Blelock Street, four in Laurel Street, three in Shepherd Street and one each in St John's Place, Willow Street, Brewery Street, and Leeming Street. In the 1870s there were six in Blelock Street, five in Laurel Street, four in Library Street, three in Shepherd Street, one in Rose Street and one in Old Cock Yard. There certainly would have been more than this in other areas.

Phillipus ends his article with:

> Let us hear no more about the deplorable spiritual conditions of people in far-off climes when we have a criminality in a monster form at our own thresholds. Would to God that our spiritual advisers would be more active in home missionary work, that they would visit these dens of iniquity and reclaim their occupants from their vicious life. When we have purged our own shores of vice, then we may with better

> grace whisper into the ears of far-off brethren the Great Truths and point out their iniquities.

A similar sentiment was expressed in the *Herald*'s editorial of 29 August 1863 where various groups were criticised, such as the Quakers, the Peace Society and the Preston Foreign Affairs Committee for involving themselves in areas such as the American Civil War

> and getting up memorials about some victim of whom no-one ever [had] heard before ... while the social degradation and moral defilement of Queen Street and it neighbourhood are ignored ... for they are too busy with evils in distant lands to think of anything so commonplace as the ignorance and crime at their own doors.

The writer of the *Builder*'s second article entitled it 'The Black Parts of Preston', an expression reused as a heading for the reproduction of the article in the *Chronicle* with a probable further intention, that of pressing for serious change. The *Builder*'s black parts comprised of just streets and buildings, but other aspects of the town were worthy of that description – some of its people, their behaviour and the desperation that caused it and the depression that accompanied it. Whether the magistrates' inability, or lack of will, to improve the situation came from a lack of money during the Cotton Famine and its attendant financial pressures or simply an attempt to contain the problem into a few areas, the situation had got out of hand. Over the next two decades there would be a gradual improvement, but not entirely as a result of legislation either local or national.

Trials were held at Lancaster Castle

6

'My Character Is Too Bad'

VIOLENCE OF ALL TYPES WAS a constant theme of life in the Sandhole and its surrounding area for four decades or so. Many instances had robbery at their core, such as the 'Murderous Assault' in Leeming Street which was reported in the *Chronicle* of 14 April 1860. William Bradley, 'a notoriously bad character', had assaulted Michael Clare ten days earlier. While Clare was living in James Traynor's lodging house in Leeming Street, Bradley came to know that he had received his Army discharge and offered him 'half a gallon of ale' if he handed it over to him. Naturally, Clare refused, so Bradley grabbed him, threatening to choke him. Traynor managed to separate them, allowing Clare to leave but Bradley followed him and violently kicked him on the legs. He was arrested but had to be remanded three times as Clare could not attend court because of his injuries. Doctor Corless said that Clare's lip was split, his forehead swollen and his leg had a bad contusion on it. When Clare was found, he was conscious but unable to speak because of concussion and was in a dangerous state for three days. Bradley was committed for trial at Lancaster.

Another cause or source of violence was the presence of a bully, some of whom were more active than Bracebridge Heminge's generalised description. Ellen Berry, a prostitute, was challenged to a fight in the Lodge Bank Tavern by another prostitute called Ann Moore between eight and nine o'clock on Thursday 17 October 1861.[1] When she refused, she was set upon by Moore and a man called Roscoe, a known thief of the area called Abraham Roscoe, who was probably her bully. As a result, Berry was badly scratched about the face and severely beaten. The case failed because of a lack of witnesses, possibly because they were frightened or unwilling to come forward.

Some women were not just 'unfortunates' in the Victorian sense, but also unfortunate to become attached, or fall into the grip of, a bully who used them mercilessly. One such woman was Mary Heap who became involved with William Ireland, a violent thug, who made no attempt to support himself or even fend for himself. The *Chronicle* of 11 March reports that she charged him of hitting and kicking her several times in the Lodge Bank Tavern in Water Street, for reason unknown, but they became clear later. Eighteen months later they were married at the Parish Church on 26 December 1866. He aged 26, gave his occupation a piecer in a cotton mill, living in Clayton's Court. She, aged 22, gave her residence as 22 Hopwood Street. Neither could read nor write. Up to this time, Ireland had been constantly in court for theft, and this continued for the rest of his life.

Seven weeks after the marriage, in February 1866, Margaret Ireland charged her husband with assault. At this stage they were living in Blelock Street. While in the Black Swan Inn in Water Street, they quarrelled about their lack of money. In desperation she grabbed the cap off his head to go and pawn it to get something to eat. It turned out that he had already eaten. He kicked and thumped her for her trouble. During the court case, Mrs Ireland declared that she had kept her husband from her earnings as a prostitute and she assumed that he did not have a trade because he had never attempted to ply it anywhere, ever. The court found him guilty, and he was sent to prison for a month.

Three months or so later, at the beginning of June 1866, William Ireland, described by the *Chronicle* as 'a stupid looking fellow', was charged with assaults on his wife and threatening to kill her. 'only been married five months' and she described her life as a 'misery'. On this particular occasion he arrived home, this time in Shepherd Street, and demanded that his wife, who was in bed at the time, should get up and make his supper, but there was only a piece of bread in the house. On realising this, Ireland seized her by the throat and tried to choke her. The marks were still clearly visible in the court. The Bench were so incensed that they told Ireland, as they sentenced him to three months' imprisonment with hard labour, that they were very sorry that they could not have him flogged. This is not as fanciful as a threat as it might sound nowadays as the Royal Navy only suspended flogging in 1879. The older people in court and readers of the *Chronicle* may have remembered or even witnessed, the last public flogging in Preston in 1827. Two men were tethered to carts and dragged along to various corners and public places such as the Market Place where they would be stopped and whipped on their bare backs. The last woman to be publicly flogged in Preston was Christine Fellows in 1786. This type of punishment 'was not uncommon before these dates'.[2]

The older people in court and readers of the Chronicle may have remembered or even witnessed, the last public flogging in Preston in 1827

At the end of the *Chronicle*'s account of this court session, a commentator, possibly Anthony Hewitson, added a paragraph of comment.

> There is scarcely a day passes without a case being brought before the Bench in which one or more 'unfortunates' appear as either complainants, defendants or witnesses, or mention is made of rows having occurred at brothels. Prostitution is alarmingly on the increase in Preston and we would remind the police that something can be done to check it by putting in force the bye laws referring to night walkers and brothels. (8 June 1867)

Sometimes a bully would step in to protect his source of income. On 22 January 1864, a prostitute called Elizabeth Fielding was arrested on the corner of Greaves Street and Shepherd Street for being drunk and disorderly by P.C. Kenny and P.C. (later P.S.) Keefe. On their way to the police station, Edward Fielding made a serious attempt, as did another prostitute called Isabella Slater, to free Fielding from custody, but failed. He was fined ten shillings (£48 in 2018). Fielding was sentenced to a month in prison, while Slater was discharged. In court it became obvious that the Fieldings had led her into a life of prostitution.

An incident occurred on Tuesday 29 March 1870 which was nothing in itself but gives a wider picture of the area, the time and the expectations of those involved. George Smith was summoned to court for 'harbouring lewd people in his house', the Rifleman Inn in Water Street where several were found to be drunk, there was singing and it was very noisy. P.S. Keefe and P.C.s Burns and Watson had gone into the vault and saw nineteen prostitutes and named four bullies in court, namely Gillespie, Bell, Forest and Brown. This must have been a tactic to have the men's names mentioned, but not their forenames as they were not being charged. Giving a definite number to the type of women present also shows the police officers' good knowledge of the area and its inhabitants. P.S. Keefe also stated that there were 'some convicted thieves' present which included Gillespie who was a 'returned convict', a person who had returned from Australia after being sent there to the penal colony as a punishment.[3] It is worth noting that he did not take his chance to reform and make a better life for himself, but gravitated back to the Sandhole where he presumably resumed his old way of life. The defending solicitor maintained that the noise was 'not very great' and that people of that type lived in the neighbourhood and could not see why they 'should not have enjoyment like other people'. The Bench decided that the presence of nineteen prostitutes constituted an offence and fined Smith two pounds (£118) and costs (16 April 1870).

Four weeks later, James Shorrock, the landlord of the Black Swan public house, also in Water Street across from the Rifleman Inn, was summoned to court by the police for keeping a disorderly house. When P.C.s Higgins and Machonachie entered the premises at quarter to nine, they found several drunk men and some prostitutes. In his defence,

Shorrock said, 'I have tried to keep an orderly house, but it is about two hundred yards off the worst neighbourhood in town. I have always done my best and I am very sorry [but] I am situated in that neighbourhood'.

Bullies were often elusive, slippery characters who avoided notice where possible and evaded arrest for the worst and more violent crimes. Good examples are the ones reported in an article in the *Herald* on 17 June 1871. One night during the previous week, P.C.s Watson and Butler arrested George Melly, John Gardner and Thomas Catterill for loitering in Fishergate at 10.30pm in Fishergate. Their real purpose becomes obvious when the woman who was accompanying them, Mary Wolly (also Wooley), who was a convicted thief, approached 'two gentlemen' possibly to set them up for a robbery of some sort, but one of the bullies spotted the police and shouted, 'Hallo![4] Look out!'. P.C. Butler told the court that Wolly, 34, was a prostitute and the men were 'always in the neighbourhood of Water Street and were the associates of prostitutes and thieves.' To avoid punishment, the defendants all promised to leave town. The three bullies, all in their mid-thirties, appear in the 1871 Census, declaring respectable trades and two of them gave addresses at nearby Fishwick (London Road and Grosvenor Street). The third, Catterill, lived in Melbourne Street in St Peter's District, which was fifteen minutes' walk from the Sandhole. Wolly (or Wooley) does not appear in the 1871 Census, but she was arrested in Chorley a few weeks later with George Wooley for robbing William Booth of twelve shillings and sixpence (£57). Both were sent to prison for seven years under the cumulative provision of Section 7 of the 1871 Prevention of Crime Act. In the prison records she was described as a hawker, born in 1837 and she could read. She had been in prison five times previously, but not specifically for prostitution.

However, subtlety was not the watchword with some bullies whose rapacious nature soon boiled over into violence. In April 1871, the *Herald* reported a case where Elizabeth Ann Clark, 22, charged William Lever with assault. She testified that during the two years they had cohabited together Lever had done no work and she had kept him with her earnings from prostitution. On 11 April, at 28 Shepherd Street,[5] Lever had demanded money from her but she said she had none, even though she was hiding a half sovereign in her mouth (£45).[6] She said her brother had given it to her. Enraged at having no money, witnesses said Lever pulled her to the floor, hit her with his fist across her mouth, jumped on her and kicked her. The Chairman of the Bench described this as an aggravated assault, totally unprovoked. It was Lever's eighth appearance in court, three times for felony, and on the last occasion he had served six years. He was sentenced to four months with hard labour in the House of Correction. Before he was taken down, Lever defiantly thanked the court.

A year later, in March, James Judge, described by the *Chronicle* as a 'notorious character', was summoned to court with having no visible means of subsistence. The *Herald* declared Judge to be a 'rogue, vagabond, associate of thieves, constantly with them and had never attempted to work', although he had told the Census enumerator and the prison authorities that he was a piecer in a cotton mill. Chief Inspector Dunn's charge was backed up by Inspector Oglethorpe who had arrested Judge on two occasions (theft and felony) and Sergeant Byrne who testified that he associated with prostitutes and was living at 23 (though more likely 3) Laurel Street. Other previous convictions were for vagrancy (twice) and desertion (three times). At the time of his last conviction in 1869 for theft, witnesses had seen him daily in Water Street and after release after nine months with hard labour, he immediately returned there and continued associating with thieves and prostitutes, who were all named in court. He was detained for a time under the Effectual Prevention of Crimes Act of 1871, but after release he went to prison in October for six months for felony and a further six months for assault in 1873. After maliciously wounding P.C. John Forest in 1875 he finally served five years.

In the society of the time, women were second class citizens, though they were slowly emerging to a greater position of strength later in the century and into the

Edwardian period. Taking this into account, the women in this line of business were vulnerable to unscrupulous men who were hardly more than thugs. Occasionally, some women were the victims of ruthless violence. In July 1866, an Irishman called Michael Chester was charged with the brutal assault of Bridget Commoford. The two, who were said to be lovers, were drinking in the Griffin Inn when Chester asked Commoford for money and she gave him all she had. He was obviously her bully. He decided that it was not enough and he wanted more. When she was unable to give him any more, he hit her in the face with his fists, knocked her down and kicked her outside into Water Street where he kicked her in the head. Between his arrest and the last week in August, Chester was remanded until Commoford was well enough to attend court.

The town surgeon, Edwin Moore, examined the victim and found that her scalp had separated from the bone and three quarters of an inch of the skull was exposed. There was also a bruise on her spine in the small of her back where Chester had stamped his heel. He also found numerous old bruises. When she finally appeared in court, Commoford's head was bandaged all over. Mr Moore stated at the trial that when she was first seen by him that she was 'in a dangerous state'. After the evidence had been heard a verdict of guilty was returned. The court was told that Chester had already been in prison at Kirkdale for six months and at Preston for one year, where his status was recorded as 'uneducated'. The Chairman of the magistrates declared it to be the most brutal case he had ever seen and told Chester that if Commoford had died he would have been hanged. He was sentenced to eighteen months with hard labour. All this did not seem to upset Chester unduly because just over ten years later he was arrested twice for drunkenness and twice for assault, resulting in four months' imprisonment in total. In October 1878 he attacked his common law wife, Catherine, at their home in Cobden Street, Accrington, more brutally than he had attacked Bridget Commoford. For unlawful and malicious wounding, he received eighteen months' hard labour.[7]

Occasionally, a prostitute would try to rescue a bully from arrest

Occasionally, a prostitute would try to rescue a bully from arrest. One such incident occurred in October 1876 when Thomas Scanlon, described by the *Chronicle* as a 'disreputable fellow', was found guilty of violently assaulting P.C. Simms at three o'clock on Saturday afternoon, 7 October. The police were called to the Black Swan where Scanlon and others were causing a disturbance. When Simms removed Scanlon from the premises, he ran at the police officer, hitting him on the side of the face and kicked him several times. An unnamed prostitute handed Scanlon a knife who cut Simms' hand twice while trying to defend himself and 'continued to kick unmercifully'. P.C. Upton came to assist and Scanlon was arrested. On the way to the police station, bricks and stones were thrown at the policemen. Scanlon was sentenced to three months' imprisonment. It was his eleventh conviction.

During the same week, Thomas Taylor and James Turner were arrested in Water Street by P.C. Forest for being drunk. In court, the officer stated that they were bullies and depended on prostitutes for a living. He expanded further by saying that there were about thirty 'such fellows' in the neighbourhood of Water Street. As a result, the Bench ordered the police to keep a sharp look out for young men like these who 'frequented such places'. This ties in with a general tightening up of the bye laws from this point on.

Groups of soldiers on a night out in Preston, especially in the Sandhole and surrounding areas, sometimes turned out badly, but individual soldiers also caused havoc and injury. James Scully, a private of the 8th (King's, later King's Liverpool) Regiment, attacked Maria Kenyon, aged eighteen, in what the *Herald* described as a 'shameful assault' in its edition of 7 June 1873. Kenyon, described as 'a poor unfortunate girl' of Leeming Street, was kicked in the head and lower abdomen by Scully. When he tried to escape, he was 'stopped by a crowd'. When the case came up in court, Kenyon was still in the Infirmary because of her injuries, which prompted the Chairman of magistrates to describe Scully as 'hardly to be called a man' and the assault as 'dastardly'. He was remanded until 13 June, then 21 June and again until 24 June because Kenyon was still ill. Finally, on 30 June, Kenyon attended court 'still not quite recovered and ... still a patient at the Infirmary for a further week'.

At the outset, Mr Watson, the prosecuting solicitor, requested that Scully be sent to Quarter Sessions, but this was refused. The whole business started on the afternoon of the 5 June when Kenyon entered the Lodge Bank Tavern with two Lancers, just as Scully was leaving. He had been with Kenyon the previous evening and seeing her with the other two soldiers inflamed him with jealousy and he wanted revenge. Swearing, and without warning, he rushed forward and kicked her in the abdomen. She fell and began to bleed profusely and was rushed to the Infirmary. There she was examined and was found to have coagulated blood on her thighs and there was a contusion at the junction of her thigh and her buttock. 'There was also a contusion wound on the abdomen in the lower parts' such as might have been produced by a kick. After this, Scully was committed to Quarter Sessions where he was found guilty and sentenced to six months' imprisonment with hard labour.

Such were the dangers that these women were vulnerable to, but life had to carry on, as it did for Maria Kenyon. A year later, she became involved in a case where two prostitutes, Mary Ann Blue and Margaret Connor, and a thief called James Leonard, were charged with passing counterfeit coin. This was a fairly common crime in Victorian times, but it came with a heavy punishment. Most of the evidence was given by Agnes Smith and Thomas Smith of the Bear's Paw in Church Street. Leonard was later tracked down and arrested by P.C. Brown in a cellar in Blelock Street. Kenyon, who was living in Leeming Street testified that Blue had asked her to retrieve the three counterfeit coins from the bed of 'old Mrs Whittle'[8] where she had hidden them. William Peatfield, a barman at the Bear's Paw, also stated that Connor had attempted to pay him with base coin. As a result, she and Blue were also arrested by P.C. Brown. Leonard and

Connor were sentenced at Quarter Sessions in Lancaster to five years' imprisonment each and Blue received five years for concealing the coins.

By the mid-1870s, Maria Kenyon was still, after her serious injuries, living and working in the Sandhole area. On 15 November 1876, then aged twenty-one, she was arrested for being drunk and riotous in Oak Street and fined ten shillings (£46). A year later, she found herself the victim of another attack, together with another prostitute called Elizabeth Haynes. James Parker, and convicted thief and warehouse breaker, tracked down the two women to the Globe Inn in Grimshaw Street and assaulted them for giving evidence against his friends in a recent trial. He was pursued by the police and arrested in the next street and was found guilty of violence in court. He was unable to pay a surety of £5 (£462) and so served a month's imprisonment with hard labour instead.

Despite the police's best efforts and, to a lesser extent, the magistrates', violence was quite a common occurrence in this area bearing in mind that most of its population were without education, without family and genuinely caring friends (because they had been alienated) and without hope. Add to this desperation and alcohol and the result was often explosive. Disputes between prostitutes could be vicious. In August 1872, Mary Ann Bury (or Berry) charged Lucy Ann Stephens of assaulting and stabbing her, causing a one and a quarter inch cut on her left breast. She had to be rescued by the brothel keeper at 2 Laurel Street, Elizabeth Hurst. In court, Stephens denied that she had intended to stab Bury and the charge was dismissed through lack of hard evidence, but she received one month's hard labour for assault. Incidentally, this case exposed the nature of the house and Hurst was charged in November with running a brothel at 2 Laurel Street and selling ale without a licence. On Saturday 16 November, the police watched a man enter

Despite the police's best efforts and, to a lesser extent, the magistrates', violence was quite a common occurrence in this area

the house three times and found out that he had obtained three quarts (six pints) for sixpence (£2.20) a quart. A search revealed an empty three-quart bottle under the stairs. She did not attend because she had absconded, which was not an uncommon event at that time in that place.

On 25 January 1873, the *Chronicle* reported that Mary Thompson was found guilty of running a brothel at Shepherd Street and, as it was her fourth offence for the same premises, she was fined twenty shillings (£87). Six weeks later, she and Elizabeth Brown were ejected from the Black Swan by the landlord, James Shorrock for fighting. They continued in the street, using obscene language and were eventually arrested. The court ordered them to pay sureties of ten shillings each (£43) or one month in prison. Shorrock, in a different case, took Brown to court for the damage she had done to the public house after he had ejected her. Enraged, she returned and threw glasses at him, shattering some plate glass in the process. It was her eleventh appearance in court, so she was sent to the House of Correction for two months with hard labour. Brown is a good example of the flotsam and jetsam found in these streets in this period. Born in 1838, she had no trade whatsoever and had had an 'imperfect education' which probably meant that she was very basically numerate. Between June 1870 and 1881, when she was imprisoned for wounding Annie Percival, a known thief, she had been in prison thirty-five times for damage, running a brothel, drunkenness, assault and want of sureties.

Mary Thompson and Elizabeth Brown were ejected from the Black Swan for fighting. They continued in the street, using obscene language and were eventually arrested

Emily Brand suggests that women working in a brothel often shared clothes, especially dresses, as a way of pooling resources. However, this arrangement could go wrong, as it did in a Shepherd Street brothel in July 1873 when Margaret Wilding attacked Elizabeth Harrison during a quarrel over shared clothes. The dispute quickly escalated into violence, coming to a climax when Wilding threw a teapot full of hot water at Harrison who was lying on a sofa. Harrison raised her leg to defend herself and was severely scalded. Wilding was found guilty and fined eleven shillings (£43). Born in 1858, she was convicted over the next ten years of drunkenness eight times, resulting in two periods of imprisonment. In 1885 she was imprisoned with hard labour, along with two other women, for stealing ten shillings (£53) from a man called Henry Hudson Thomas. Harrison, born in 1855, was assaulted by Robert Denwood, a cotton operative from Salford, when she opened the door to him in January 1875. An unnamed witness in the house gave supporting evidence and Denwood was fined ten shillings (£46 in 2018). At this point, the *Herald* reports, Denwood's friend shouted, 'They're two common prostitutes!' The magistrate, Mr Pedder, called him to the witness box, saying, 'What business is it of yours to interfere business of this court? You will get yourself into trouble if you do not mind! Stand down!' This illustrates that the court was fair, at least, to the more despised members of society.

An example of a violent incident which had the mark of revenge or retribution on it occurred in Turk's Head Court in October 1875. Bridget Shearns, also known as Thompson, was found guilty of assault on Elizabeth Greenwood. The *Chronicle* describes Shearns as 'one of a gang of prostitutes which infects Cock Yard'. She assaulted Greenwood as she was putting up the shutters of the Turk's Head Inn. Described as 'beastly drunk', she made this unprovoked onslaught by dragging Harrison to the ground, kicking her round the head and body and jumping on her. It is worth remembering here that most people wore clogs at this time. The attack left Harrison severely hurt and bleeding badly. As a result, Shearns, who had just been released from prison, was committed to Lancaster Castle prison for three months with hard labour. The prison records show that she had been born in 1853, had no trade or employment and was completely uneducated. Her crimes up to this point included wilful damage, drunkenness (9 times), riotous behaviour (2), running a disorderly house (4), assault, prostitution and indecent behaviour.

In September 1878, the *Chronicle* reported that Annie Bell, 'an unfortunate', had been summoned by another prostitute, Elizabeth Jones in a house where they both lived at 3 Laurel Street. Somehow, Jones had transgressed and breached one of the house regulations, causing a furious argument which provoked Bell to hit her over the head with a poker 'causing blood to flow profusely'. Another prostitute, Bridget Connolly, who was living next door, ran in and saved Jones from further damage. Other women who were present acted as witnesses and Bell received six months' imprisonment.

It is surprising that, less than two years later, Bell and Connolly, both aged around forty, were living at 3 Laurel Street, with Bell named as the head of household. In fact, Annie Bell had lived there for some years, having been fined ten shillings (£46) in October1876 for running a brothel, under threat of being sent to Sessions for any further appearances on the same charge. It is also ironic that Bridget Connolly should be the saviour in 1878, because two years earlier she had been the perpetrator of a similar attack, 'a disgraceful assault' the *Chronicle* called it, on a sixteen-year-old prostitute called Margaret O'Brien. Then she was living at the same address as Connolly – 30 Water Street – and an argument started over cleaning. O'Brien refused to help Connolly, so she threw her to the ground and bit a piece out of her forehead. On 30 November, O'Brien was still being treated by Dr Oliver and was still unable to attend court on 7 December but Connolly, on her twenty-fifth court appearance, was sentenced to six months' imprisonment.

At a time when the population in the area round the Sandhole was itinerant for many reasons – legal, financial and family – Bridget Connolly was an almost permanent fixture in the Sandhole community. Born in Chorley, Connolly is recorded in the 1871 Census as living at 5 Blelock Street, the house where Ann Collett and Barbara Marchant were living at the time of James Steanson's murder. She declared herself to be a cotton weaver and twenty-two years of age, both of which are highly suspect as she had been fined for running a brothel there in 1871. In the 1881 Census she said she was thirty-eight. In November 1877 she was fined forty shillings (£184) for selling beer without a licence at 30 Shepherd Street at three o'clock in the morning. She had been seen by P.C. Walmsley, looking through a keyhole, filling three men's glasses and taking money. With her was another prostitute, Kate Matthews (see below). On the same day she was fined ten shillings for being drunk and incapable. In April 1879 she was involved in a violent incident at the brothel she was running at 3 Laurel Street involving a sailor from Freckleton called John Council.[9] During a drunken brawl at the house, Council hit Connolly in the face. In retaliation, Connolly smashed a jug across Council's face and continued to hit him with the handle. As a result, he had to be taken to the Infirmary. However, he had been so drunk that he could remember nothing of the incident, so Connolly was discharged. At the 1881 Census she was living with a bully called Joseph Hutton who said he was a labourer in a coal yard.

Violence among prostitutes was not uncommon, though only the worst or more public cases came to court. The main causes were arguments over territory, clients or disagreements in a brothel or some imagined slight when drunk. Two cases which fell in these categories during August 1879, were contended in public, one of which caused extra comment in the Magistrates' Court. On 16 August, Mary Cogan and Mary Jane Conor (or Connor) were found guilty of fighting in Water Street when drunk. This was Cogan's twenty third conviction and by 1888 she had been found guilty of drunkenness on thirty-three occasions. Conor already had convictions in Liverpool and Wigan.

> *On 16 August, Mary Cogan and Mary Jane Conor were found guilty of fighting in Water Street when drunk ... by 1888 Cogan had been found guilty of drunkenness on thirty-three occasions.*

In the first week of the same month, the *Chronicle* reported a case in court under the headline 'Prisoners from East Lancashire'. On the evening of 1 August, Mary Burke and Rose Ann Mitchell, both prostitutes, were charged with drunkenness and fighting in Water Street, more than likely over territory. Mitchell was from Burnley, while Burke had only been in Preston a short time and was originally from Liverpool. Mitchell had been arrested in Burnley and sentenced to a prison term in the Preston House of Correction. On release she had made her way to the Sandhole, as Burke had done slightly earlier. Coincidentally, tried on the same day was another prostitute, Sarah McDonald, who was released on the same morning – 31 July – was arrested the same evening in the Sandhole for drunkenness. All three were sentenced to fourteen days with hard labour. At the end of the session, the Bench openly wondered why Preston had so many prostitutes. Mr Oglethorpe, the Chief Constable, replied that on release from prison the prostitutes stayed in the town and plied their trade. He explained further by saying that when prostitutes were released, they were just turned out into the street. At one time they had been given an allowance to return to their own towns, but a recent change in procedure had meant they were given nothing and found their way down Church Street to the Sandhole.

When prostitutes were released, they were just turned out into the street. At one time they had been given an allowance to return to their own towns, but a recent change in procedure had meant they were given nothing and found their way down Church Street to the Sandhole

Occasionally, violence spilled onto innocent families. Bridget Chester was seen one day in September 1879 beating a boy, the son of Walter O'Donnell of 32 Shepherd Street, by Mary Jane Smalley of 7 Shepherd Street while sitting on her front doorstep. She ran into the kitchen of number 32 to alert the boy's mother, Ann O'Donnell, who ran out to stop the assault. Chester saw Mrs O'Donnell, drew a knife and slashed her around the head including on the left temple. Her wounds 'bled profusely'. The outcome would have been far worse if Smalley had not snatched the knife away. The *Herald* reported that, in court, Chester had said she was in a

Chester saw Mrs O'Donnell, drew a knife and slashed her around the head including on the left temple. Her wounds 'bled profusely'

drunken temper and apologised. However, she was sent to Sessions where she was found guilty and sentenced to eighteen months' imprisonment with hard labour.

For whatever reasons, people ended up living and working in the Sandhole and similar areas nearby and the fact is that they more than often had to survive without the benefits of education, trade or skill, or any semblance of care or sympathy for the unemployed on a State or local level. Under the dark shadow of the workhouse and the threat of penal sanctions for begging, they were just a small section of 'a large part of the population [that] was all the time under the menace of total destitution' (Kellow Chesney). The grim and grimy world of prostitution with its attendant diseases and dangers led many to dull the pain, both physical and psychological, with alcohol. This led to dependency which often resulted in violence. One way to make money more easily was theft.

One of the annual occasions which was a draw for pickpockets and prostitutes was the Horse Fair held in January. The police patrolled it carefully to frustrate this sort of criminal, but in 1862 the *Chronicle* reported an incident where prostitutes showed themselves to be astute opportunists. John Ormerod, a farmer from Bentham in Yorkshire, he had had a successful day at the Fair and by seven o'clock he 'was the worse for wear for drink'. He was carrying £105 (£11,000) in a secure waistcoat pocket but had £35 (£ 3,700) in a canvas bag in his trouser pocket. He was accosted by two prostitutes, no doubt in a friendly fashion, and while they walked and talked, one of them removed the bag. He did not realise his loss until the women had gone. The women went quickly down Fox Street, followed by some boys who were seen in Union Street. Searches by the police revealed nothing.

One case of theft, which opened up to view the workings of brothels but rebounded on the person who brought the charge, concerned a woman called Mary Jane Watt. This eighteen-year-old was a native of Oswestry, who had lived from the age of sixteen with her uncle, Henry Wilson, a fruit seller of the town. At that age she went into service in a house in Bolton but left after two years when she took up employment, in March 1877, at the Clarence Hotel in Grimshaw Street. In the second week of that month, she encountered Kate Matthews (see above), a thirty-three-year-old prostitute who ran a brothel at 22 Rose Street.

Matthews had been mentioned in a case reported in the *Herald* on 30 September 1871 when a Blackburn draper, Philip Atkinson of 65 Darwen Street, was allegedly robbed of one £20 note, one £5 note, two promissory notes and several letters amounting to £50 (£4,573) at 17 St John's Place. The four women accused were Jane Almond[10] who ran the house, Elizabeth Heyes, Matthews and Elizabeth Brown. Atkinson stopped at the house from Friday 22 September to Monday 25 September, mostly in the company of Heyes, who is described later in the article as 'only following her occupation and receiving money from that man's hands'. Heyes revelled in a special nickname – 'Prince Paul' – that prostitutes seemed known by in those days. Atkinson spent most of his time in Preston throwing his money around, going to public houses down by the river and drinking champagne and brandy in great quantities both there and back at Almond's establishment, where all five of them joined in. Twice he went to bed early, and fully clothed, which suggests he was drunk or perhaps not completely confident that his money was safe, or both. When he finally went to bed normally, money went missing and he accused the four women. The magistrates were 'not sympathetic with such a fellow as that because he had lost £20 (£1,829) in idleness'. St John's Place runs round two sides of St John's churchyard, the other two sides being bounded by Stoneygate and Church Street, and number 17 was obviously a brothel. Jane Almond, aged 51, classed herself in the 1871 Census as a confectioner and Elizabeth Heyes described herself as a dressmaker, that well-worn euphemism often passed on to the enumerators by prostitutes. Although Kate Matthews

Atkinson spent most of his time in Preston throwing his money around, going to public houses down by the river and drinking champagne and brandy in great quantities

was at the premises in September, she was not present when the Census was taken, nor was she in the 1881 Census. The reason for this will become obvious and explain the itinerant nature of some of these people.

St John's Place is near to Rose Street where Kate Matthews had set up her own house sometime before the winter of 1872 when she was found guilty of running a brothel at number 22 in November, fined twenty shillings (£88) and again two years later. In March 1877, Matthews decided that she needed a new girl and planned to invite a young barmaid, working in Grimshaw Street, enticing her with the usual promise of easy money and 'finery'. The young woman, Mary Ann Watts, aged nineteen, joined Matthews on 11 March and three days later absconded with clothes and a purse worth £6 (£548) and containing six shillings (£27). Matthews decided to recoup her losses by reporting Watts to the police and charging her in court with an action which would rebound on her somewhat. The case was covered by the *Herald* in detail and by other newspapers.[11]

Watt was arrested in her hometown of Oswestry, brought back and taken into court on 28 March where 'she wept bitterly through the whole proceedings'. At the start, Matthews admitted that she ran a brothel in Rose Street and that she had met Watts in the Clarence Hotel. Mr Blackhurst, a local solicitor defending Watts, carried out a prolonged line of questioning against Matthews, implying that she had enticed Watts away from her respectable job by making her promises of better money, getting her drunk in the process and that she had told Watts on Thursday 14 March to put on her (Matthew's) clothes and go to the end of Rose Street to entice men back to the house as she herself was unwell. This may have been a ruse on Matthews' part to get her working. Matthews gave flat denials to all the solicitor's questions.

Mr Blackhurst then portrayed Watts as recently orphaned and had led a blameless life until Matthews had got her drunk, taken her to Rose Street and 'led her astray'. Having been 'ruined', she was told to go out and bring men back so that Matthews would 'reap the benefits of the girl's shame'. As a result, Watts took the clothes, found new lodgings and earned money in the way 'that besom' had taught her, in order to escape. For good measure, the solicitor added that Matthews was 'one of the vilest characters on the face of the Earth'. Character witnesses, including her uncle, attested to Watts' previous 'most irreproachable' character. The magistrate, Mr Pedder, turned on Matthews, saying that her actions were disgraceful and that he hardly knew what to say except that it was 'the most disgusting case that had ever come before the court'. Because Watts had committed a felony, he had to commit her to prison for seven days, but he ruined Matthews' business by ordering Chief Inspector Oglethorpe to direct his attention to Matthews' house in Rose Street and to watch it closely.

There is no further mention of Matthews in Preston from this point. She must have decided to carry out the threat she probably made to Watts when she hesitated to go out and do her 'work', or try to escape, using an old device common in the Georgian period, as explained by Emily Brand. 'Girls belonging to a brothel were bound by its rules and bawds made escaping as difficult as possible. Absconders were often charged with the theft of the clothes belonging to the "house"'.

Her further comment is also pertinent to Watts' case: 'Those who did escape the bawdyhouse did not necessarily renounce the life of prostitution entirely. With professional opportunities severely restricted for most women, while there was demand for sexual services, virtue continued to be overthrown.'

It goes without saying that the only thefts and robberies which are reported are the unsuccessful ones, but the prevailing impression is that theft of all types was rife in Preston in this period. One of the more adept and prolific thieves was Mary Tallent (also Talent and Tallock) who, in a period of over ten years was only arrested five times. In November 1851, she and another prostitute called Ann Dawson stole two pounds and five shillings (£242) from, according to the *Chronicle*, 'a simpleton from Dutton called Thomas Dewhurst'.

The prostitutes' usual plan was to shepherd a victim into their area, be affable, then friendly, encouraging, then amorous and possibly making promises or creating a fantasy of pleasure to come

The Preston newspapers at this time were free and easy with their comments and descriptions. The prostitutes' usual plan was to shepherd a victim into their area, usually after the man had been selling and buying at the market or the horse fair. Some obviously rolled up of their own accord. The second stage was to be affable, then friendly, encouraging, then amorous and possibly making promises or creating a fantasy of pleasure to come. The third stage was the technique of getting the duped man to buy all the drinks and to become drunk at his own expense. Dewhurst sat and drank with Tallent and Dawson in an unnamed tap room in the Sandhole and, when Tallent judged that the time was right, she pushed her hand into his pocket, lifted his money and ran off with Dawson. The police eventually caught up with them and Tallent was sentenced to three months in prison. Dawson, however, was awaiting sentence for another theft and, as a result, taking other offences into account, was transported to Australia for seven years. She sailed on the prison ship *Sir Robert Seppings* on 16 March 1852 from Liverpool.

Tallent robbed a man called Hugh Spencer a year later but was luckily acquitted because the latter did not turn up to court, possibly because of embarrassment, and the case was dismissed. Four years later, she was lucky again when the 'farm servant from Thornton', who accused her of stealing two sovereigns (£183), did not press charges. According to the *Chronicle* of 17 March 1855, the unnamed victim had drunk three glasses of ale in the afternoon of Saturday 10 March and went to a 'house of ill fame in the Sandhole', where Tallent lived with two or three others. He paid for three gills of rum[12] 'and dallied with the girls'. Eventually, he realised that his money was missing. Tallent pretended to find it in a back room and gave him one sovereign back. Obviously deciding to retreat, cutting his losses, he allowed her to keep the other. He alerted P.C. Hillson and she was

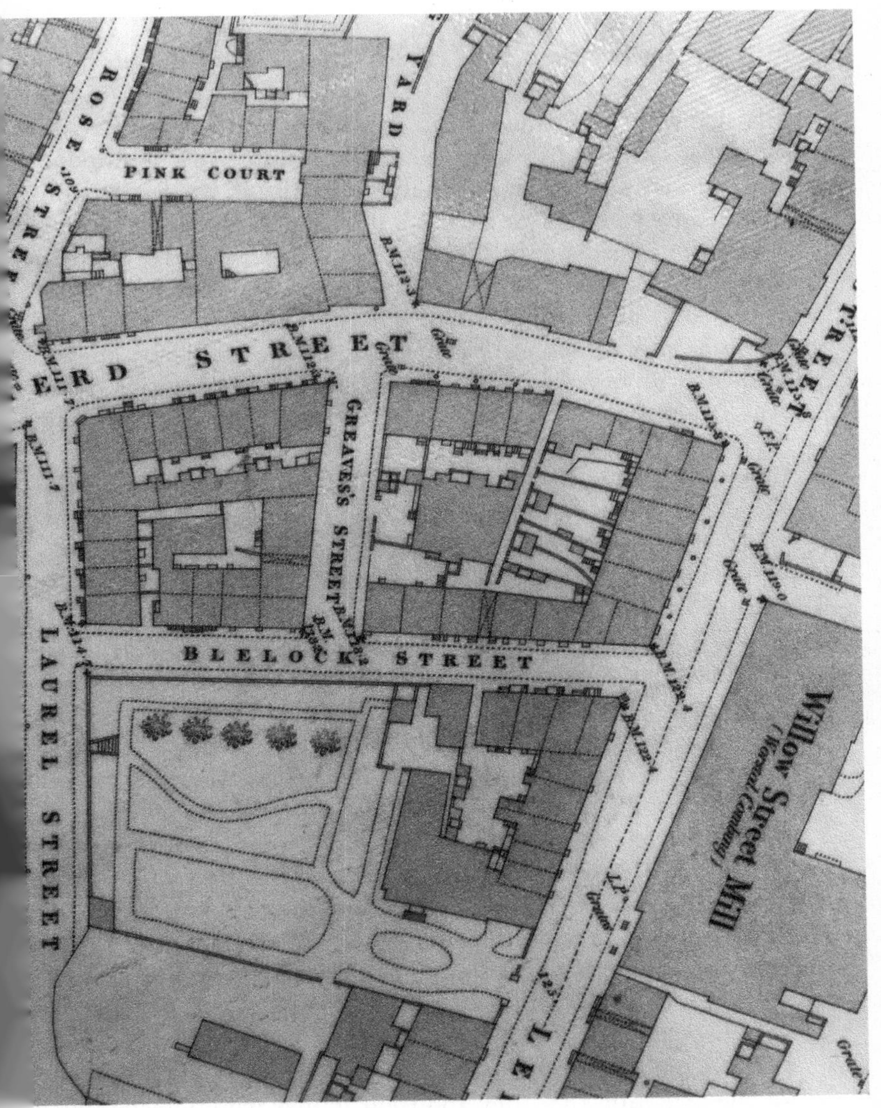

Blelock Street and Laurel Street showing old handloom weavers' cottages.

arrested but did not turn up to court. In June 1857, Tallent was having her head bandaged in the White Lion on Syke Hill[13] by Ann Cross who was probably a woman of the district who performed basic medical care to avoid paying doctor's fees. While she was performing this kindness, Tallent showed either deplorable ingratitude or desperation or both by picking Ann Cross's pocket and lifting her purse which contained six shillings (£28 in 2018). She was arrested, sent to Sessions and sentenced to a year in prison and was lucky to avoid transportation.[14]

Some prostitutes were adept in spotting would be clients who had money, usually strangers to Preston. One of these was Mary Ann Fisher who enticed John Smith in January 1857 into the brothel where she lived and there knocked him down before taking nine sovereigns from his pocket (£843). When arrested, she denied having ever seeing Smith and that she was 'up t'street talking to a policeman'. The other women in the house backed her up. As a result, the case was inconclusive. Earlier, in 1855, Fisher, who was described by the *Chronicle* as 'a notorious prostitute' was charged with stealing thirty-seven sovereigns (£3,400) from William Bee, a drover from Garstang who turned up at 11 Blelock Street where Fisher ran a brothel. He took off his waistcoat, hung it up behind a door and went up to bed where he stayed until two o'clock. He was called for by a friend, James Cowell, and they went to the Legs of Man public house in Fishergate, just before it becomes Church Street. Here, Bee found that his money was ten pounds short, but revealed to his friend that 'twenty pints of rum' had been drunk at the brothel that morning. Fisher was arrested but the jury at the Midsummer Sessions acquitted her of stealing £18 4*s*. (£1717).

It beggars belief that so many outsiders made their way to the Sandhole to find some action yet were so ill-prepared for the reception that they and their money would encounter, knowing the reputation of the place. One slightly different example of how stupidity could be trounced was a that of Richard Dover who was in Leeming Street at quarter past eleven on Saturday night, the 5 July 1856. He came across a prostitute called Isabella Cogan who pretended to be drunk and asked him where the Sandhole was(!). She was accompanied by Margery Bradshaw. When they reached Blelock Street, Cogan threw her arms round him in an amorous embrace, performing the 'bug hunting' technique before eventually lifting Dover's money which she passed to Bradshaw. He went to the police and P.C. arrested both women. At trial, Cogan received six months' imprisonment for larceny while Bradshaw got twelve months because she was awaiting sentence for a previous conviction.

As discussed earlier, the 1870s were a financially difficult period for working-class people because of the Great Depression and the Agricultural Depression, made more acute in Preston by the unrest over the cotton operatives' wage cuts, the second coming in April 1878. There was a noticeable rise in prostitute violence and theft at this time, probably caused by desperation. In December 1871, five prostitutes, Agnes Ann Hornby, Alice Fielding (known as 'Big Alice'), Ann Miller, Ann Batty and Theresa Sheerens 'pounced on William Francis', a weaver from Blackburn, and stole sixteen shillings (£73). Foolishly, they all met up later for a drink in the Black Swan in Leeming Street, where they were arrested. When searched at the police station, there was money on all of them amounting to seven shillings (£32), which may or may not have been the money they had stolen from Francis. The missing amount, some of which will have been spent on drinks, may have also put into rent and contingency funds. Incidentally, female suspects were searched at the station by Mrs Dawson, the wife of P.C. Dawson. The five were tried at the Preston Sessions on 3 January 1873 but were all acquitted because their accuser did not turn up to court.

Of this group of five, 'Big Alice' was the most notorious and served sentences for keeping a brothel at 11 Blelock Street, wilful damage, prostitution (four times) and the theft of a watch in April 1872 for which she served two years in Lancaster Castle with hard labour. Ann Batty (born 1852) was involved with Catherine Smith (born 1852) and Emma

Pimley (born 1855) in a robbery at a brothel, possibly 11 Blelock Street, in May 1874. All three of them set upon Joseph Ellis, seizing hold of him and forcibly taking four pounds (£364) from his pockets. P. D. Watson arrested them and all three were found guilty at the Preston Sessions two weeks later. Batty received nine months in Lancaster Castle with hard labour; Pimley was sent to the same place for four months with hard labour; Smith, who had done prison sentences at the ages of twelve and sixteen for theft, was sentenced to twelve months in Preston Gaol, also with hard labour. Incidentally, the prison records show that Smith could read while the other two had never received any education.

In December 1873, Ann Davis and Annie Miller (see above) came across Alfred Gallagher in the Rifleman Inn. He had only just arrived from America and was looking for accommodation. The two women were only too happy to oblige. They took him to a house, possibly in Leeming Street, where they knocked him down before stealing a bag of silver coins containing fifteen shillings and six pence (£67). At Sessions they both received four months' imprisonment.

Two well-known characters, Edward Leonard (aged 20) and Catherine Beisley (23), bully and prostitute, worked together in December 1876 to rob Joseph Knowles of his money at a brothel in the Sandhole. Despite his youth, Leonard was already covered in scars, especially around his face and neck. According to prison records neither he nor Beisley had had any education. During an intense argument, Leonard hit Knowles on the head with a poker and, while he lay on the floor bleeding, Beisley stole his money – two pounds, sixteen shillings and six pence (£261). After arrest, both were sent to Sessions in Preston where they were found guilty. Leonard, who had spent numerous short periods in prison for minor felonies, was sentenced to seven years. Beisley, who had spent thirteen periods of time in prison for prostitution, was sentenced to one year with hard labour. Just taking this one case into consideration, Rev. John Clay's recommendation, forty years before, that education might break a circle of crime certainly rings true.

Other mundane crimes were being committed in the Sandhole and the surrounding area, such as theft of shoes, boots, sheets and clothes from brothels and lodging houses, petticoats, shawls, dresses, bonnets, neckerchiefs and lead from roofs. For instance, lead was stripped off a roof in Rose Street, close to where Kate Matthews set up her brothel later.[15] All through this time, there was a steady stream of men who ventured into this area, looking for entertainment, excitement and action. Some of them were too trusting, some of them thoughtless, and other plainly stupid enough to enter this well-known den of thieves while carrying purses, wallets and pockets full of money, usually made from business made at market. Many of them, though not all, came from out of town, only to fall under the knowing scrutiny of prostitutes and their bullies.

Some of them were too trusting, some of them thoughtless, and other plainly stupid enough to enter this well-known den of thieves while carrying purses, wallets and pockets full of money,

The *Herald* reported, on 11 August 1866, one such case where Thomas Simpson of Harrington Street was relieved of his watch by Elizabeth Ann Whalley and Emma Taylor in a classic piece of opportunism. Simpson told the police that he had gone into the Rifleman Inn between eleven o'clock and midnight to buy wine. It should be made clear here that Harrington Street ran across Adelphi Street, a good fifteen minutes' walk away. At the Rifleman he struck up a conversation with Whalley and Taylor, who later took him to a private house where whisky was drunk (no doubt at Simpson's expense) and he fell asleep, intoxicated. When he woke up his watch and chain had gone. The two women attempted to pawn it at Mr Hayhurst's pawnbroker shop, but the assistant refused it and reported them to the police. At Sessions, eleven days later, Taylor and Whalley were mysteriously acquitted. Perhaps the court had little sympathy with Simpson.

Less than four months later, the *Herald* reported that Mary Mawdsley, a prostitute who was on remand, had stolen twelve shillings (£54.60) from John Hilton of 12 Albert Street. At half past six on the evening of 27 November 1866, Hilton was in the Griffin Inn and treated Mawdsley to a glass of beer. When they left the beerhouse they went to a brothel in Blelock Street 'where he fell asleep'. He woke at five o'clock the following morning to find Mawdsley and his money gone. She was eventually tracked down and sent to Sessions in Lancaster. Here she was sentenced to a year in Lancaster Castle prison with hard labour, as she was on remand for an earlier theft of silver coins from Joseph Holden amounting also to twelve shillings. It was also revealed in court, at the end of the case, that Mawdsley had only just been released from a four-year term in prison for theft. This is just one more example of the vicious circle of crime Rev. Clay warned about.

The ability of prostitutes to spot a man of means and then work on him is illustrated by an incident which occurred in May 1875. Policemen on their rounds of the Water Street area went into the Black Swan and spotted Ralph Yates, 'a respectable looking middle aged man', surrounded by prostitutes 'who seemed to be aware that he had a large amount of money one him'. The police officers arrested him for drunkenness, but they got a surprise when he turned his pockets out at the station. He had £62 (£5,737) on him in cash. When he was fined five shillings (£21), the magistrates commented that the constables 'had done him a kindness in bringing him to the station for safety'.

A robbery case which may reveal what a prostitute charged for her services was heard in October 1854 when Joseph Holden, a weaver from Blackburn, came to Preston to look for work. He left his bundle at a beershop in Butler Street, adjacent to the railway station, and wandered the streets. Eventually 'he found his way to that den of iniquity in Shepherd Street called Liverpool House' where he encountered 'two notorious characters' (*Chronicle*) – Mary Ann Hanlon and Ellen Brown. After drinking a glass of ale, Hanlon put her hand into his pocket

He found his way to that den of iniquity in Shepherd Street called Liverpool House' where he encountered 'two notorious characters

and stole six shillings (£28) and ran off. Holden returned to Butler Street, sold a pair of trousers from his bundle and returned to Liverpool House to retrieve his money. There, an unnamed man (possibly the landlord, John Proctor or a bully), knocked him down and Brown took his wallet. He summoned the police and P.C. Park arrested the women and they were searched at the station. Brown had nothing on her person. Hanlon had sixpence (£2.30) 'in her bosom', and one shilling and ten pence, probably in one of the many pockets in her underskirts where most prostitutes kept their money secret and safe. (They were 'dressmakers' were they not?) That last amount, taking labour earnings and value into consideration as opposed to the going price for staple foods etc would be worth £67 in today's money. The original six shillings may have been 'tipped up' back at her house for rent and the fine contingency fund so, possibly, the money found on her might have been earned through 'business'. In the end, the case was dismissed 'because of mistaken identity'.

It is easy to forget that children and young people lived and worked in or near the Sandhole. In a letter to both the *Chronicle* and the *Herald*, published on 2 July 1881, 'A Sufferer' engaged the readerships with a complaint about 'the overflow of Water Street blackguardism into Grimshaw Street'. The two streets were joined by a large passage called Back Grimshaw Street, which still exists. The letter was a plea to the authorities in letter, petition and deputation form for the magistrates to take action. The writer gives details such as 'exhibitions of sin and vulgarity' being witnessed often. Later, he reminds the authorities about the people most affected, among them, children. He talks about Grimshaw Street School 'with its nearly four hundred scholars', 'young boys and girls belonging to respectable parents' who should not have 'exhibitions of sin and vulgarity forced before their eyes in the street where they attend school'. He also points out that workers, many of them half-timers up to the age of twelve and others not much more than that, had to walk up to Anderton's Mill, Sharp's Gold Bobbin Works and Dryden's foundry past 'uproar and bawdy talk'.

During the nineteenth century, one person in three in Britain was a child under the age of fourteen.

During the nineteenth century, 'knots of children crowded the Victorian landscape',[16] as one person in three in Britain was a child under the age of fourteen. However, as far as newspapers and other records are concerned, children feature little in the comings and goings of the Sandhole and its associated areas. Some, with their poor families had to live in houses mostly to the southern end of the area around and beyond Queen Street. Occasionally, children would steal items and take them to the pawnbrokers in Church Street and Water Street where the assistants would send them on their way. However, in one case, the boys who stole brass door handles were caught and sent to reformatory schools for five years. Occasionally a boy under the age of sixteen was birched at the police station for theft, but far fewer received corporal punishment in Preston than some people may think.

One girl who was sent to a reformatory in 1870 was thirteen-year-old Martha Kennedy, who arrived in the Sandhole in August, trying to sell some items which she had stolen the day before. When she approached Martha Wignall of 3 Leeming Street, she said she wanted to buy a 'brat'. In its mid-Victorian sense, a 'brat' meant the child of a degraded person or beggar, so what Kennedy intended to do with this child is anyone's guess, but it is unlikely it would be for moral purposes. She herself was above the age of consent – twelve – and some prostitutes in Preston were under the age of sixteen, and Kellow Chesney states that a quarter of prostitutes in York were all younger than that. Earlier that day, Kennedy had stolen a locket and chain from Mary Peacock, a woman who had found her sitting on a doorstep in Walker Street, taken pity on her and given her a bed for the night. Martha Wignall called the police and P. D. Dawson arrested Kennedy who was found guilty, sentenced to one month's imprisonment then sent to reformatory for five years.[17] The *Chronicle* reports that 'She cried for her mother and was removed with difficulty from the court'.

One child, designated for reformatory school through no fault of his own, was eight-year-old Robert Johnson. In October 1878, application was made for his removal from his mother, Mary Johnson, who was a prostitute living in a brothel in Water Street (later reported as Shepherd Street). The Chief Inspector of police, Mr Oglethorpe, probably with the best of intentions, decided that Robert should go to an industrial school to remove him from evil influences. This was related to the 'muscular Christianity' approach becoming prevalent at the time. The magistrate, Mr Pyke, agreed but wanted further enquiries to be made and called a week's adjournment. Seven days later an order was issued to remove the boy in order to take him from 'the company of prostitutes and thieves' and send him to St George's Catholic Reformatory School in Liverpool. However, careful and extensive reading of the school's registers show no mention of him. In addition, he and his mother are not on any Preston records after this date. Perhaps they moved on during the week's adjournment.

Child abduction was not uncommon in the Victorian period

Child abduction was not uncommon in the Victorian period, especially where the victim was put to some purpose for the gratification or financial betterment of adults. In August 1854, while walking his beat, James Steanson found a young boy wandering around in the rain at one o'clock in the morning in High Street. He had been snatched with violence from Toxteth Place, in the township of Toxteth, by two men who had taken him in a gig, a fast two-wheeled carriage. For reasons unknown, he was dumped in Preston, but these abductees were often put to criminal acts. In April 1870, Mary Walmsley abducted a nine-year-old girl, Mary Cowell, from Chorley railway station, brought her to Preston and forced her to beg. The police were alerted and, eventually, P.C. Beardwood found them at Wearden's lodging house in Water Street. Unsuccessful rescues, or none at all, would often result in a life of adult crime, as Kellow Chesney says, quoting Thomas Archer,

> Their downward path was 'expedited by old debauchees … to whom indecent language and abandoned indifference to modesty have been a fresh stimulus and gratification'.[18] No-one remotely acquainted with the subject will doubt that small boys were active in the same way.

Earlier in this project, mention was made of Sarah Gee, a well-known prostitute and vagrant of the 1840s, taking in young girls and teaching them to be prostitutes. In May 1876, Edward George Smith, the proprietor of a cap and hat shop in Friargate, was accused in the Police Court of 'criminally misconducting himself towards a little girl'.[19] According to the evidence, he was in the habit of paying girls around ten years of age a halfpenny or a penny (19/38 pence) to go upstairs where he would have intercourse with them. At Sessions, after a defence run on the idea that the evidence of mere children could ruin a respectable tradesman, the jury found him guilty of 'having carnal knowledge with a girl under twelve'. The judge declared that Smith had been 'deliberately training up these children to become prostitutes'.[20] He went on to describe him as 'a brutal, cowardly man … who was undermining the morals of children'. He was sentenced to two years' hard labour.

A child living in the Sandhole, eight-year-old Jane Banks, the daughter of Joseph Banks, landlord of the Black Swan in Water Street, was indecently assaulted on Avenham Park in May 1868. She and some other girls of her age had been on the park with a pram which John Hoyle had helped to wheel to the top of the hill to the main entrance. Here, he lifted Jane Banks up 'to have a view of the railway engines and, in doing so, he committed a very indecent assault on her'. (*Chronicle*) He proceeded to assault all the others in the same way, and he gave them all halfpennies 'not to mention the affair to anyone'.[21] He promised more money if they would meet him again the following day, but the girls told their parents and Joseph Banks was a former policeman. The following day, P. D. Brown arrested Hoyle on the park and, it turned out, he had been imprisoned for six months in Blackburn for similar offences.

A few years later, a similar offence took place in the Sandhole. Peter McLaughlin was arrested in February 1872 for indecently assaulting Isabella Hayes, the daughter of Thomas Hayes, a pawnbroker in Water Street. While she was 'doing domestic duties' at the top of a ladder at the shop on 3 February McLaughlin 'took liberties with her'. After he was taken into custody, his manner was said to be 'impudent and outrageous', laughing and joking and refusing to take the charge seriously, claiming he was drunk at the time. He was found guilty and spent a month in the House of Correction. Unfortunately, not all crimes of this type resulted in conviction. In 1863, William Thompson was charged with attempting to indecently assault twelve-year-old Mary Smith, but he was discharged.

A general view of the Sandhole and the immediately surrounding area was, by the 1870s, that it was a place to be avoided by decent people though it proved to be a magnet for men who wanted some excitement or action. Certain soldiers who had been 'roughing it' in various locations in the Empire and men from the country who possibly lived more primitively, seemed not to be deterred by the less than salubrious conditions. It is true that some country people migrating to towns, brought with them more uncouth ways of life, for example, Margaret Boylan and her pigs.

By the 1870s ... the Sandhole was a place to be avoided by decent people

In a time when women were seen as second-class citizens, the general impression is that women held most of the influence in the Sandhole and its satellite streets. Of course, some women chose to work in 'partnership' with a bully, but the general trend for decades was that women were in charge of the houses and therefore of recruitment and finances. When the grip of the law grip began to tighten after 1870, these women tried methods to avoid longer prison sentences. Also, their association with public houses and beerhouses was threatened, a development to be considered in the next section.

Tom Sayers (1826–65)

7

'Places of Ruinous Resort'

For almost thirty years after Reverend John Clay's death in 1858, his comment held true. The public house and beerhouse were, in their time, an important social centre which '… offered warmth, gossip, information, entertainment, meeting rooms and comradeship …'[1]

But these good points of social interaction were outweighed by the fact that the same establishments were instrumental in '… disrupting family budgets, promoting fighting and rowdiness and, critics alleged, nurturing most of the crime, vice and poverty in the country.'[2]

Within a few limits, the same could be said of the licensed premises in the Sandhole and surrounding area, some of which has been touched on in this study already. For nearly fifty years, this area continued its grimy existence, promoted by various landlords and licensees who carried on their businesses with little restriction from the authorities. In the days leading up to the annual Brewster (Licensing) Sessions at the Town Hall, usually held at the beginning of September, certain groups, often made up of Anglican and Nonconformist representatives, would meet in places like the Temperance Hall in North Road. Here they would discuss the Superintendent of Police's annual report, specifically to examine anything which pertained to alcohol. The attendance at these meetings varied from fair to 'sparse', but the discussion culminated in 'memorials' (a form of memorandum) to be read out to the Mayor and Licensing Committee before they considered their licensing decisions. These memorials often chimed with the Superintendent's report but, consistently, over a thirty-five-year period from about 1835 to 1873, the Committee made its own decisions, despite what had been put before them. In fact, reports in the *Chronicle* and later the *Herald*, give the distinct impression that the Committee were going through the motions of listening before getting on with their own agenda, which was usually just to censure the worst offenders.

There were 432 licensed premises in Preston, a dozen or so situated in the Sandhole and the area surrounding it.

Today, people in Preston may be amazed to know that there were 432 licensed premises in the town, a dozen or so situated in the Sandhole and the area surrounding it. The main ones, the Griffin Inn, the Rifleman Inn, the Black Swan, Liverpool House and the Lodge Bank Tavern were all integral to the lives of many in the nearby streets, especially those who lived for the day and never looked much further than the day after that.

From 1836 until 1869, Liverpool House carried on a charmed existence while being known as the most notorious beerhouse in the district. As early as 1849, the landlord, Samuel Leighton, was charged with permitting drunkenness on Sunday 18 March, which seems severe, in hindsight, compared with some of the behaviour perpetrated in later years in other licensed premises in the area. However, on that day, police officers found the place full of soldiers and prostitutes, most of whom were in a 'beastly state of intoxication and conducting themselves in a most riotous and disorderly manner'. Leighton was fined forty shillings (£203) and the Mayor, James German, said that the town authorities were determined to 'put down these disorderly houses'. Another forty years would pass before this happened.

From this time on, Liverpool House was the centre of illegal and immoral activities. An incident which led to further trouble was when Private Thomas Shepherd assaulted P.C. Atherton because he thought that he was part of a piquet which had been sent by the 85th (Bucks Volunteers) Regiment, searching for absentees and deserters in the Sandhole. As a result, the Colonel of the Regiment stated that there was too close a bond between soldiers and public house keepers and accused Leighton of allowing Shepherd to change into civilian clothes. In his defence, Leighton said he had told P.C.s Hoole and Leach and had tried to prevent it. In the end he was discharged because the evidence was inconclusive. Liverpool House was, therefore, an early runner in the Sandhole as a centre of crime, much of which took place on the premises, such as orgies, beatings and theft, examples of which have already been discussed. Despite the licence passing from Leighton to Proctor, there was no improvement. Once Proctor got into his stride and tried to extend his influence[3] (see earlier) his licence came under scrutiny on a number of occasions until being refused for the last time in 1869 when the premises were sold.

Once the glory days of the handloom weavers were past, the area gradually, then steeply declined in every way, and with it did the licensed premises. The Griffin Inn, the Rifleman Inn and the Black Swan were situated in Water Street, the first two almost facing each other, only yards away from Church Street. The Black Swan was on the same side as the Griffin Inn and faced the eastern end of Shepherd Street and was described by some newspaper reports as being in Leeming Street, Water Street's continuation. Its site is now occupied by the boarded-up Balmoral Hotel premises, the only definite Sandhole landmark still in existence.

The Balmoral Hotel

The Griffin Inn, in the two decades up to the late 1850s was a reasonably quiet place for a town-centre tavern. There had been minor incidents such as when Ann Burgess, in a drunken state on 1 December 1859, had fallen out with the landlord

The character of the Griffin Inn deteriorated further during the tenure of Joseph Banks as licensee

and got her revenge by smashing the main window. It resulted in her sixteenth summons for drunkenness and resulted in six months in the House of Correction. The character of the Griffin Inn deteriorated further during the tenure of Joseph Banks as licensee. Banks was a former policeman who had left the force to take up a position at the railway station but turned up shortly afterwards in charge of the public house in August 1861.

Within twelve months, Banks was summoned for having in his house a large number of soldiers and prostitutes. When he visited on 13 July 1862, Detective Beckett found thirteen men and six prostitutes in the house and three prostitutes in another room. Banks was charged court costs, which would amount to about three shillings (£14) and was given a warning. In October 1861, a married couple, Thomas and Mary Greenwood, lured P.C. Gould into the Griffin at half past one to have a drink after he had moved them on earlier in the day. Martha Banks later testified in court that the policeman had not taken a drink, but the Greenwoods assaulted him in revenge. Both were sent to Sessions. In January 1863, Joseph Banks, who brewed his own ale like many other licensees, was taken to court for brewing irregularities. He was summoned by Mr Lane, the superior of excise, under the new Excise Duties Act (1862) in the first case of its kind to be brought in Preston for neglecting to enter twelve bushels (64 pints or 36 litres) of malt he had brewed the previous October. In his defence, Banks stated that his wife usually kept the brewing records but had forgotten because one of his children was ill. Mr Lane did not believe him and doubted that this was Banks's first offence. He was found guilty and fined fifty pounds (£4,700).

So, as far as Banks was concerned, 1863 had not started well, but it was to continue in much the same way. The following month, the Griffin was named as the place where five men planned to rob a man of his money. John Brockbank, a sailor, had been drinking there and was followed across Church Street by Joseph Alston (18), a blacksmith; Christopher Rogerson (18), a blacksmith; Thomas East (21), a stonemason; William Jackson (22), a brickmaker and John Tootle (20), a self-actor minder (cotton weaver), who attacked him in St John Street. As a sailor he would be a target for robbery because of the way seamen were paid. For her part, Alice Ann Aspden (20), who described herself as a factory hand, was found guilty and sentenced to eighteen months' imprisonment. The men were sent for trial at Sessions later in the month where they were all found not guilty, surprisingly, probably through lack of evidence. It is interesting to note that Alston, East, Tootle, and Jackson all lived in the Adelphi area of the town which was at least fifteen minutes' walk from the Sandhole. Rogerson managed to run shy of the law, being twice acquitted of felony later in 1863 and in 1865, but with ten summary offences including theft, drunkenness and assault, one of which was on his wife in the Griffin, he was sent to the House of Correction for twelve months with hard labour in 1869 for theft 'from the person'.

The next public event to hit Joseph Banks in 1863, and one which sheds more light on the workings of the area, was the report of Chief Superintendent Dunn, delivered at the Annual Licensing Sessions. In it he said that the Griffin had 'given the police a great deal of trouble' (*Herald* August 1863). He declared the place to be the cause of a great deal of prostitution. It never closed, being open from Monday morning to Saturday night, i.e. all week. The tripe shop next door had a communal door to the Griffin which Banks used to frustrate the police as they tried to stop drinking during prohibited hours. He continued by saying that his officers had been careful about Sunday drinking (prohibited before one o'clock in the afternoon) but they had found that the Griffin, and other premises, had 'spies and observers to deceive the police'. The Griffin had a concert room, which may have prompted Dunn's next remarks. He said if that these rooms, if properly run, were all right, but dancing rooms where 'youths and girls of a tender age are allowed to assemble' were an 'intolerable nuisance'. He continued, saying that the Griffin's licence had been suspended in 1862 but it had been allowed to continue. By August 1863 he declared it to be 'a great nuisance', especially that it still had a dancing room attached to it. After twenty minutes' deliberation, the Bench suspended the Griffin's licence and those of the Lodge Bank Tavern and the Turk's Head for a month for reconsideration. Within four weeks the licence was restored under strict conditions.

Over the next six years, until Banks lost his licence for good in 1869, the premises were a base for theft and violence both inside and out. It became common practice to size up a quarry in the Griffin to rob later. In 1864 a prostitute was arrested for meeting up with William Bond of 37 Oxford Road, as he left the house at one o'clock in the morning and enticed him to a nearby house where she relieved him of his money. Jane Overend, already mentioned, did the same in August 1867. Having met Henry Hall in the Griffin and drinking at his expense, she took his money from his waistcoat 'when he went to the yard' (*Chronicle*). After a lifetime of lawbreaking, Overend went to Lancaster Castle prison for twelve months. December of that year was particularly fertile for this type of crime. John Hilton of 12 Albert Street had twelve shillings (£57) stolen from him on 7 December. He had met with Mary Mawdsley in the Griffin at half past six and drank with her until late when she took him to a brothel in Blelock Street. Here he fell asleep until five o'clock the following morning when his money and Mawdsley had gone. Another man, William Wignall, was not as lucky as Hilton when he met Mary Ann O'Connor (aka Thompson) in the Griffin on 28 December. After drinks, O'Connor took him to her house where she seized him round the neck, hit him with a poker and stabbed him on the side of the head, presumably because he was too muscular in protecting his money. She was arrested and dealt with at Sessions.

After drinks, O'Connor seized him round the neck, hit him with a poker and stabbed him on the side of the head

True to the nature of the area was the theft, petty and otherwise, which seems to have been committed by people who were desperate or just downright immoral. In January 1865, Richard Bonny walked into the stables at the Griffin, calmly untied a horse belonging to Mark Law, a farmer from Burscough, and walked off with it. He sold the animal, which was said to be worth five pounds (£478), and sold it to William Gillibrand for a pound. The police were called, witnesses questioned and the two men were arrested, separately, in the Bear's Paw in Church Street.

While it is obvious that Banks ran a disorderly house and was making money, a little sympathy must be reserved for the Banks family. In the earlier period, two of his children became seriously ill and his daughter, Jane, was indecently assaulted on Avenham Park in May 1868. His house was also a target for theft on a fairly regular basis, such as in 1868, his charwoman, Mary Walker, made off with a sheet, a bonnet, a chemise, a bolster, a silk dress worth ten shillings (£44) and a petticoat. As she had performed other thefts in the past, she received a prison sentence of three months with hard labour. In August 1867, Richard Rogerson and James Evans entered the Griffin and stole Banks's tools which they were trying to hawk round the town when they were arrested. Both were sentenced to six months. A measure of the type of person who was liable to turn up at the Griffin was William Taylor who, in an act of revenge or in an attempt to entertain the regulars, put the Banks family cat on the fire. The cat survived. Taylor received a fine of forty shillings (£190).

In the lead-up to the 1869 Brewster (Licensing) Sessions of September 1869 there were some disastrous events for Joseph Banks as far as the magistrates were concerned. The first, in May 1868, the police raided the Griffin on a number of occasions, and he was charged with running a disorderly house by P.C. Walton. When he visited the place on 25 May, just before midnight, he counted forty to sixty people in the vault, of whom twenty to thirty seemed to be prostitutes. One of these was fighting with a man. As soon as Mrs Banks saw him she turned off the gas lighting, which accounts for the inexact numbers in the evidence. The case was deemed inconclusive and was dismissed. At this point in the court proceedings, Banks spoke up and complained about police raids which was noted by the magistrates. The second, which happened less than three months before the Brewster Sessions was a serious case of assault. In June 1869, Cornelius Sharples (21) and Christopher Rogerson (25) (see earlier), described by the *Herald* as 'a viciously disposed character', assaulted a prostitute called Isabella Robinson in the Griffin before stealing tenpence (£3.80) and her front door key. Both were found guilty: Sharples was sentenced to six months' imprisonment and Rogerson to a year with hard labour because of his previous convictions. At the end of the case, the magistrate, Mr Thomas Batty Addison (1787–1874) referred to the 'disreputable character' of the Griffin.

That year, the Beer and Wine Act was passed which, among other terms, ruled that all sellers of alcoholic drinks had to obtain a licence at the discretion of the Justices of the Peace, thus strengthening their hands at the Brewster Sessions. In mid-September 1869, the Preston Sessions took place and, unsurprisingly, the licence for the Griffin Inn was suspended. Reports said that in the previous two years a number of felonies had taken place there and the perpetrators had been convicted. Police Sergeant Upton stated that he regularly visited the Griffin and he often saw prostitutes and known thieves, sometimes as many as twenty. Police Sergeant Keefe had visited fourteen or fifteen times in the previous month and agreed with Sergeant Upton's statement. As a result, the Griffin licence was suspended.

In mid-September 1869, the Preston Sessions took place and, unsurprisingly, the licence for the Griffin Inn was suspended

Joseph Banks appealed against the suspension on 21 October. In this session, magistrates Addison and Gorst argued that the original charge against Banks of harbouring prostitutes could hardly be helped because of the nature of the prevailing circumstances of the Sandhole, i.e. the prevalence of brothels and low lodging houses. If a landlord did not let locals drink there, they would drink elsewhere. So, here again, is the argument for containment. The statement continued by saying that the magistrates had allowed the licence for forty years and women did not go there to commit crime, they went there for a drink. They said, '... he [Banks] would not allow anything improper in his house. There has been no complaint against him and no-one told him he might lose his licence.'

They went on to assert that Banks had spent time and money keeping his house orderly and other houses in the street were frequented by the same sort of people. Positive statements were given by a solicitor called Oakey and a doctor called Haldan about Banks's character. Among the comments made was that the Griffin could accommodate two hundred people and he knew that 'low characters' drank there and no-one could stop them going in, including the police.

The prosecuting solicitor, Mr Hawthorne, stated that the house had been a resort for 'low characters' for years and that it was 'a pity that the magistrates had tolerated the nuisance for so long and there had been many complaints'.

After due deliberation, the licence was refused. The owners proposed a man called George Kirk in September 1870, after the house had been closed for a year., for a beer and cider licence but it was not granted. The Griffin became a lodging house and acquired a more notorious reputation than it had as a public house. Joseph Banks became a beer agent for a number of licensed premises before becoming the landlord of the New Legs of Man and the Mitre Inn, both in Fishergate, the Red Lion in Church Street and then the Plough at Ashton, now known as the Lane Ends.

The Lodge Bank Tavern stood just north of Queen Street on the east side of Leeming Street. And had been a near neighbour of the Baptist Chapel until the congregation moved to Fishergate, a move partly caused by nature of the Tavern. The establishment does not feature in any documentary way until the Brewster Sessions of August 1852. After the customary depositions and memorials presented to the magistrates from the Temperance Society and delivered by Reverend John Clay, appeals were made by Nonconformists and Quakers not to grant any new licences. After consultation, the magistrates granted eight new licences out of twenty-one applications, reprimanded Charles Swift of the Black Swan for 'irregularities' before suspending the licence of the Lodge Bank Tavern, run by John Younghusband. There had been no mention of the public house in the depositions and no explicit reason was given for the suspension. Two weeks later, Younghusband successfully applied for a renewal. Again, no details or reprimands were given.

The usual occupation of many people of the Sandhole, thieving, went on near or in the Lodge Bank Tavern. The laissez-faire of two landlords, Younghusband in 1853 and John Fielding in 1863, allowed customers to be drunk and sleep in the house. Elizabeth White, in the first instance, was arrested in the Tavern for picking the pocket of Reuben Snape, 'a rather soft looking individual' (*Chronicle*) from Whittle-le-Woods while he was drunk and asleep. In the second instance, William Mansergh was also drunk and asleep when Mary Ann Waddington, Ann Callaghan and Jane Naylor relieved him of his bank book and three pounds in cash (£282).

In 1852, John Younghusband trustingly hired out a hurdy-gurdy[4] to a 'foreigner' (*Chronicle*) called John Keefe. Judging by his name he was more likely to be Irish. When he did not return it, a search was made and it was found in a pawnshop where Keefe had received thirty shillings for it (£160). He was arrested, found guilty and fined five pounds (£533) or serve three months in prison. Between 1850 and 1865, stealing lead was very prevalent in Preston. Thieves would strip lead from almost any roof anywhere. Notable buildings which suffered in this way were the railway station, St Thomas's School and the stables in Church Street which had once belonged to Patten House, the Derby family's town residence before they left Preston for good in 1835. In November 1856, the Tavern suffered the same fate When Edward Burns and William East (see earlier) were sent for trial for stripping lead from an outhouse roof. They both were sent to prison for two months. East, aged fifteen, was too old to be birched, but this misdemeanour started a life of crime over a twenty-year period which included nine assaults, four thefts, drunkenness, five militia offences, bastardy[5] (for which he served three months) and a final theft for which he served ten years under the Habitual Criminals Act of 1869.

A robbery in the Tavern in April was one of the incidents which put the most recent licensee, John Fielding under scrutiny and damaged his reputation. Mary Ann Lawson robbed William Mercer of Chipping, 'a simple looking fellow' (*Herald*) of all his money on 10 March 1863. Lawson, who had worked the streets of Preston for about six years and had been in custody five times since 1857, was sent to prison for three years. At the Brewster Session of August 1863, the licence for the Tavern was suspended because Fielding had allowed prostitutes to assemble there. Police officers reported that it was 'an extremely bad house'. The Chairman of magistrates decided that the landlord was very unfit and the licence was suspended. Yet, four weeks later, Fielding was back in business. The licence was approved 'after good reports' (*Herald*).

Earlier in this study, an act of wanton violence was described where William Ireland had attacked his cohabitee, Margaret Heaps, in 1865. This took place in the Tavern in full view of all and was one of the reasons why Fielding came under further scrutiny. Although the Tavern somehow escaped suspension in that year, the picture of it painted by Chief Constable Dunn of the area in the September Sessions is a grim one. He mentioned no specific establishments but decided to quote statistics instead. At that time there were four hundred and seventy-five licensed house in Preston (221 public houses, 254 beerhouses) which was a ratio of one to every thirty two dwelling houses in the town. Forty-nine licensees had been reported for violating the law, some of them three times. Gambling was allowed in six places and twenty-eight were described as the resorts of thieves and prostitutes. For some reason, he blamed drunkenness 'as a possible cause of prostitution' and the Shepherd Street area was cited as a centre of this.

The summer of 1867 marked the beginning of the end for the Tavern as it and neighbouring buildings were advertised for sale in the *Herald* on 20 July. The property was split into three lots. Lot 1 was the Tavern itself 'occupied by John

Fielding'. Lot 2 was made up of 'land and offices adjoining' used as joiner and builder's yard, and Lot 3 was a bakehouse and a cottage 'abutting Lot 2'. The advertisement went on to state that the properties should all be sold in one lot, described as 'very valuable land for building purposes and has an outlet onto Blelock Street, Laurel Street and Leeming Street'. This overblown and over optimistic advertisement came to nothing, no small part due to the fact that Fielding was, with others, objected to at the August Sessions, though he was later reprieved. That year, the Wine and Beerhouse Act gave magistrates more power and the police more confidence. In his submission, Chief Inspector Dunn boldly states,

> There are a number of publicans and beersellers who encourage thieves and prostitutes and persons of bad characters ... who are unfit to hold a licence. I have reason to complain of the encouragement given to Sunday drinking and many publicans and beersellers, especially the latter, employ scouts to watch for the police which makes them almost impossible to detect, and the fine is so small that they can indemnify themselves in a few hours. (my emphasis)[6]

In the last week of August, a public meeting was held with representatives of all the town Protestant churches and chapels present. All new licences were opposed including seven in the Sandhole, one of which was the Lodge Bank Tavern. At the Sessions, all seven were suspended until the middle of September. In the meantime, on 4 September, the *Chronicle* decided to intervene with its own criticisms in a rare editorial on the subject. Although not sympathetic to teetotallers, it complained about drunkenness and badly regulated licensed premises. It looked forward to 15 September when the new Act would be applied against certain establishments. There was a particular snipe at beersellers

> who have the commonest and worst portion of trade to deal with and ... are more liable to get into a vicious way of managing it – have been able to snap their fingers at magisterial jurisdiction and console themselves with the fact that, however wrong they get, nothing beyond a fine, which could be made up in a matter of hours, could be inflicted on them. But now the new law gives power over licences.

On 15 September, the licence for the Tavern was upheld despite it being described as 'a resort for prostitutes'. The defending solicitor, Thomas Edelston, said that if the licence was refused then the trustees for the property would take it up. They issued a statement saying that they knew nothing of the place being used 'to allow such persons to resort there', which is hardly credible as the town had four newspapers and the Sandhole was hardly ever out of the news. The following year, which turned out to be the Tavern's last, Fielding was summoned before the magistrates for keeping a disorderly house and there was a weight of evidence.

At half past eleven on 31 March 1870, Sergeant Hornby and Constable Burns walked into the Tavern and found a prostitute and a man called Steele with glasses of ale in front of them. In the back room they found three prostitutes with three men and in the kitchen they found two more men and two more prostitutes. When the landlady, Mrs Fielding was asked about this situation, she replied, 'I know them'. In addition, Hornby had visited the Tavern on 10, 14 and 29 March, always finding the same class of people there. Fielding was fined twenty shillings (£94) and costs. As a result, the Brewster Sessions in August went badly for him because the police regarded the Tavern as a resort for 'a good many prostitutes who live in the houses of ill fame' nearby and 'no steps had been taken for their suppression'. The verdict was that the landlord was 'very unfit' and the licence was suspended. There had been an attempt by an accountant, Thomas Fletcher of Cross Street, to put this 'old established inn' out to let and more serious attempts were made in October, advertising in all the newspapers. On 3 December, James Fletcher passed the Tavern onto James Turner, formerly of the Weavers' Arms.

By January 1872, the Tavern was put up for sale as part of an auction comprising of four lots and it was Lot 3. The first was a foundry with workshops, offices, showrooms, a cottage and stables which had access from Leeming Street and Grimshaw Street. The second was classed as 'valuable land' which was occupied by a timber yard, workshop, boiler house and office on the north side of Laurel Street and on the east side (i.e. in the middle of a clutch of brothels). The Lodge Bank Tavern, on the southern end of Leeming Street, was described as a 'well established inn or public house'. Nothing was said about its reputation, of course. The fourth lot comprised a cottage, dwelling house and bakehouse at 42 and 43 Leeming Street. The advertisement was run in the *Herald* on 6 January 1872 and repeated in the next three weekly editions. Whether the Tavern was closed during this period is unclear, but on 15 February 1873 the *Herald* reported that it had been bought by the Anglican parish of St Saviour to be opened as a school next to the church on the corner of Queen Street.

The Rifleman Inn[7] stood on the northern end of Water Street, close to Church Street and opposite the Griffin Inn. The early period of its existence seems to have been fairly quiet, being the venue for formal dinners and celebrations. The deterioration of the area changed all this. The first notable crime reported in this place was perpetrated by the landlord, David Mellor, on a prostitute called Ann Collett. He attacked her and knocked her down one night when she was leaving in March 1860 (see earlier chapter). There was the usual ever-present thieving, even from the licensee and his family. In March 1860, 'a rather wretched looking woman' (*Chronicle*) called Mary Ann Jackson stole a woollen scarf, the property of Mrs Mellor and pawned it for tenpence (£4) for which she received a month's hard labour. Three months later, 'a respectably dressed young man' (*Chronicle*) called John Hayhurst and Mary Helm were arrested for stealing a pair of trousers from the landlord.

The first notable crime reported in The Rifleman was perpetrated by the landlord, David Mellor, on a prostitute called Ann Collett

Most robberies took place in the streets outside after a rendezvous in the Rifleman, such as when, in 1866, Elizabeth Ann Whalley and Emma Taylor managed to get Thomas Simpson drunk at his own expense so that they could steal his watch (see earlier). A year later, Margaret M'Kown, convicted three times for theft, became acquainted with John

Breakell of Emmett Street on the other side of town, on an April evening. In Leeming Street, she amorously threw her arms round his waist and lifted his watch. However, when she tried to dispose of it, none of the women in her Blelock Street house would have anything to do with it. After further drinking in the Rifleman she decided to hide it under some stones in Leeming Street. When it was discovered she was arrested.

The last year of Mellor's tenure was coloured by a growing poor reputation for the Rifleman, including robbery and violence. In May 1865, Thomas Nixon robbed Robert Huston after Huston had bought him and Elizabeth Berry some beer. When Huston was drunk, presumably at his own expense, Nixon got him down and stole his money which he passed to Berry. Both were arrested and after witnesses had testified against them, they were both found guilty and were sent to Sessions. There followed, after Mellor, three quick changes of landlord, firstly George Crook, secondly Ralph Spencer and thirdly James Pitcher. Two weeks into Crook's time, there was a serious case of actual bodily harm in the building. Ann Hall, a prostitute, was sent to prison for one month with hard labour for a vicious assault on another woman. After an argument, Hall forced the woman into a corner where she repeatedly hit her in the face; the marks and bruises were clearly visible in court. The *Chronicle* states that Hall was 'said to have the ability of Sayers'.[8] She had already served two long sentences for violence.

Ann Hall, a prostitute, was sent to prison for one month with hard labour for a vicious assault on another woman... she had 'the ability of Sayers'

While Spencer and Pitcher were the landlords, the reputation of the Rifleman, already tarnished, deteriorated further as a constantly disorderly house. The police were called thereon the night of 19 November 1867 when the place was in uproar as two drunk prostitutes, Alice Booth and Ellen Stephens were fighting. After this incident, Spencer was fined ten shillings (£43.50) for running a disorderly house, but the worst part of this was the bad publicity.

The *Chronicle* called the Rifleman 'a resort of convicted and known thieves and prostitutes' (30 November 1867). All this happened after the tenure of George Crook came to an end by losing his licence at the August Brewster Session. The licence was only restored to Spencer after this incident on assurances of better management.

Two years of rowdiness and general lawlessness under a man called George Smith brought a suspension of his licence at the 1869 Sessions, At these, Sergeant Keefe said that he had visited the Rifleman twelve times during August and 'found there prostitutes, drunken characters, low characters and thieves'. Thomas Edelston, the defending solicitor, took Smith's suspension as an opportunity to bring in a new angle on the recent Act of Parliament. He maintained the police evidence did not

> maintain a fair trial and that the licensees only heard of these accusations when they arrived at court. The police should have summoned the landlords to court to allow them chance to defend themselves. Society called landlords into being and they were not to be put down just on the statements of the police.

He went on to ask what prostitutes were, and that some people who had been named would be 'aggrieved' if they knew. He asked if prostitutes were allowed to go into these places simply for a drink. He added that 'if persons of high rank would be unlikely to frequent such places as the Rifleman Inn and the Griffin Inn, so does it follow that prostitutes and such like go in for a drink they are committing an offence?'

The result of deliberations was that the Rifleman licence was reinstated with a new landlord, James Pitcher, taking over with a caution. On 24 September 1870, a year after taking up the position, Pitcher was summoned to court under the new Habitual Criminals Act passed on the 4 August 1869. This Act was designed to curb the careers of persistent lawbreakers through an accumulation

The Rifleman licence was reinstated with a new landlord, James Pitcher, taking over with a caution

or 'totting up' of misdemeanours over the years into a heavy sentence for a recent, sometimes fairly minor offence and seven years' supervision by the police.

Two good examples are the criminal records of two prostitutes who were active in the Sandhole area which are taken from the ledgers of Preston Prison/House of Correction.

The first is of Bridget Dolan who was born in Ireland in 1848 and spent her early years in the workhouse at Chorley. She gave her trade as card room worker, though this is probably what she did as a child. It was a junior's job. She had had no formal education, but she could read.

Her criminal record:

22 February 1864 Felony – 14 days' imprisonment

15 February 1865 Drunk and disorderly – 7 days' detention[9]

13 October 1865 Wilful Damage – 2 months' imprisonment

11 June 1866 Assaulting a constable – 1 month's imprisonment

1 April 1867 Drunk and Disorderly – 7 days' detention

19 October 1867 Theft at Burnley with Ann Lee (30) of a wallet from John Lord containing 18 shilling (£78) Lee – 18 months' imprisonment Dolan – 4 months' imprisonment both in Lancaster Castle

31 March 1869 Theft in Blelock Street brothel with Agnes Lewis of £7 15*s.* (£703) from Thomas Holmes Lewis – 12 months' imprisonment Dolan – 2 years' imprisonment Both with hard labour in Lancaster Castle

31 August 1869 Assault (in prison) – 6 weeks' imprisonment

16 May 1871 Drunk and Disorderly – 14 days' detention

6 June 1871 Theft of £3 from Richard Cook of Mawdesley in the Rifleman Inn – 7 years in the House of Correction and 7 years' police supervision.

In the 1881 Census, Bridget Dolan was recorded at a brothel at 6 Blelock Street. She got married in 1883.

The second woman, Ellen Dunderdale is an interesting case and rather an enigma. Unlike Bridget Dolan, Dunderdale came from a comfortable home. Born in 1834, the 1861 Census records her at home with her parents and siblings at 3 St Austin's Road, only yards away from St Augustine's Church. Her father is recorded as a 'Banker's Clerk' and the house the family lived in was new, having been built around 1858. Coincidentally, my great great grandfather, John Garlington and his sisters were living at 11 St Austin's Road, having moved there from Walton-le-Dale only recently. He was a cabinet maker by trade.

What went wrong with Ellen Dunderdale? She could possibly have disgraced herself somehow. Ben Wilson[10] quotes Christian Goede from his book *The Stranger in England*, saying that Goede was amazed that English people were proud of their morals when there were so many prostitutes, many of whom were so because they were outcasts from society – '… in England, one false step is never pardoned.'

On the other hand, she may have been a renegade, a 'wrong-'un' on 'whose nature, nurture can never stick'.[11] Kellow Chesney has an opinion on this. 'The fallen girl from a decent family was less likely to be restrained than encouraged to promiscuity and the rewards of prostitution.'[12]

As it was, her education was imperfect and she had no trade or profession.

17 January 1863 Want of sureties[13] – 7 days' detention

26 January 1864 Felony (unspecified) – 1 month's imprisonment

23 June 1864 Drunk and Disorderly – 7 days' detention

17 August 1864 Theft of a shirt from Evis Lever – 12 months' imprisonment

12 March 1869 Drunk and Disorderly – 7 days' detention

8 March 1870 Want of sureties – 2 months' imprisonment

9 March 1871 Prostitution – 1 month's imprisonment

4 October 1871 Theft of a shawl from Louisa Whittle of Everton Gardens with Jane Atkinson – 2 months each with hard labour in Lancaster Castle

13 January 1872 Theft of seven shillings (£30) from Robert Rigby – 12 months' hard labour and seven years' supervision

13 June 1873 Running a disorderly house – 7 days' detention

19 July 1873 Running a disorderly house – 7 days' detention

20 October 1873 Running a disorderly house – 1 year's imprisonment

28 November 1874 Running a disorderly house – 18 months' imprisonment

15 November 1877 Receiving stolen brushes from John Bretherton, the property of Charles Legge – Bretherton 6 months with hard labour – Dunderdale 2 years' hard labour with seven years' supervision.

At the 1881 Census she was living with her widowed mother at 10 St Austin's Road and in 1891 she was living in Carr Street, off Manchester Road.

The problem arose when the Preston magistrates used this Act against Pitcher and, judging by the context of the above examples, it was a poor decision. The reason why they went ahead with it was probably the weight of criticism they were receiving in official proceedings, letters and newspaper editorials, and they wanted to show they meant business. Such an editorial had appeared in the *Chronicle* on 18 September 1869 where the police and magistrates were at odds.

> How could constables tell that immorality named [in the licensing session] existed at all if they had not seen it? … why have they not taken the course the law directs … summoning the landlords before the magistrates … [but] they seem to have allowed the evil to go on quietly under their very eyes and nose ends for months and years.

The magistrates dealt out punishments which were not much more than slaps on the wrist, which must have been demoralising for the police

This opinion is unfair on the police of the time. They patrolled the area twenty-four hours a day, arrested and charged miscreants of all types, and their Chief Constables, Dunn and Oglethorpe, gave realistic and incisive reports at each licensing session. The magistrates dealt out punishments which were not much more than slaps on the wrist, which must have been demoralising for the police.

The editorial continues by criticising the magistrates. 'Magistrates are often fettered by interest, direct or indirect, or led away, perhaps by whet we may call unconscious particularities, as the proverb says, "a rich man may steal a horse whilst a poor man may look over the hedge."'

The writer then looks forward to the future. 'It is not until the new Act comes into force that they (police and magistrates) arrive at a healthy state of consciousness, begin to think what a dreadful thing they have been permitting to openly exist for such a long time ...'

The writer did have some sympathy for the landlords because many were 'pounced upon' though they had 'never received a caution.'

It is against this backdrop that action was taken against James Pitcher.

Tension had been very much in evidence at the licensing session of August 1871. In a joint memorial agreed on at a public meeting, intention was shown much more strongly than in previous years. There were comments about brothels – sixty-one houses acknowledged by the police 'to be the resort of thieves and prostitutes'. The authors could not understand why proceedings had not been brought against those placed and recommended that the police should collect evidence and take proceedings against the offenders. In reply, the Mayor said that the magistrates were independent and there was no collusion with the police or anyone else, that they had to work within the law, but had come under fire from all sides, although they arrived at decisions 'through mind and conscience'. At the sessions, the licences for the Rifleman Inn and the Black Swan were suspended and proceedings against Proctor came to nothing.

Four weeks later, the licences objected to in August were reconsidered in a new meeting. One of the solicitors, Mr Watson, underlined the importance of the independence of magistrates and that the powers of licensing had been put into their hands in the reign of George II (1727–60).

He stated that if those who made petitions 'objected to vice and immorality, they should follow their vocation and visit the houses themselves', which was as much a criticism of the inactivity at the Parish Church as anywhere else. He continued by say they would never stop immorality by making speeches at it. 'They would never do it by preaching on platforms – they must reach the people themselves – go to the source of the evil itself.'

During the meeting, which lasted seven hours and thirty-five minutes, the licences objected to – the Lodge Bank Tavern, the Rifleman Inn, the Black Swan, the Bear's Paw and two beerhouses – were all considered and evidence examined. Despite police officers reminding the Bench that 'a good many prostitutes live in "houses of ill fame" in the area and no steps had been taken for their suppression', Pitcher and the others receive a renewal of their licences with a caution. So, nothing radical had been done to change the situation in any way.

The friction between the newspapers, the police and the magistrates must have rumbled on in the background because the situation resulted in a letter being written to the *Chronicle* by Thomas Edelston.[14] Published on 5 November 1870, it is an important exposition of the working of the courts, the magistrates' court in particular. In it he cites the summons of James Pitcher, its reasoning, its weakness and its unfairness. This friction must have affected Edelston as letters of this kind are uncommon almost to the point of uniqueness.

He begins by going back just over a year to the licensing session of 1869 where he and Robert Watson[15] (working as prosecuting and defending solicitors) had objected to publicans and beersellers being deprived of their 'certificates in an arbitrary and unfair manner'. He continues:

> The magistrates at this meeting had the power for the first time of withholding beersellers' certificates. The police had collected reports over a varying length of time which could have shown a breach of the law if they had been summoned. The offenders could have been convicted and punished, but they could have called witnesses, marshalled evidence and cross examined. These matters, brought up unexpectedly after

> a lapse of time, made it impossible for the person objected to to produce witnesses and defend themselves.

At this point, he quotes W. H. Higgins, the Chair of the Salford Sessions, who was of the same mind as he and Robert Watson. He uses lines which have more drama than his own.

> Nothing can be more unfair … than for the police to go spying on other people's premises … keeping them [i.e. facts] by them, then blurting them out just at the time when a man applies for a renewal of his licence, when his memory might be dead … nothing could be more unfair than that.

He moves on to a matter where he, his colleagues and the magistrates must have been criticised, that of obstructing or misusing the law.

> (Mr Watson and I) … were looked on as having come to court, not to discharge important duties but to thwart the Bench as if the "ex parte"[16] statements had been before the magistrates (as is done in some places) and a course of action resolved upon before the session started. Mr Watson stated the law clearly and lucidly but some of the members of the Bench made comments which led to angry words.

He goes on to cite the case where an unnamed innkeeper was summoned under the Habitual Criminals Act for 'permitting persons of bad character to assemble in his house'. The magistrates had gone ahead with the idea that the customers in question had used the premises for illegal purposes, but Messrs Watson and Edelston had argued that they had gone there for refreshment. The he turns to the case of James Pitcher at the Rifleman Inn.[17] The magistrates wanted thirteen cases of the above charge bringing against him, even though these had been objected to twelve months before. Then he turns to answer those outside the court who were agitating for change.

> The public seemed to expect that there was some means or other, no matter whether legal or not, for a diminution of the number of beerhouses … and magistrates conceived the impression that they were invested with power that they might exercise at pleasure, without hampering themselves

> with law and other considerations due to the holders of the licences.

He then turns to some people's misperceptions of the police, the way they carried out their job, but mostly the leadership of James Dunn[18] who made representations at all these annual sessions.

> I deny that anything like hue and cry was or could be raised against Mr Dunn or any other person. Mr Dunn was doing what he believed to be his duty and we were doing ours. I know not from whom he got his instructions or whether he got any; but it was the mode of proceeding and not Mr Dunn that we were hostile to.

The final part of this unusually candid and important letter shows the tack that Edelston and Watson were undertaking and how much, in the writer's opinion, the magistrates had been going wrong.

> It ought to be remembered that there is a great difference between granting a new licence and taking away an existing one. In the one case, the magistrates have discretion, in the other they have not. They have no right to deprive a man of his vested interest except on clear proof that he has broken the law and brought himself within the Act of Parliament.

This previewed arguments to come with the new Licensing Act in 1872, but it was the end of the road for James Pitcher as he was replaced by John Smith.

The modern observer may see the site of the last of the notorious Sandhole public houses, the Black Swan, in the shape of the rebuilt but now boarded up Balmoral Hotel in its last guise as a café. The Black Swan faced west up Shepherd Street; the short Water Street ran away north, to Church Street on its right. On its left, Leeming Street ran south to join King Street then the later developed Manchester Road which became the official name for the whole road from Church Street to Frenchwood in 1887. In the small web of

In the small web of streets which made up the Sandhole, the Black Swan sat on the side like its spider, notorious in its presence and position

streets which made up the Sandhole, the Black Swan sat on the side like its spider, notorious in its presence and position. Before other houses acquired their dubious reputations, The Black Swan had made an early start.

In more innocent times, the Preston appetite for theft, especially lead, manifested itself again when Thomas Kellett, labourer, walked off with a hundred and eleven pounds of it which he had stripped from the Black Swan's brewhouse roof in 1840 while he was working there. He tried to sell thirty-five pounds of it to Joseph Walmsley, a pawnbroker of North Road, offering it for three shillings (£13.30). He was committed to Sessions for trial where he received six months' imprisonment. Almost two years later, almost to the day, Kellett was caught stripping lead off the roof of the former stables of Lord Derby[19] where he had worked as an ostler. This time he was transported to Australia for seven years.

The 1850s opened unpromisingly with the landlord, Charles Swift, being charged, in October 1850 with running a disorderly house. By 'knowingly allowing bad characters to assemble in a dramshop belonging to his house'. P.C.s Poole and Thornton went in the week before and saw a number of soldiers and 'abandoned women' in company. They were orderly and sober, so Swift was angry that the police had picked him out because there was a beershop on the opposite side of the road which had 'similar company at the same time', but the police had taken no notice of it. In his opinion, they had 'negligently acted in their duty'. He was fined ten shillings (£52). Nearly two years later he was warned at the Brewster Sessions about infringing the Sunday licensing laws, i.e. selling alcohol before one o'clock to 'disorderly characters'.

The Black Swan seems to have come in for a fair amount of damage over the years, which gives some indication, if any were needed, of the type of customer who frequented it. Already quoted was the 1854 systematic smashing of the place by Catherine Ward and a soldier called Richard Hothersall of the 66th Regiment, all because Swift had prevented Ward from entering. Hothersall tried to intervene and, as a result, the main window, door panels and some glasses were broken before gas fittings were partly pulled down. Two years later, a character by the name of Francis Englishby broke twenty-three squares of glass on the premises, causing seventeen shillings and threepence worth of damage (£80) for which he was sentenced to two months' imprisonment. The passage of time did not bring improvement or progress in the Sandhole, as shown by the fact that, in 1864, two prostitutes called Ann Brown and Hannah Topping, were charged with being drunk and disorderly and smashing glasses. They were cautioned and made to pay for the damage. In 1876, a prostitute called Harriet Ann Marsden was put out of the Swan at 5.30pm for being drunk and riotous. In revenge, she found two bricks and threw one at the front door before putting the other through the front window. She had to pay for the damage which amounted to one pound (£180). These incidents are the ones which came to light. How many others remain unreported?

The main window, door panels and some glasses were broken before gas fittings were partly pulled down

Theft in and around the Black Swan began early. In 1849, two prostitutes called Emma Holden and Mary Smith picked out their mark, a man who was not named in court, sat on either side of him and rummaged through his pockets, removing four half crowns (£50) and ran off. Although he was drunk, the man managed to alert P.C. Stirzaker who arrested the women in Water Street. However, the court dismissed the case because of the man's inebriate state.

Emma Holden and Mary Smith picked out their mark, sat on either side of him and rummaged through his pockets, removing four half crowns, and ran off

Another example of choosing a victim occurred in 1862 when Mary Coates (26) was charged with stealing fifteen shillings (£69) from Joseph Bretherton from Longridge. He had visited a number of alehouses before meeting up with Coates and another prostitute in the Black Swan, for whom he bought drinks. Later, he and Coates left together and went to a house in Blelock Street where they 'went upstairs'. Here,

Coates, and probably others, made fun of Bretherton's dialect and strong accent, in particular his use of 'hoo' instead of 'she'. In fact, he seemed more annoyed by this than the loss of his money which Coates had removed from his pocket before running off. To evade capture, she called in somewhere else and changed her dress, but she was still arrested. On the day of the trial, she did not attend and the case was adjourned. Eventually she was brought up, found guilty and sentenced to two years' imprisonment.

Occasionally, stolen goods would turn up at the Black Swan. Just before Christmas 1857, three privates from the 7th (Royal Fusiliers) Regiment, Isaac Green, James Proctor and William Gibson, stole a roll of linsey woolsey[20] from Mr Jones's draper's shop in Church Street. The following day, Proctor and Green went to a brothel in Shepherd Street, run by a woman called Lennon because Proctor wanted to hide it there. None of the women would have anything to do with it so they went to the Black Swan and hid it under a form in the parlour. Eventually, Mrs Swift, the landlady, noticed it and told the police. The three soldiers were arrested, though Gibson was discharged. The other two received three months' imprisonment in Lancaster Castle at the Quarter Sessions the following month.

The police constantly identified the licensed premises in the Sandhole as venues where thieves congregated, made their plans and divided their spoils. One example of the Black Swan being used for this purpose occurred in February 1864. Solomon Sharples and George Ainsworth had bought some articles from a coal dealer called Thomas Watmough in the Black Lion beerhouse in Richmond Street, off Lark Hill Street. When Watmough fell asleep, probably drunk, Sharples and Ainsworth made off with his purse containing seven pounds and eight shillings (£707). Later in the Black Swan, another man, called Joseph Ashton, was asked to share it but Police Detective Swift tracked them down. One pound and fifteen shillings

The police constantly identified the licensed premises in the Sandhole as venues where thieves congregated, made their plans and divided their spoils

(£167) was found on Sharples; fifteen shillings and three ha'pence (£73) was found on Ainsworth. A year later, on 9 August, in the Black Swan itself, John Charnley's slumber provided the opportunity for Cornelius Monaghan to relieve him of three shillings (£14).

Like other premises in the area, the Black Swan was used as a base and a drinking hole by prostitutes, as the police knew and repeatedly reported to the magistrates and as observation posts for their stock-in-trade – theft from victims who showed that they had money, possibly the more they drank. On Saturday[21] 13 February 1869, Richard Tomlinson, a farm labourer from St Michael's, was drinking in the Black Swan when he met Mary Woods (19) and Mary Ann Clark at seven o'clock. 'After a while', the three of them went to a house in Laurel Street where Tomlinson paid for a quart of ale which was drunk by Clark, Woods and some other girls. He had a bag with him, which the women must have seen in the Swan, which contained two pounds and three shillings (£195). Some time later, Clark 'forced' him upstairs, seized him round the body and snatched the bag from his waistcoat, probably in a short version of the 'bug hunting' method. When he accused her of stealing, she struck him and, when they both ran down the stairs, Clark locked the door and when he threatened to call the police she struck him again, shouting, 'I'll give you policeman!' Woods, in the meantime, had escaped through the back door.

After Tomlinson finally got out of the house, he found P.C. Helm, pointed Clark out and she was arrested, still in Laurel Street. At the same time, Woods had gone back into the Swan and offered a sovereign (£90) for a few drinks to the landlord, James Shorrock. Then she thought better of it, asked for it back, and paid for the drinks with a florin (£9).[22] After that, she asked Shorrock to keep a sovereign and six shillings for her until the following morning and to give it to no-one else. When Shorrock saw P.C. Helm he handed over the money, no doubt taking the opportunity to curry some favour with the police. This resulted in Woods being arrested in Laurel Street. The following evening, they were both charged. At first, Clark said, 'I never had a halfpenny of the money. I know nothing about it.' Later, when Woods was charged with receiving, Clark said, 'I took the bag, but I did not know what it had in it. I gave it to her (pointing to Woods).' At the police court, both of them were committed to Sessions for trial. On hearing this, Woods pointed at Tomlinson and shouted, 'I'll give it to your devil when I come out for sending me to the Sessions, but I hope you will be dead before I come out!'

At Sessions, both were sentenced to six months with hard labour in Lancaster Castle.

The first part of 1872 proved to be an unhappy time for men from out of town visiting the Black Swan. In January, Robert Mercer, a quarryman by trade, came across Catherine King there and bought drinks for them both. Later, she asked him to go to her house at 28 Shepherd Street, which was a brothel for well over twenty years. He had a sovereign in his purse (£87) and three shillings in silver (£13) in his waistcoat. After drinking more beers, Mercer went upstairs with King and, after a time, he gave her the sovereign to change. She demanded five shillings (£22), presumably for her services, but he only gave her four. When he tried to leave, the other women in the house pounced on him, forced him into a chair and took all his money. He called the police and P.C. Byrns arrested the women. The female searcher at the police station, Isabella Dawson, the wife of P.C. Dawson, found two shillings and fourpence on Bridget McCormick (£10.26), four shillings and sixpence on King (£19.73), three shillings on Mary Ann Lewis (£13.16) and nothing on a fourth prostitute, Bridget Shearns. All were committed to Sessions where Shearns and Lewis, both aged 19, were acquitted. McCormick (21) had been found guilty of larceny in Blackpool in 1869, was found guilty of theft and sentenced to a year's hard labour in Preston Prison with seven years' police supervision on release. King, also 21, had been found guilty of theft in Wigan a year earlier and so was sentenced to seven years' imprisonment and seven years' supervision. For a woman so young, King had an astonishing

> *For a woman so young, King had an astonishing number of convictions while working under three aliases*

number of convictions while working under three aliases, including eleven times for drunkenness, twice for assaulting the police, twenty-one days for causing damage, a month for prostitution and fourteen days for indecent behaviour.

During the week after Easter in 1872, on Tuesday[23] 9 April, Richard Brindle, Edward Whittle and Peter M'Loughlin robbed a labourer from Longton called Richard Hall after he left the Black Swan at ten o'clock. Like many robbery victims, he must have been picked out because he had given the impression of wealth, possibly being more generous the more he drank. They followed him, caught him up in North Road near the junction with Church Street, knocked him to the ground, tore his jacket and waistcoat and made off with three pounds and thirteen shillings (£333), possibly the profit from selling at the market.

An interesting case which, like the others, started at the Black Swan and came as the area was beginning to crumble as a centre of vice. On 20 June 1885, Annie Winders (23) and Annie Jackson (27) were accused of stealing one pound two shillings and threepence from Eli Margerison, a joiner from Brook Street. At two o'clock in the afternoon he met Winders and Jackson in the Black Swan and got into conversation. Drinks were bought, presumably by him, and later the three of them, together with another man, went to a brothel in Shepherd Street. Margerison went into the backyard and 'his suspicions were aroused' when Winders and Jackson both appeared. He tried to escape through the front door, but it was locked. He ran back to the backyard and tried to climb over the wall but failed. He turned to face the women and tried to engage with them but 'they got hold of him, banged him against the wall and took the money from his pockets'. Jackson took it and Winders received it. The police were called and P.C. Inman arrested the two women. At the court, the magistrates listened to the evidence and sent the defendants for trial at Sessions.

It is worth showing at this point how low these two young women had fallen. Both had a string of offences to their names. Annie Winders, who was uneducated and had been classed both as a 'factory operative' and 'no trade' in prison records occasionally used the alias 'Pallester'. From her first offence for theft in 1881, aged seventeen, and the present case, she had been found guilty of five crimes including drunkenness, running a brothel and theft. Annie Jackson, described as 'imperfectly educated' and having 'no trade', had a longer list of offences to her name. From her first in 1873, aged 16, to the present trial she had been found guilty on fifteen occasions, including theft, drunkenness, riotous behaviour, running a brothel, assaulting a constable and prostitution. Her last conviction for drunkenness had been given only three weeks before the Shepherd Street incident.

At Sessions, on 1 July, all the evidence was heard again before Mr James Hall, the presiding magistrate. To everyone, the outcome must have seemed a foregone conclusion, even to the defendants. Twenty-five years earlier they would have been expecting transportation to Australia. At the present time they must have resigned themselves to seven years' imprisonment. This time, however, the defence counsel proposed that Margerison had been drunk and 'that in all probability the sovereign had been spent in the Black Swan before he went to the brothel'. As a result, the jury found the women not guilty and they were discharged, which must have been a surprise to most people present. What is more surprising is that Mr Hull addressed Annie Jackson saying, 'that if she were sincere in her wish to lead a better life, he was authorised to say that means would be afforded her to do so in another place. Jackson thanked the Chairman and withdrew'.

Despite extensive research, it is unknown whether Jackson, or even Winders, returned to their lives of crime or changed their lives completely, but their names do not appear in newspapers or prison lists again. The remarkable aspect of this case is not just the surprising verdict, but that there was an offer which encompassed much of what Rev. John Clay had advocate fifty years earlier, i.e. education and a new start. The process of 'reaching the people' had started.

In its time, the Black Swan, being centrally located, came in for its share of violent conduct, both inside and outside the premises. Charles Swift, the landlord, became embroiled in a fight in November 1861 with hawker called John Leary, who was a stranger to Preston. Witnesses said that Leary quarrelled with some men, went out, returned and attempted to rob a man. When ordered off the premises by Swift, he refused, striking and kicking him, then hitting Swift's wife, Ann, and daughter, Elizabeth aged 19. Both Swift and Leary ended upon the ground. Leary's account began with him seeing a man bleeding when he entered the Black Swan and advised him to summon his attacker. Swift then set on Leary, kicking and striking him before running in with a knife in his hand. Swift was charged with stabbing Leary, though witnesses said when Swift hit Leary he cut his head on a coal box. 'After a long and tedious enquiry', the magistrates sent the case to Sessions where Swift received three months for 'malicious cutting and wounding'.

In the sad saga of the domestic violence involving William and Mary Ireland, a further vicious episode was played out in the Black Swan in February 1867. In full view of everyone he attacked her (see earlier account) for which he was given a month's imprisonment. A third episode, nearly four months later, earned the husband two months with hard labour, though the magistrates would rather have had him whipped instead.

In the sad saga of the domestic violence involving William and Mary Ireland, a further vicious episode was played out in the Black Swan in February 1867

A similar, deplorable incident took place in September 1875 when William Thomson violently assaulted Elizabeth Cook, 'a single woman of Water Street'. Thomson, who was probably a bully, demanded money from Cook at five o'clock in the afternoon of 8 September but she said she had none before she walked into the Black Swan. He followed her there and demanded money again. Somehow, she escaped to the Bear's Paw in Church Street where he followed and kicked her violently. She ran off, but he cornered her in her lodgings and assaulted her again, this time witnessed by Elizabeth Carter, after which he made off, probably to avoid detection. When the town's medical officer, Doctor Pilkington, examined Cook he found bruises all over the lower half of her body, and teeth marks on her lip. The police tracked Thomson to Blackburn where he was arrested. For his assaults he received four months' imprisonment with hard labour. Six months later, a similar assault by a bully took place. As Michael Leonard, described by the *Chronicle* as a 'bad character', was leaving the Black Swan with an unnamed woman on the afternoon of Tuesday 14 March when he turned and punched her on the head with his fist. P.C. Simm saw this and arrested him. For disorderly behaviour and assault, Leonard got fourteen days in prison with hard labour.

One of the disadvantages of running a public house in this district at this time was having to remove characters who were aggressive, drunk, desperate and felt they had nothing to lose. One such character was Catherine Beasley. Aged twenty-three in 1876, she had, up to that point, been convicted seven times for being drunk and disorderly, three times for assault, three times for prostitution and had served twenty-one days for lack of sureties. During the week ending 20 May 1876 she created trouble in the Black Swan and the police had to be called to put her out. She refused to go, making an even greater scene, both loudly and entertaining enough to attract a crowd. As a result, the police had to arrest her whereupon she attacked P.C. Walmsley, which was added to the original charge of drunk and disorderly. At court she was sent to prison for a month. Just over six months later, on 2 December, she was found guilty, with Edward Leonard, of robbery with violence in Leeming Street where they took two pounds and sixteen shillings (£261) from Joseph Knowles. For this she was imprisoned at Preston for twelve months with hard labour. In the prison records she is recorded that she was a weaver, which is patently untrue. She was also recorded as completely uneducated and therefore, from a young age, likely to be condemned to a vicious spiral to the bottom.

She was recorded as completely uneducated and therefore, from a young age, likely to be condemned to a vicious spiral to the bottom

It is hardly surprising then, that in view of the general situation in the area, that the *Chronicle* reported on 1 January 1875 that at the Police Court the day before, Mr Robert Watson (see earlier) made an application to extend the closing times of licensed premises from eleven o'clock, as stipulated by the 1872 Licensing Act, to midnight in view of the imminent Horse Fair on account of stabling for horses and beds for visitors. The Chief Inspector, James Oglethorpe, took the list, looked through it and immediately struck off the names of seven premises, including the Black Swan and 'others at the back of St John's Church'.

Being the landlord of a public house in the Sandhole must have been a stressful job and the activities described so far are just a digest of incidents. It must have taken its toll on Charles and Ann Swift as they both died suddenly in 1866, she on 22 February and he on 25 March, both aged sixty-two. In the *Herald* of 31 March, 7 April and 14 April an advertisement was published which, it might be said, was an excellent example of the advertiser's art, namely,

> To Let, with immediate possession, in consequence of the death of Mr Charles Swift, that well known inn by the name of the Black Swan, Water Street.
>
> This house is situated in a very populous district and has long been noted for doing a very remunerative trade. Any enterprising party desirous of embarking in the public business will find this an eligible opportunity, the house being admirably adapted for an increased trade, by the formation of a commodious spirit vault and other improvements.
>
> Apply to Mr Richard Robinson, spirit merchant, Avenham Street.

It is inconceivable that anyone who lived in Preston, read the newspapers, talked to anyone at work or in their neighbourhood would recognise this description of the Black Swan, but James Sharrock became the next landlord and stayed until 1874. He was a thirty-three-year-old native of Preston, with a wife, Ann and two children.

A year later, almost to the week, the establishment was put up for sale again. This time, a shorter advertisement was used, describing the place as 'the old, commodious and well built public-house' together with 'the cottages behind'. This time, the agent was a Preston solicitor, John Ambler. Whether a buyer came forward is uncertain, but James Sharrock continued his tenancy.

Whether Sharrock had less control over his customers than Charles Swift or whether the area became more lawless, probably the latter, his time in charge was peppered by incidents and was infamous in the minds of the authorities. At the Brewster Session of 26 August 1869, the renewal of the licence was objected to and suspended. At a hearing on 18 September to reconsider his and other suspensions, Sharrock had his licence restored without comment, along with George Smith at the Rifleman, while others, including the Griffin Inn, were refused a second time. P.C. Williams had given evidence that he had visited on a few occasions in the month leading up to the Sessions and had found prostitutes and men of bad character there. P.C. Watson supported him, but there were no complaints about the landlord.

P.C. Williams had given evidence that he had visited on a few occasions in the month leading up to the Sessions and had found prostitutes and men of bad character there

However, seven months later Sharrock was charged with keeping a disorderly house on 28 April 1870. On Monday 18 April, P.C.s Higgins and Machonochie had visited at quarter to nine in the evening and found four men and several prostitutes. Two of the men were drunk and two militiamen were cursing and swearing. Sharrock told the court that he had tried to keep an orderly house 'but it is about two hundred yards off the worst neighbourhood in town'. It was, actually, much less than that. Mr Dunn, the Chief Constable told the magistrates that Sharrock had been cautioned two or three times in the past. In turn, the magistrates told Sharrock that 'they were quite determined to put down the assembling of prostitutes and drunken men together in the house and we make every allowance for the character of the neighbourhood'. That determination did not start here, however, as Sharrock just had to pay costs and not a fine. He received a caution 'and any others will be brought up on licensing day'. At the end, he said, 'I have always done my best and I am sorry I am situated in that neighbourhood'.

Sure enough, at the Brewster Session of August 1870, Sharrock's licence was suspended because the Black Swan was 'a resort of thieves and prostitutes'. Four weeks later, it was restored with a warning. There was a report by the *Herald* of this second session and the statement the magistrates made about the Lodge Bank Tavern applies also to the licences suspended in the same earlier session.

> They had no other course but to grant the licence because it had been proved that prostitutes had gone there for refreshment, not for the sake of prostitution.
>
> Under the circumstances – how much they might regret the state of Preston in regard to these kinds a of characters – and one could hardly walk through the streets at night without meeting some of their fellow creatures in a most disgusting state in mind and body – how much they might lament the state of things – they felt that the man had not committed any offence against his licence and they were bound to grant it.[24]

It seems rather strange these days to find out that public houses (but not beerhouses) did not have to close overnight until the 1864 Public House Closing Act forced them to close from one o'clock in the morning until four o'clock, three hours later. The Wine and Beerhouse Act gave some control over licensing to the magistrates. Also, by this Act, existing licences could be challenged: firstly by not providing enough evidence of good character; secondly, the house was of a disorderly character or frequented by thieves or prostitutes, fifteen minutes being deemed long enough for 'refreshment'; thirdly, that the licensee had had a licence forfeited for misconduct; fourthly, the premises or applicant were not properly qualified by law.

Closing time was set nationally at midnight, though the Preston magistrates decided on eleven o'clock

Three years later, the 1872 Licensing Act, enacted on 10 August, incorporated all these regulations and applied them to public houses. In addition, closing time was set nationally at midnight, though the Preston magistrates decided on eleven o'clock and the contents of beer, often brewed on the premises, was to be pure and unadulterated. Other provisions of the Act, outlined by the *Herald* a week after it became law, included a penalty of twenty shillings (£88) for sell spirits to anyone 'apparently under sixteen years', which must have been comfort to the journalist 'B' (see earlier) who had seen children in an intoxicated state in the 1860s. The sale of spirits was to be done by a standard measure and the licensee's name was to be put over the front door. Any licensee who allowed 'drunkenness or violent or quarrelsome of riotous conduct to take place on his premises, or sell intoxicating liquor to and drunken person shall be liable to a fine of ten pounds (£880) for the first offence'. Therefore, drunkards could be excluded from licensed premises. These regulations were enforced by the police force, which must have rejoiced, knowing that the Act gave them and the magistrates the power they wanted.

James Sharrock has the dubious honour of being the first publican to be charged under this Licensing Act. The *Chronicle* reports that in November 1872, he was summoned for permitting prostitutes in his house and allowing them to stay longer than was allowed for 'refreshment'. P.C. Dugdale stated that he and P.C. Beardwood entered the Black Swan on Thursday 22 November and found nineteen men, including two bullies, and thirteen prostitutes in the vault. They had 'watched and counted'. Three prostitutes had remained on the premises, one for half an hour, one for thirty-five minutes and the third for a full hour. The defending solicitor, Robert Watson, said it was unfair that the landlord,

P.C. Dugdale stated that he and P.C. Beardwood entered the Black Swan on Thursday 22 November and found nineteen men, including two bullies, and thirteen prostitutes in the vault who could not keep them out, had been summoned and the prostitutes had not. Sharrock claimed that he had turned them out when the police pointed them out. The new Chief Inspector, Mr Oglethorpe, was of the opinion that if the prostitutes were driven out of this area they would 'scatter among the respectable population'.

The case was remanded for a week until 7 December when the magistrates found Sharrock guilty, but they decided to be lenient because he had come forward of his own accord 'in order to find out what he must do'. He said he had done his best and could do no more and that it was impossible to tell how long prostitutes had stopped in at one time. He was fined twenty-three shillings (£100), the lowest fine the magistrates could impose rather than ten pounds. Sharrock paid the fine in full on the day. The leading magistrate, Miles Myres, the Mayor, said that if Mr Oglethorpe found the law broken by prostitutes then 'he must bring them up'. The way this case, and others like it, were conducted was probably the reason behind Margaret De Lacy's remark, 'The Preston justices had never been great reformers'.[25]

Sharrock was consistent in showing annoyance every time his licence was challenged. In this last episode he was not consoled at all by being fined the least a Bench could impose, and he made it clear in the court. His mood did not improve in the aftermath either. He wrote to the *Chronicle* on 13 December 1872 from 'Swan Vaults, Water Street', protesting his innocence and deploring the fine placed upon him.

> I beg to state that prostitutes are not harboured by me. No doubt most of the public know where my house is situated. It is not in Winckley Square but in Water Street where most of that class reside. It has been altered to suit the neighbourhood in the shape of a vault at the front and not at the back, where it would be difficult for the police to find any secret snug drinking. All is fair and above board. It is visited by all classes and is capable of accommodating 150 people when full.
>
> As a rule, the prostitutes do not stop long, but are constantly on the move when they are in the place. I can assure you that

> they must behave themselves in a proper manner or they are instantly put out. If I cannot manage, the police can and do.

In the next part of the letter, Sharrock shows his anger and criticises the prevailing thought and opinion, shared strongly by Chief Inspector Oglethorpe, that prostitutes and thieves should be corralled into this small area between Queen Street and Church Street.

> In my case of summons I was led astray by the Watch Committee[26] deciding to let this class alone in this locality, or I could have brought sufficient witnesses to prove they did not stay longer than the police say. I evidently made too light of my case. Two or three weeks before, I volunteered to be summoned to see what we must do with this class of people. I got summoned and had to pay. Everyone knows this is a sad disgrace to me; but I can assure you that I have not had anything of the sort to pay before. I also wish the public to know that to this house there is a private entrance, up which no prostitute or bad character is allowed to enter; in fact, this establishment is conducted on a principle that cannot be mended by man. Hoping this will meet the eye of everyone who knows how I am situated. I remain, yours etc
>
> James Sharrock

Sharrock does seem to have been let down by the authorities in that he had cooperated with them. But there is a touch of hubris when he states that his system could not be bettered. In addition, he must have been naïve to think that prostitutes were 'constantly on the move' as they used the Black Swan and similar establishments as place to pick up likely customers or identify likely victims for robbery. As we have seen, there always seems to have been a crowd on certain nights, as recognised by the police and backed up by this research.

The next eighteen months passed without any reported incidents. On 21 February 1874, an advertisement appeared in the *Herald* for a sale of properties which had been instructed by the executors of the will of the factory owner whose factory, Willow Street Mill, stood on the southern end of Water Street, Edward Swainson.[27]

Lot 1: Freehold Worsted Spinning and Weaving Mills in Water Street with two cottages – 2 Leeming Street and 5 Factory Brow

Lot 2: House at 17 Grimshaw Street – warehouse and stable

Lot 3: Two cottages at 30 and 31 Willow Street

Lot 4: The Public House 'Black Swan' occupied by James Sharrock

Five months later, presumably because there had been no buyers for the Black Swan, the *Herald* carried another advertisement on 29 July for the house to be let 'with immediate possession', then another on 1 August, this time for sale. This time it was offered at the same time as two lodging houses for 57 and 33 lodgers with land to build another shop on Water Street. There were no takers, but a year later, the Black Swan was offered for sale 'as the owner and tenant were retiring'. Again, the persuasive vocabulary of the advertiser was very much in evidence, employing words such as 'commodious', 'centrally situated', 'well accustomed', topped off with claims such as 'No business house in Preston has so rapidly and successfully increased the value of its connection' and 'For the last year the consumption has exceeded 12 barrels a week with takings of £120[28] (£11,000) a month and trade is still increasing'. There was a further claim that the 'premises have been thoroughly and substantially renovated and the arrangements for accommodation are considered the most perfect of the kind in the country'. This, it has to be remembered, was a public house 'not in Winckley Square but in Water Street where most of that class reside', as Sharrock had stated in his letter in 1872.

The person who took over the tenancy was 42-year-old Stephen Cranshaw, a native of Blackburn, who was living with his family in Greaves Street which is adjacent to Laurel Street and Blelock Street. In other words, he knew what the area and its inhabitants were like and knew what to expect. Not long after he took over, the Black Swan was mentioned in relation to the January Horse Fair of 1875 and by July he was up in court. On Sunday 27 June, Cranshaw had served two policemen during duty and prohibited hours, namely P.C.s Farraday and Lawrenson. It is not clear whether this was entrapment of the policemen or Cranshaw, but Inspector Dawson, watching through a ventilator, saw a young woman serve them beer at half past ten. Drinking on duty was a reason for dishonourable discharge from the force. There is no record of this in the Superintendent's Log Book, so this was a trap for Cranshaw, who was fined ten shillings (£47) for a second offence.

Apart from a few incidents, which have been covered in earlier sections, the public house and its licensees kept out of court for the rest of the century. The building was demolished around 1890 and on its site was built the Balmoral Hotel. Looking at that site today, it is hard to imagine that the Black Swan was ever 'commodious' as claimed by the 1874 advertisement. None of the Sandhole licensed premises survived into the twentieth century. The reason for this included greater surveillance and supervision by the expanded police force and legislation such as the 1869 Wine and Beerhouse Act, the 1872 Licensing Act (with its later additions), the 1864 Public House Closing Act, the 1869 Habitual Criminals Act and the 1879 Habitual Drunkards Act.[29]

None of the Sandhole licensed premises survived into the twentieth century

The change of attitude and habit was gradual in Preston and in the nation as a whole. Gourvish and Wilson[30] state that a rise in consumption between 1865 and 1879 was caused by rising wages for many workers and there was little in the way of amusement or leisure but drinking. They credit the gradual decline 'not so much the success of the temperance movement or stricter control'. Tea was the most popular domestic drink by 1880 and there were other demands on money such as 'consumer goods, imported and manufactured food products, factory made clothing, furniture, newspapers, music halls, sports, travel and holidays'. Outside agencies started to promote other and healthier pursuits such as gardening, allotments, parks, team sports, libraries and reading rooms and cooperative societies. Heavy drinking and drunkenness were no longer seen as remotely 'respectable'. That said, these changes would be far slower in an area like this, requiring firm control well into the twentieth century thereby retaining its poor reputation.

When Rev. John Clay spoke of 'places of vicious and ruinous resort', he may not have had lodging houses in mind, but they were certainly part of the Sandhole's grimy tapestry. As in other industrial towns of the North, many respectable people in Preston took in lodgers to supplement their income. Their clients may have come from different areas and backgrounds such as those itinerants who moved about for work, or from an overcrowded family home. In the latter case, the older children of large families living in a small, terraced house would live elsewhere to make room. The official Censuses would record all these as either 'boarders' or 'lodgers'.[31] The common lodging house, of which there was a number in Preston, was defined as 'a house … where persons of poorer classes are received for gain, and in which they use one or more rooms in common with the rest of the inmates who are not members of one family, whether eating or sleeping.'[32]

As in other industrial towns of the North, many respectable people in Preston took in lodgers to supplement their income

For many, it was the worst or last resort for the homeless or poor before landing at the dreaded workhouse. As such, these lodging houses formed a microcosm of the Sandhole itself, where the deserving poor were forced to live cheek-by-jowl with the dregs of society. The journalist, whose nom-de-plume was 'B', gave a glimpse of what lodging house were like in his descriptions in the 'Life In Preston' series of articles (see earlier), but a more general view is provided by Kellow Chesney.

> Here were to be found specimens of all the types of the social sump … [it] might harbour a shifting collection of casual labourers, hawkers, beggars, thieves, street performers and more or less unspecifiable riff-raff … Some were literally thieves' kitchens, chiefly frequented by pickpockets, house

> robbers and their confederates while others were chiefly tenanted by beggars.[33]

Before the 1851 Common Lodging Houses Act (and its amendments over the following two years) the standard of accommodation ranged from fair to foul with people being packed into rooms, many to a bed, especially children, and on available floor space. As for cleaning, washing and the toilets,

> The sanitary habits of most of the lodgers were disgusting, but washing might be possible under a tap or pump in the stinking back yard where there was also some kind of privy – a collection of buckets or a hole over a cess pit … (children) often relieved themselves all over the stairs and passages.[34]

One of the lodging houses was owned by James Traynor, situated at 20 Shepherd Street. He also had another, smaller house in Leeming Street. On the night of Sunday 2 April 1871, the night of the Census, forty people were in the Shepherd Street house, eight members of the Traynor family and thirty-two lodgers. Traynor and his wife, Mary, gave their ages as forty when, in fact they were forty-nine. They had both been born in Ireland, but all their six children, ranging in age from seventeen to one, had been born in Preston.

The thirty-eight lodgers were made up of nineteen men, six women, five boys and two girls. There was a family of six, two of whom, the father and the eldest son, were musicians, all from Glasgow. The rest were small family groups, including one young couple and two children with mothers but no fathers. Ten of the lodgers had been born in Ireland, but only five in Preston. The rest had been born within a thirty-mile radius of the town. Twenty-one gave a trade or profession, eight of which were labourers, or so they said. The life expectancy of women in the 1870s was forty-four and none of the women was as old as that. On the other hand, the life expectancy at birth of men in 1871 and one man was older than that, aged sixty. He appears as one of a group of single men at the bottom of the list, five of whom were born in Ireland. They could have been

Forty people were packed into a fairly small town house

regulars; they could have been ne'er-do-wells though none of them had a criminal record, or they could have been a gang of workmen. The fact remains that forty people were packed into a fairly small town house.

James Traynor first came to Preston in 1856 as part of the Royal Irish Regiment. In March, there were two instances where he was named in the *Chronicle*, firstly as part of one of the regiments involved in fighting in the Black Swan and secondly in a case of street theft which came to nothing. While at Shorncliffe in Kent in 1860, Traynor resigned as a Colour Sergeant in the Regiment's Second Battalion and bought a lodging house in Preston with his wife, Mary. Later, he bought the one in Shepherd Street.

Lodging houses were largely unregulated until 1851 when the above Act, promoted strongly by the Earl of Shaftesbury, came into law. Each house had to be registered with the local authority which was useful in times of epidemics when unregulated houses were breeding grounds for disease, even though 'fever' was a constant visitor to these sorts of places. The police were given an automatic right to inspect but did not have the authority over a house when it was let out room by room, so prostitution could go on. The police did the next best thing by arresting unmarried couples found sleeping in the same room, thereby, in Preston at least, breaking the bye laws. Rooms, stairs, yards and landings had to be swept by eleven o'clock and the windows had to be opened twice daily at ten o'clock and four o'clock, bad weather or sickness permitting. The house had also to be vacated between ten and four, which caused hardship for some people.

Rooms, stairs, yards and landings had to be swept by eleven o'clock and the windows had to be opened twice daily at ten o'clock and four o'clock

As with all parts of the Sandhole and in the town in general, theft was rife because many people were desperate. In February 1864, Catherine Fleming stole a watch from Traynor and passed it to Michael Chester (see earlier), her bully and cohabitee. Both received a year's imprisonment. In 1878, Chester received eighteen months' hard labour for maliciously wounding her in Accrington. Two years later, in March, Alice Dunkley stole three sheets from Traynor's in Leeming Street and tried to pawn them. It is unclear whether they came from one of the rooms or from a secondhand-clothes shop he used to run as a sideline. A shawl and other articles of clothing were stolen from the Water Street house in July 1868, by Eliza Brown, who received a month in prison for her trouble. Her husband was discharged through lack of evidence. Thirteen years later, in 1881, Brown got five years for maliciously wounding another prostitute. In November 1868, William Whitehead stole a silk dress worth ten shillings (£44) from the Leeming Street house and sold it for sixpence (£2.20). Born in 1836, Whitehead, who was a notorious thief, received two months in prison. Between 1852 and 1868 he had spent a total of nine years and five months in prison.

It seems that if items were not nailed down in the Sandhole they had a good chance of being stolen. Alice White, a fifty-six-year-old washerwoman, described by the *Chronicle* as 'an old woman', was sentenced to two months' hard labour in November 1871 for stealing a basket, a hat and a candlestick from the Leeming Street house. Emma Whitewright, a twenty-one-year-old mother of two, was sentenced to fourteen days' hard labour for stealing a pair of boots from Traynor and pawning them at Mr Carter's in Church Street for one shilling and sixpence (£6.50). A year later, two sheets, a petticoat and a shawl were lifted from the Shepherd Street house by Alice Ann Atkinson, a twenty-one-year-old tobacco worker from Saul Street, and received by seventeen-year-old Mary Cosgrove, a linen spinner of Dunderdale Court (near Saul Street). Atkinson received three months and Cosgrove one.

Two sheets, a petticoat and a shawl were lifted from the Shepherd Street house by Alice Ann Atkinson, a twenty-one-year-old tobacco worker from Saul Street

A variation on the confidence trick theme involved the use of Traynor's Leeming Street lodging house in December 1873. William Cummings, a recruiting soldier, met Mary Jane Jones (30) and Mary Ann

Feeney (55) on the Preston to Chorley road. Cummings was a native of Liverpool, billeted in Blackburn. In the conversation which followed, the two women told him that they were very tired and hungry so, when they arrived in Preston, he treated them both to a meal. Later he went to Traynor's where he slept with Jones, thereby breaking the law. When he woke up, Jones had gone and so had Feeney with his money, amounting to one pound and eleven shillings (£134). The police managed to find the women and when they were searched, Jones had no money on her, but the police searcher found one pound and eight shillings on Feeney (£121). Both were found guilty at the Sessions on 8 January 1874; Feeney got three months' hard labour in Lancaster Castle; Jones received six months' imprisonment in Preston Prison, also with hard labour.

Because Traynor was a secondhand bedding and clothes dealer in a low area, some thieves thought he would be interested in buying goods they had 'acquired'. If the price was right, he sometimes was. In December 1871, a youth called Peter O'Brien turned up at Leeming Street with a five-pound cheese he had stolen from Alice Reeder's new provision dealer's shop in Ribbleton Lane.[35] He persuaded Traynor to buy it for tenpence (£2.35) when it was worth at least seven shillings and sixpence (£35). The police got involved and O'Brien ended up with a month in prison. Traynor got a court reprimand. In 1863, Robert Marsden tried to persuade him to buy a pair of shoes which he had removed from James Thompson while he was asleep in the Bear's Paw. They could still have been warm! As late as 1880, Traynor was being brought stolen goods. On 4 September, Ann Dawson brought him six and a half yards of woollen cloth that she had stolen, but he called the police and Dawson was sentenced to a year in prison and three years' police supervision.

Sometimes, thieves used Traynor's premises as a refuge. In April 1867, Francis Smith, described by the *Herald* as 'an old man', (he was 62) was arrested by P.C. Pilkington at the Shepherd Street house for stealing items

He may have been a nuisance when drunk, but his wife, Mary, was positively frightening when she was

from a hawker called Andrew Gilligan of Union Street and selling a pair of boots to a tripe dealer called Thomas Beardwood of Water Street. Up to this point, Smith had been in prison twenty eight times. Sometimes the audacity of some thieves has to be admired. In September 1871, Elizabeth Thompson (25), described by the *Herald* as 'a notorious character', risking the wrath of Traynor, she lifted a shawl and a silk dress from the Shepherd Street house where Mrs Mary Traynor had hung it up to dry in the kitchen. She lent Thompson, who was lodging there, the shawl. After the dress was missed in the evening it was reported to the police. Not long after, Thompson was seen wearing the dress, having pawned the shawl at Sarah Worden's secondhand clothes shop and lodging house round the corner at 5 Water Street! She was found guilty and given seven years' imprisonment.[36]

A persistent theme in Sandhole life was violence and Traynor was no stranger to it. The *Chronicle* reported on 14 April 1860 that he had stopped William Bradley from attacking and robbing Michael Clare in the first instance (see earlier chapter). The *Herald* reported in February 1866 that 'a dirty looking woman' called Sarah Mullen was charged with attacking her husband, John, at Traynor's lodging house. In the first week of November, later that year, two cases were started on the same day which both involved Traynor. In the first, William Sandham accused him of violence; in the second, Joseph Banks of the Griffin Inn accused him of assault. Both cases were dismissed through lack of evidence, but they show that Traynor was no saint and that life in the Sandhole was uncompromising at best.

A 'dirty looking woman' called Sarah Mullen was charged with attacking her husband, John, at Traynor's lodging house

Exactly three years later, Traynor was involved in a serious incident at 3 Laurel Street, which was adjacent to Shepherd Street. The brothel here was well known for well over twenty years and was run at that time by Sarah Norton.[37] Between one and two o'clock in the morning of Sunday 14 November 1869, Traynor stormed over to Laurel Street and demanded half a gallon (four pints) of beer. Elizabeth

Parker,[38] an inmate of the house, answered the door and told him that none was available. Undeterred, he barged past Parker, threatening to smash everything in the house. At this point, Norton appeared and an unnamed 'young man' who was with Traynor warned her that he had a knife up his sleeve. Getting no further with Norton than he had done with Parker he brandished the knife and threatened to cut her throat. P.C. Clark was called in just as Traynor began smashing windows and damaging other items. In court, Parker testified that Traynor was going to run Norton through when the constable arrived. Parker witnessed the damage and arrested Traynor who kicked him several times on the way to the police station. At court, the magistrates imposed two sets of fines. The first was to cover the damage; one shilling (£4.50) for committing damage and one shilling and eightpence (£7.50) or one week in prison. The second was to cover the assaults; five shillings (£23) or a week in prison. Traynor paid up in full on the day, six shillings and eightpence, the equivalent of two and a half days' pay for a builder's labourer. He said he was drunk at the time, but it also shows he had a serious alcohol problem.

In August 1871, Traynor was imprisoned for two weeks after he assaulted a man called James Berry. The details were not reported, but it may have been an alcohol-based incident. Up to 1881, Traynor had been in the police court fifty-three times for being drunk and disorderly and his wife, eleven times. In February 1866, he had been fined five shillings (£23) for being disorderly and assaulting P.C.s Whittam and Wilson. As well as being regularly drunk and badly behaved in Preston, he was arrested by police in Blackpool in March 1872 for being intoxicated and misbehaving at two o'clock in Lytham Road, 'cursing, swearing, annoying passers-by and knocking on doors'. He got away with court costs on the promise to leave town.

He may have been a nuisance when drunk, but his wife, Mary, was positively frightening when she was. In November 1873, she was charged with assaulting her husband at the Shepherd Street premises. The evidence[39] given was that she was 'perfectly quiet', but recently she had 'become addicted to the habit of drinking'. In drink she became like a 'perfect virago' and beat her husband unmercifully. Traynor stated in court that she hit him with an iron and a tailor's goose.[40] He had nine wounds on his head and five on his lips. On the night of Tuesday 11 November, after thrashing him with various weapons, she threw a kettle at him which had been heating on the fire. Found guilty, she paid sureties rather than go to prison for seven days.

They produced a number of children, one of which, James, turned out to be what might be described as a disappointment. He married a girl from an Irish family called Mary Kelly and together they became town nuisances and vagrants, constantly in trouble for pilfering and begging. Eventually, they both ended up with serious prison sentences, the husband for five years for stabbing and the wife for twelve months for manslaughter. She was a member of the Kelly family who lived in Moor Lane. On the evening of 11 December 1880, when her husband was in prison, the younger Mary Traynor, drunk, decided to walk down North Street where the Mundle family lived. She went to their house and swore, cursed and threatened them, to which they instantly reacted. Others from the Kelly family turned up and there was a pitched battle, 'a general fray', during which she and her brother ended up with bloody faces. At one point she hit Thomas Mundle (19) on the back of the head with a kettle and he died, almost instantly. At the inquest, the coroner explained that Mundle had had a very thin skull, which had been a contributory factor in his death.

Traynor may have been an incorrigible drunk, but he was incorrigible in other ways, including the keeping of pigs. In September 1871, when Traynor was in prison for assaulting James Berry, Mr Marriott,[41] the Nuisance Inspector visited. His 'attention was drawn to the state of the Water Street lodging house'. When he had visited a week earlier, there had been 'only two pigs on the premises'. The night before Mr Marriot's second visit, Inspector Oglethorpe and another officer had visited and reported that four large pigs, two sows, sixteen piglets and a donkey in the yard. The Mayor was of the opinion that there was 'enough to generate a fever'[42] (*Chronicle*). He wanted them removed. Eight weeks later, Traynor was summoned to court by Mr Marriott for continuing to keep pigs in his back yard, 'in such a state as to be a nuisance to his neighbours' (*Herald*). There were six large pigs and young ones kept in a dirty state. The court ordered him to clean the yard up and 'a number of pigs removed before the second review'. Three weeks later, at the inspection, the pigs must have been moved but he was summoned for breaking the Common Lodging Houses Act. Inspector Oglethorpe visited 20 Shepherd Street and 55 Leeming Street on 17 November and found that bedrooms in both houses were very dirty. Traynor promised to remedy this situation and got away with just court costs!

Inspector Oglethorpe and another officer reported that four large pigs, two sows, sixteen piglets and a donkey were in the yard

Traynor's life was made up of trying to dodge the law, getting drunk and being fined for misbehaviour. On Sunday 14 September 1879 he was arrested for being drunk and disorderly for the forty eighth time and fined twenty-one shillings (£105) and costs. The magistrate, Mr Birley, said he was 'a disgrace to the town'. At the same time, he was summoned for keeping pigs, contrary to the Swine Order of 1879 'so as to be a nuisance'. Mr Marriott visited the Leeming Street premises and found a sow, seven piglets and two others in the back yard. They were allowed to run anywhere and the yard was very dirty. Repeatedly, Traynor had been told to keep it clean, the court was told and, as a result, Doctor Pilkington, Preston's Medical Health Officer declared the area as a nuisance and was no longer to be used for pigs. The case was adjourned while the pigs were cleared out, but an inspection on 18 October revealed that the pigs were still there, so Traynor was fined twenty shillings and costs.

On Sunday 14 September 1879 he was arrested for being drunk and disorderly for the forty eighth time

Although Traynor looks like he had cornered the

lodging house market in the Sandhole, there were other, smaller premises such as Worden's, Day's, Becket's, Slater's, Shorrock's, Wearden's, Taylor's and Smith's, all with their own troubles, most of them self-inflicted. During the same week in February 1871, two lodging housekeepers had their house inspected. John Worden of 14 Water Street was summoned for a breach of the Common Lodging House Act. The Chief Inspector, Mr Dunn, told the court that there had been a great number of complaints made about the state Worden kept his house in and had been officially cautioned twice. Inspector Oglethorpe had visited on 27 January at eleven o'clock and found the floors unswept; they should have been swept by ten. Worden promised to improve and was charged costs. The same round of inspections by Oglethorpe brought a summons for Margaret Boylan, whose case has been quoted already. He found she was keeping 'swine in a filthy state' and that her house was not registered. On the same day, he visited Worden's where he found two pigs in the cellar and two more on the cellar steps. 'The smell was offensive and the rooms throughout the house were in a very filthy condition'. Boylan was ordered to pay costs and to keep her house in a cleaner state. Less than seven weeks later, the 1871 Census shows that Boylan's house had seven lodgers.

One of the main reasons that the Common Lodging House Act was passed was to establish some order and level of cleanliness in those premises to avoid the spread of diseases like cholera, typhoid and typhus. Lodging houses of the lowest type were always regarded as breeding grounds for infections of all types, including a generic illness known as 'fever'. At the beginning of March 1866, the *Chronicle* and the *Herald* both reported the rise in cases of a fever which was distinct from scarlet fever. It was reported as 'virulent in lodging houses, even well kept ones'. Becket's of Foundry Yard, Water Street was badly affected and had to be closed down, by request of the Guardians of the Poor as they said the fever was 'virulent' there. Even Mr and Mrs Becket were ill with it. On 10 March, there were forty-two people in the House of Recovery with the infection, which was declared to be of a 'dangerous type' (*Herald*), and six people who had smallpox. Three weeks later, the Beckets' son succumbed but all the family recovered eventually, which was better than some, like the lodging housekeeper in Main Sprit Weind who died from it.

The usual Sandhole themes repeated themselves in other lodging houses where a variety of crimes and misdemeanours were committed. In September 1869, Henrietta Boyle was caught walking out of William Slater's lodging house in Foundry Brow, Leeming Street with a quilt. She was given a week in prison by the court. Seven months later, Mary Walmsley turned up at Wearden's lodging house with a nine-year-old girl, Mary Cowell, whom she had abducted from Chorley railway station. It seems strange that no-one asked who they were. Perhaps they were just happy to take the money. So how surprising was it when P.C. Beardwood arrived to make an arrest?

Mary Walmsley turned up at Wearden's lodging house with a nine-year-old girl, Mary Cowell, whom she had abducted

A month later, John and Mary Ann Walmsley where indicted for the manslaughter of their ten-month-old son, James, on 8 May 1870 at Simon Shorrock's house at 37 Shepherd Street. They had arrived at the house, 'located in a disreputable neighbourhood' (*Herald*), had drinks and argued before going to bed. Mrs Walmsley stated that her husband had struck her 'two or three times' before retiring. All three slept in the same bed. In the morning, the child was found to be dead. A surgeon, Richard Allen, inspected the child and said he could find no marks of violence on him; he was well formed, though his stomach was empty, even though his mother insisted she had breast fed him and given him milk in the day. The coroner declared manslaughter and the case was referred to Sessions in July. There, some emphasis was placed on the fact that the parents were drunk but no-one could find any sign of foul play or intent and the child had been 'overlaid'. Due to lack of substantial evidence to convict either of the parents the case was dismissed.

Simon Shorrock was summoned in September 1877 for allowing people who were not married to sleep in the same bedrooms in his house

Simon Shorrock was himself summoned in September 1877 for allowing people who were not married to sleep in the same bedrooms in his house. The magistrate, Mr J. Pyke, condemned 'this disgraceful mixing of the sexes'. Shorrock was fined twenty shillings (£93) and costs. Three weeks earlier, another lodging housekeeper, called Harrison, was summoned for the same reason, contrary to Section 14 of the Lodging House Bye Laws, which was there to prevent prostitution. Sergeant Dugdale and Inspector Brown had visited and found several men and women together who were not married. Harrison brought witnesses forward who testified that he had asked them all and they had affirmed they all were. Nonetheless, he was fined ten shillings (£47). In March 1878, possibly when he thought he could get away with it, Shorrock was again summoned for the same offence and again fined twenty shillings. The bottom line of all this was making money and the risks taken to bring it in. Like those who ran brothels in the Sandhole and elsewhere, they would probably have a contingency fund for fines.

Lodging house keepers were fairly vulnerable to attention from violent characters. Sergeant Dugdale was called at half past eight in the evening of Saturday 26 September 1874 to 54 Leeming Street,[43] next to Traynor's, because the keeper, Elizabeth Taylor (29) had been assaulted by William Robinson, 'a powerful looking man' (*Chronicle*). He was drunk and the sergeant had to handcuff him on account of his violence. In the ensuing struggle, the policeman's coat was torn and Robinson was repeatedly aggressive on the way to the police station. In court, Robinson said he had been drunk and could remember nothing. He was ordered to pay restitution and ordered to find bail to keep the peace.

There are reports of incidents where trouble and violence invaded a lodging house. One example in 1875, quoted in the last chapter, was where Bridget Chester, angry at being reprimanded for hitting a boy in Shepherd Street, attacked

Ann O'Donnell, cutting her round the head with a knife. In consequence, she received eighteen months' hard labour. A year later, Mary Jane Wilson was charged with attacking Mary Jane Quigley on Monday 15 March at a Shepherd Street lodging house. At eleven o'clock. Wilson walked into the house, calling Quigley's husband foul names and then grabbed a candlestick but it was snatched from her. Quigley went to bed, but later felt sick and went downstairs to the kitchen for a drink of water. Unfortunately, Wilson was there and attacked her, throwing her to the ground, scratching her eyes, kicking her and hitting her violently with a basin. Quigley was so badly injured that she had to be taken to the Infirmary. In court, the magistrates had no hesitation in sentencing Wilson to eighteen months' hard labour.

From the time just before the handloom weavers fell on hard times to the early 1880s, the Sandhole had prospered as a place for every low-level criminal, where the worst in Preston society existed and worked. It was also a place for outcasts, the unfortunate and those who never prospered. In the late Georgian period, the view that society was made up of 'civilised' and 'barbarous' people still had some currency at least in mid-Victorian Britain, so some people never had a chance. As Charles Dickens wrote in *Bleak House*, '... a shameful testimony to future ages how civilisation and barbarism walked this boastful island together.'

From the time just before the handloom weavers fell on hard times to the early 1880s, the Sandhole had prospered as a place for every low-level criminal, where the worst in Preston society existed and worked

Naturally, the people of the Sandhole would be thought of as 'barbarous' – outside polite society and never likely to lift themselves above their 'barbarity'. These were the uneducated, the unsophisticated and the badly brought up, who had to fend for themselves to survive and to avoid the workhouse at all costs. The situation would change, gradually, with outside assistance.

Rose Street (1937) showing handloom weavers' cottages with number five on the far right.
(by permission of the Harris Museum)

8

'Go to The Source of Evil'

STRANGELY, THE CONSUMPTION OF BEER and spirits grew after the 1872 Licensing Act, rising to one and a half gallons in 1874 and 1875 for every person in the country[1] rising 'to a peak in the decidedly drink sodden year of 1879 when the consumption of alcohol reached an all-time high.'[2]

The rise, starting in 1865 and ending in 1879 was caused by 'rising wages for many workers and little in the line of amusement or leisure but drinking.'[3]

Of course, there were well run public premises in better areas which provided entertainments such as singing, dancing, and social gatherings, and were often the focus for goose clubs (a goose club was a savings club that enabled the poor to save money to buy a goose at Christmas), mutual associations and celebrations. The worst run establishments in poor areas were often 'centres of debauchery and brawling, and helped to promote the temperance movement.'[4]

The process of getting to the source of evil in the Sandhole had been started at national level by the legislation such as the Licensing Act, the Wine and Beerhouse Act and the Public Closing Act. This was borne out by the report published by the *Herald* on 19 October 1878 of the Chief Constable of Lancashire, Colonel Robert Bruce.[5] He stated that the above Acts had had 'a marked and beneficial effect in checking disorderly conduct at night.' The police had had trouble getting thoroughfares clear before one o'clock in the morning and even later. More recently they had been clear by half past eleven. The number of cases of drunkenness, assault and breaches of the peace had not declined but he considered the closing of premises 'for several hours every night prevented persons from staying in a drunken state for days together'. He had also been informed that the more respectable licensees were anxious to maintain order in their houses.

In parallel with all this, moves were being made to hit evil at its source with tougher policing and punishment with the Habitual Criminals Act as a deterrent. Preston Borough police force, which had a strength of fifteen men in 1850, had grown to sixty-eight by 1869 and to ninety-eight in 1883 under the leadership of Joseph Oglethorpe, the more recent Chief Constable. The attention of the local constabulary slowly intensified after the summer of 1871. At a meeting of the Watch Committee in September, the then Chef Constable, Mr Dunn, reported that 'the natives of Water Street had been reduced to a state of ordinary civilisation by the regime put into operation, namely, the constant supervision of a corps of officers specially told to attend to the requirements of that interesting district.'

Preston Borough police force, which had a strength of fifteen men in 1850, had grown to ninety-eight in 1883

Their patrols round the licensed premises have been discussed and the police's work with Mr Marriott and Doctor Pilkington, inspecting lodging houses was intensified. Mr Dunn's optimistic comments were commendable but there was a long way to go, and the process would not be brought to any sort of completion until long after his death. The main obstacles were the brothels and the women who ran them.

An interesting comment on this subject was presented as a memorial at the Brewster Session of 1872 by Rev. George Alker,[6] Vicar of St Mary's Anglican Church[7] and Rev. Christian Benzing,[8] junior curate at the Parish Church. Instead of repeating the same facts and sentiments which had been presented every year for the previous two decades and more, purporting them to be the demands of 'the people of Preston' when only sixty or so were ever present at the Temperance Hall in North Road, this was different. It was signed by 1,900 people and the subject was the character of the Sandhole and the language used was more forceful and straightforward than previous memorials, right from the start.

> We the undersigned, grieved at the terrible amount of demoralisation and disorder caused by the increasing number of houses of ill fame in certain notorious districts, and especially in the district of St John, beg most earnestly that you would enforce with greater rigour the laws which the legislature has put in your hands for the suppression of their houses. The publicity and shameless effrontery with which the inmates of the houses ply their trade; their drunken habits; the blasphemous and indecent language which they are in the habit of making; the freedom with which they mix with the more respectable portions of the inhabitants in districts swarming with children have made these notorious districts schools of vice, profligacy, laziness and seduction, and are daily doing an incalculable amount of harm to the moral training of the young.

This was a worthwhile and heartfelt departure from the mixture of hyperbole and statistics shovelled at the magistrates at previous licensing sessions which, in turn, the magistrates chose to ignore while presenting a thin veneer of concern. Here are concerns for other, innocent, mostly poor inhabitants of the Sandhole, as there always were, trying to lead decent lives and, among them, children.[9] Alker and Benzing go on to describe the effect of brothels on the local people.

> Many people are obliged to move away to avoid contamination. Much of the property, except for the houses of ill fame, have deteriorated in value.[10] These notorious places are situated in a very central position, daily traversed by great numbers of young people going to and from mills, day schools, Sunday schools and churches. People who have engagements in the district are daily sickened by the spectacles they have to witness.

Although the next strand of the argument had been put forward before by journalists and lawyers, Alker and Benzing saw fit to make it again.

> Your petitioners regard as a great mistake the opinion[11] that it is better to let evil remain in one part of the town than by breaking in on it to cause its removal to other places. By its location in one district these exhibitions of immorality become necessarily more conspicuous, the contaminations more certain.

The attention of the magistrates was finally drawn to the licensed premises in the Sandhole in a short but telling paragraph. 'Your petitioners would beg to draw your attention to the low character of numbers of public houses and beershops which are almost wholly supported by the custom of these women and their associates.'

If Revs Alker and Benzing thought that their sharply argued, cogent and eloquent memorial was going to provoke the magistrates into positive action they were, like others in the past thirty years, doomed to disappointment. The magistrates decided that no action should be taken as they wished to see how the new licensing law would run for a year. Although there was no immediate sign of action, it is probable that the reports of Chief Constable Dunn, Colonel Bruce and this forceful petition delivered by prominent clergymen prompted the authorities to embark on a systematic operation of brothel raids in the Sandhole.[12]

In the early period of this red light district, Shepherd Street became synonymous with the Sandhole itself in some commentators' minds and writings. The street, which had such an auspicious start, being the location where Doctor Shepherd's Library could be visited, soon gained its bad reputation because of the notorious Liverpool House beerhouse and the brothels at Nos 15 and 4. In the 1861 Census, brothels were in full swing at number 28 and 29 where ten women in total lived, the oldest being thirty and the youngest eighteen, all from different parts of the country. By 1871 there were brothels at 28, 29 and 30 Shepherd Street. Number 30 was occupied in April 1871 by a well-known prostitute, Elizabeth Ann Clarke and her lover/bully, William Cleaver. Cleaver had already served four months with hard labour for aggravated assault on Clarke. At the 1871 Census, numbers 28 and 29 were unoccupied because they had been raided twice in previous months. In December 1870, Annie Armstrong at 28 and Emma Taylor at 29 had been charged under Bye Law 55 and were found guilty on the testimony of 'several constables' who had 'visited'. Armstrong had pleaded guilty and was discharged because she had volunteered to leave town. Taylor had paid the court costs but was not fined because she had agreed to leave the house.

Armstrong had pleaded guilty and was discharged because she had volunteered to leave town

Six weeks later, in June 1871, Elizabeth McDonald was charged with running a brothel at number 28 after Sergeant Hornby and Inspector Hornby had visited and found a man and woman in bed together. Described by Mr Dunn as 'an adept thief', she was fined ten shillings (£48) and costs. In the same court, on the same day, Agnes Worden was charged with running a brothel, location unspecified, and also fined the same. She was also charged with a second similar offence, but the Mayor simply asked her 'to give up her calling'. The *Chronicle* reports the Mayor as adding that 'they did not wish to be hard, but the eyes of the public' were on them. To put this in context, thirty-four years earlier, in July 1837, Ellen Barnes was ordered to leave her house as punishment for the same offence.

One of the mainstays of this way of life must have been a contingency fund for fines in each house because, four weeks later, Jane Pinder was fined ten shillings and costs for running a brothel at number 28. When PC Burns visited the house, he found two prostitutes downstairs and a prostitute with a man upstairs. It is highly likely that Elizabeth McDonald was one of these women because she was indicted on the same charge and was sent to prison at Lancaster Castle for twelve months with hard labour. Why did women like McDonald persist in this trade or even at this house? It has become more apparent that even paying four shillings a week rent (£20) for houses rated at two shillings and sixpence (£12), paying fines and court costs, it was worth it as long as the 'head' of the household was on a rota to take the punishment as Emma Griffin, Professor of History at the University of East Anglia says,

> 'The gender pay gap in Victorian Britain was considerable. In any kind of industry that employed men and women, women generally earned half of what the men did … it's important to remember that if women can't earn as much as men, they're never going to have as much power.[13]

So, money meant power, and the women of the Sandhole, however fallen or debased they felt or were perceived by others, they were determined to keep a grip on that power as long as they could. The rotation also meant that it gave them a better chance under the Habitual Criminals Act.

In January 1873, 30 Shepherd Street was raided, and Mary Thompson was summoned for keeping a brothel there. She had been taken to court four times before for the same offence (in different places) and was fined twenty shillings (£93). Later in that year, in June, she was sent to prison for three months for theft. In May 1873, number 30 was raided twice. In the first week, Johannah Magher was fined ten shillings. A week later, Isabella Cowell was fined for the same offence at the same house. In another Shepherd Street brothel, Jane Rowley (or Riley), described by the *Chronicle* as 'a lewd woman', took her 'turn' in February and March as head of house and was fined. Soon after, she was imprisoned for three months for theft. At the 1871 Census, Rowley was living in a brothel at 10 Blelock Street, but she was not a local. She had been born in Oldham.

There were brothels all over the Sandhole, such as in Leeming Street, Water Street, Greaves Street and Shepherd Street, and its outlying satellites like Library Street, Rose Street, and St John's Place, but none of them was in the same league either for immorality or for managing raids and their consequence like those in Blelock Street and Laurel Street. Like Shepherd Street, Blelock Street was named after a worthy citizen of Preston, George Blelock, who served the town as a respected bailiff or official of the court. By the

1870s the name of this street must have seemed so ironic. Between 1840 and 1885, every house, except number 8, had been used as a brothel at one time or another. Number 8 was occupied by a poor family, the Dewhursts, for twenty years until the late 1870s.

Between 1840 and 1885, every house in Blelock Street, except number 8, had been used as a brothel at one time or another.

Number 5 Blelock Street was raided on Sunday 8 January 1871 by two unnamed police officers who found several prostitutes with a number of soldiers. Bridget Connolly was charged on this occasion for running the house and charged costs only on condition that she left town, yet she was recorded there at the 1871 Census in April. In 1875 she was found in charge of a brothel at 30 Shepherd Street.[14] Number 5 was raided occasionally, as during the week beginning 30 November 1874 when Mary Ann Burns was in charge and was fined an undisclosed amount. Also raided that week were 28 Shepherd Street, run by Emma Corrigan, and 2 Blelock Street, run by Mary Agnes Henderson. The presiding magistrate, Mr R. Benson, seemed slightly taken aback by the cases before him and asked, 'How many houses are there in this locality?' To which Sergeant Keefe answered, 'About a score.' Then Mr Benson asked for more details.

> 'To whom do they belong?'
>
> 'To different property owners in the town,' replied Keefe.
>
> 'I suppose they get good rents?' furthered Mr Benson.
>
> To which he was informed that the tenants paid four shillings a week for houses only worth two shillings and sixpence, implying that the landlords knew the purposes that their properties were being put to. (*Chronicle*)

A very modern solution was suggested by Mary Ann O'Brien when she was fined in 1875 for keeping a brothel in Old Cock Yard. When asked if she wanted to say anything she said, 'You should give us licences for such houses.' She was fined twenty shillings (£101).

Women named as 'Head' of household, 1851–81 Censuses

Blelock Street

1 1861 Mary Ann Lawson 1871 Ann(ie) Gallagher

2 1871 Mary Jane Smalley 1881 Margaret Shaughnessy

3 1851 Ellen Garth 1861 Ann Smith[15]

4 1861 Sarah Halliwell 1871 Ann Armstrong 1881 Mary Jane Wallace

5 1881 Alice Banks[16]

6 1851 Ellen Talbot 1861 Ellen Lawson 1871 Ann Smith 1881 Bridget Leaver

7 1851 Margery Bragson

9 1871 Annie Miller

10 1861 Ellen Burk 1871 Isabella Slater[17]

11 1861 Mary Ann Fisher 1871 Mary Riley

12 1861 Betsy Fielding 1871 Sarah Smith

Laurel Street

2 1871 Jane Winstanley

3 1861 Betsy Slater 1871 Mary Mullen 1881 Annie Bell

4 1861 Mary Taylor 1871 Kate Scanlon 1881 Ellen Reed

5 1861 Ann Collett 1871 Sarah King[18] 1881 Sarah King

Shepherd Street

28 1861 Elizabeth Tonks 1881 Margaret Drummond

29 1861 Alice Porter 1881 Ann Needham

30 1871 Elizabeth Ann Clarke 1881 Jane Rowley

Women fined after raids on disorderly houses in the Sandhole 1872–79

Blelock Street

2 Mary Agnes Henderson 2 December 1874| Mary Alice Standing 7 April 1875| Elizabeth Phillips 7 August 1875

4 Bridget Shearns 1 February 1873| Mary Jane Wallace 16 March 1878

5 Jane Forrest 21 December 1872| Mary Ann Burns 5 December 1874

6 Mary Gallagher 3 February 1874| Mary Jane Pearson 5 June 1875

10 Sarah King 5 October 1872| Mary Ann Cox 14 November 1874

11 Jane Rowley 17 May 1873| Mary Ann Greenough 3 October 1874* and 14 November 1874| Jane Marsden 3 October 1874* (* on separate raids)|Ellen Dunderdale 28 November 1874 (18 months' hard labour)

Raids on unspecified addresses in Blelock Street:

Margaret Whiteside 26 July 1873

Mary Agnes Henderson 9 January 1874

Mary Jane Wallace 31 October 1874[19]

Bridget Shearns 14 November 1874

Catherine Ross 5 May 1875

Mary Shaughnessy 19 June 1875

Laurel Street

2 Elizabeth Hirst 23 November 1872

3 Annie Bell 21 October 1876

Raids on unspecified addresses in Laurel Street:

Mary Ann Berry and Mary Blue 5 October 1872 (on separate raids)

Annie Cox 14 November 1874

Bridget Shearns 10 March 1877

Bridget Connolly 5 April 1879

Shepherd Street

28 Jane Rowley 21 February 1874| Jane Rowley 21 March 1874|Emma Emma Corrigan 5 December 1874|Mary Jane Smalley 4 March 1875| Alice Jones 22 December 1875

29 Mary Ann Sharples 25 February 1876

30 Mary Thompson 25 January 1873|Johanna Magher and Isabella Cowell 17 May 1873 (separate raids)|Mary Jane Smalley 4 March 1875|Bridget Connolly 11 August 1875|Elizabeth Jones 15 November 1876|Bridget Connolly 10 November 1877| Mary Jane Bibby 22 December 1877

Raids on unspecified addresses in Shepherd Street:

Jane Rowley 14 February and 21 March 1873

Mary Ann Spencer 13 February 1875

Elizabeth Cook 30 October 1875

Margaret Kirby 21 April 1877

This shows the tightrope these women were walking with the workhouse on one side and the prison on the other

What this illustrates, apart from the workings of the rotation is that the whole brothel enterprise in the Sandhole was run by women. It was a business, illegal as it was, managed by women at a time of secure patriarchy – a man's world of economics and finance. It also shows the tightrope these women were walking with the workhouse on one side and the prison on the other. In the late 1870s, armed with the Habitual Criminals Act, the magistrates made inroads into this grimy female preserve by imposing heavier and heavier penalties, such as fourteen days' imprisonment, and more, with hard labour.[20] Gone were the days when a few days in the House of Correction would be just a break from the daily routine. The fines became greater too, such as twenty shillings by 1878 (£105). Hence there was a more zealous use of the rota and a greater importance put on the contingency fund that in previous years. However, the clouds were gathering over the area.

The Criminal Law Amendment Act, passed on 14 August 1885, had three main aims – the protection of women and girls, the suppression of brothels and 'other purposes'.[21] In the first sentence, provision was made for the punishment of any man who had 'unlawful carnal connexion' with a woman or girl he had detained, intimidated, drugged or 'stupefied'. In this section, punishments were also prescribed for men who had 'unlawful carnal knowledge' with girls under fourteen, under seventeen and under eighteen, of corresponding severity. The age of consent was raised to sixteen years by this Act. In this part also, there were further limitations put on the misuse of power, such as detaining women for sex in private houses or brothels, and rape or attempted rape. The section of the Act which was most pertinent to the inhabitants of the Sandhole was the second aim – the suppression of brothels. The actual wording is worth recording:

Any person who

1 keeps or manages or acts or assists in the management of a brothel or

2 being the tenant, lessee, or occupier (or the person in charge) of any premises, knowingly permits such premises or any part thereof to be used of as a brothel or for the purposes of habitual prostitution or

3 being the lessor, or landlord of any such premises, or agent of such lessor or landlord, lets the same or any part thereof with the knowledge that such premises ... are to be used as a brothel is liable

to a fine not exceeding one hundred pounds (£10,600) ... or imprisonment for a term not exceeding three months and

on a second or subsequent conviction to a fine not exceeding two hundred and fifty pounds (£26,500) or to a term of imprisonment for a term not exceeding six months.

While this gave the police and magistrates the spur and power they needed to attack the problem head-on and eradicate areas such as the Sandhole, it was also a timely, even unwelcome warning to land agents and landlords. Those who had feigned innocence or ignorance about the purpose to which their properties had been used and yet continued to collect the rents suddenly had to act to avoid prosecution. This resulted in a number of Sandhole properties being put up for sale rather quickly, a summary of one advertisement, which appeared on 29 May in the *Chronicle* being

'On Wednesday 26 May 1886, Mr Wm Jones put up for sale several lots of property in various parts of Preston.

Lot 1 – The old, established tripe boiling and wheelgrease manufactory situate in Greaves Street together with ... 3 and 4 Greaves Street and number 4 Laurel Street – £425 (£47,970)

Lot 2 – Three dwelling houses 31 Shepherd Street and 1 and 2 Laurel Street, producing a gross rental of £50 14 shillings per annum (£5842) were sold for £300 (£37,570)

Lot 3 – 9 Water Street sold for £192 (£22,120)

> Lot 10 – 23, 24 and 25 Shepherd Street went for £324 (£37, 320)
>
> Lot 12 – four dwelling houses 4–7 Blelock Street and three houses behind were sold for £230 (£26,500).'

Almost two years later, the older poorer houses were sold by Jabez Jones and Sons, namely 7 and 8 Shepherd Street, 31 and 32 Shepherd Street, 1 and 2 Laurel Street and 2 Blelock Street.

In 1842, Rev. John Clay had written that 'the wealthy and instructed have a great task before them, which must be accomplished in promoting education and religious knowledge among their inferiors …'

This statement was valid in both national and local contexts. It was an unusual and outstanding statement to make, almost Chartist in its sentiment. At its core is a call to those who can, to get involved as a matter of duty. In August 1870, almost thirty years later, Robert Watson declared in court that no-one would improve the situation in the Sandhole by 'preaching on platforms – they must reach the people themselves'. Some individuals did both, some organisations did both and so did the Christian parishes on the Sandhole's edge, St Saviour's and St Augustine's.

It would be appropriate here to remind readers of the problem area that these parishes had to minister to. Fortunately, there are contemporary descriptions by the renowned local historian Anthony Hewitson ('Atticus') who wrote vivid reports on Preston parishes of all denominations in 'Our Churches and Chapels',[22] including the areas and congregations they served and their staff. The idea behind the book was that 'we should be acquainted with [the] persons and priests … we should have a correct idea of their congregations … and reflect the character and influence of all.'[23] In doing this he underlines the challenge facing each parish.

St Augustine's, which stood two minutes' walk from the Sandhole, was a Catholic mission set up in 1836 and the church was finished in 1840 (see earlier). Its parish boundaries ran from Frenchwood Street in the west to

London Road in the east. Until 1860 it extended up New Hall Lane and Ribbleton Lane when St Joseph's was built. To the south it extended as far as Church Lane in Walton-le-Dale, through a rural area in the early days which rapidly became built up. To the north, the parish ran through the Sandhole and surrounding areas to Church Street. In Hewitson's description,[24]

> Only in its [i.e. the church's] proximate surroundings is the place semi rural and select. As the circle widens – townwards at any rate – you soon get into a region of murky houses, ragged children, running beer jugs, poverty; as you move onwards in certain directions, the plot thickens until you get into the very lairs of ignorance, depravity and misery ... much that smells of gin, and rascality, and heathenism may be seen in the district.[25]
>
> The congregation is almost entirely made up of working people ... On four consecutive Sundays recently ... upwards of 3,100 people heard Mass within the walls of the church.[26]

The Anglican parish of St Saviour was established in 1859. The old church, based on the old Baptist chapel, was demolished in 1866 and the new church was only completed ten months before Hewitson visited. Being so new and having little history, except for taking up the old chapel, it gave the writer a larger canvas on which to portray the full horror of the Sandhole, right from the start.[27]

> Few districts are more thoroughly vitiated (backward), more distinctly poverty-struck, more entirely at enmity with soap and water ... You needn't go to the low slums in London, you needn't smuggle yourself round with detectives into the back dens of big cities if you want to see sights of poverty and depravity;[28] you can have them nearer home – at home-in the murky streets, inner courts, crowded houses, dim cellars and noisy drinking dens of St Saviour's district ...
>
> ... Myriads of children, ragged, sore headed, bare legged, dirty and amazingly alive amid all of it; wretched-looking matrons, hugging saucy, screaming infants to their breasts and sending senior youngsters for either herring or beer or very small loaves; ... bevies of brazen-faced hussies looking

> out of grim doorways for more victims and more drink; stray soldiers struggling about beer or dram shop entrances, with dissolute, brawny armed females; and wandering old hags with black eyes and dishevelled hair, closing up the career of shame and ruin they have so long and wretchedly run.
>
> We mention this ... because it is something which exists daily in the centre of our town – in the centre of St Saviour's district [and St Augustine's – JG]. No locality we know of stands in need of general redemption as this ...

As a parting comment on the task ahead, Hewitson continues,

> ... any Christian church, no matter whatever may be its denominational peculiarities which may exist in it, deserves encouragement and support. The district is so supremely poor, and so absolutely bad, that anything calculated to improve or enlighten it in any way is worthy of assistance.[29]

And in St Augustine's description,

> There is plenty of room for all kinds of reformers in the locality; if any man can do any good in it, whatever be his creed or theory, let him do it.[30]

In 1859, there was an initiative by local and national bodies to institute a Ragged School in Leeming Street.[31] The building earmarked for this purpose was the old Baptist Chapel, a purpose 'for which it is well adapted, and for which its locality offers a wide field of usefulness'.[32] It was hoped that the thousand pounds (£109,300) needed to refurbish it would come from grants and 'local benevolence'. By 1860, the establishment was being referred to as Queen Street Ragged School and on 11 February that year a Sunday School was set up before the school was moved to Shepherd Street.[33] Another activity at this institution was reported in the *Chronicle* on 11 October 1862 when

> ... a school for reading and writing was opened ... [and] 293 young women availed themselves of the opportunity thus offered them of self improvement. We are glad to perceive that there is such a disposition on the part of females, now unfortunately unemployed,[34] to improve themselves as has

> been shown by attendance at the sewing school ... and now at this educational establishment.

The corner stone of the new church to serve the new parish of St Saviour was laid on 27 November 1866 on the site of the old Baptist Chapel which was 'erected in 1784 when there were few houses.' The *Herald* goes on to report that

> A dense population has sprung up in the neighbourhood; a great proportion of it consisted of poor people; and the district comprised some of the worst dens in the town for profligacy and drunkenness. It seems as if there were plenty of scope for any system of religion could bring its influence to bear on the masses of the people ... The Church of England has stepped in to break bread amongst the godless masses that exist in the district.[35]

The Sunday School was said, in 1866, to be 'flourishing' already with a hundred extra pupils and their teacher, Mr Edward Hall, was described as 'indefatigable'. By January 1870, the *Chronicle* reports that nearly six hundred Sunday School pupils had attended the New Year Tea Party. Three years later, in 1873, the Lodge Bank Tavern was purchased by the trustees of St Saviour's and it was remodelled as a school. The Garden Gate beerhouse was also purchased and demolished, together with two cottages. The whole arrangement had been described by Hewitson.

> At the southern end there is a wretched looking beershop, and near it a dingy, used-up cottage. These two buildings are a nuisance to the church; they spoil the appearance of the building at one end completely, and they ought to be pulled down and carted off forthwith.[36]

The area once occupied by the Garden Gate was reassigned as a school playground.

The *Chronicle* published a letter to the editor on 1 November 1873, from a person writing under the nom-de-plume of 'We Shall See'. The writer was concerned about the Ragged School which

Despite having a 'helping hand' from those people who were 'liberally disposed', there were children being sent out with cards to beg for money

had been set up in Shepherd Street, complaining that, despite having a 'helping hand' from those people who were 'liberally disposed', there were children being sent out with cards to beg for money for what was, by then, St Saviour's Ragged School. Interestingly, the writer gives us a flavour of what the children were saying to householders, and how they sounded, as they went door to door with their cards of introduction. 'Yo mun gie me twopence (pronounced 'tuppence') for t'Ragged Schoo'. Aw've getten twopennies gin me, an you mun gie me twopence. Aw've getten a card. Here, tek and look at it.'

The writer describes people being 'beset' by people begging. In short, he/she thinks it was a mistake to 'turn out a batch of children with begging cards to overrun the town'. After complaining that the churchwardens should organise it properly, he/she turns to what is probably the main reason for writing in the first place, either not knowing or refusing to acknowledge that St Saviour's was a poor parish. 'It is not fair always to rely on the rich or the habitual and well known givers. Let the working people themselves have a turn. Why should they have everything done for them in the Church of England?'

The writer is convinced that if a well-organised effort was made, the money needed could be raised and the fact that it was still needed 'is a standing reproach to the apathy of the congregation and the indifference of churchmen.'

So, the correspondent shows that being out of touch and lacking Christian charity was the norm for some people. To add to these deficiencies, he/she adds another – prediction, as the letter is concluded with the statement that the disestablishment of the Church of England was not far away!

Counterbalancing this, on the same page, is another letter written by Rev. William Dent Thompson, the Vicar of St Saviour's, concerning the re-establishment of the Ragged School as part of the parish's mission. The original premises had been sold because it was small, badly ventilated and suffocating in summer. There were 120 children on roll but realistically only room for sixty 'with little provision for separating boys from girls'. He appeals for money to set the school up in the former Lodge Bank Tavern premises, with 'parishioners, wardens, Sunday School teachers and superintendents working hard'. Taking into account the area and its character, Rev. Thompson writes with some optimism.

> Although very near Shepherd Street, our teachers and scholars will not witness the sad sights when entering and leaving the building ... The state of Shepherd Street and the immediate locality is very sad. How is this state of affairs to be remedied? It is a question more easily asked than answered. I fear that little good can be done among a certain class of the adult population with the organisation we have at present. I have ever found them respectful, willing to listen and, I believe, at times, heartily sick of the state in which they are living; but to win their way back to a better life requires effort which few, alas, seem able to put forth. But surely there is hope for the children.

He added that the teachers worked hard, six days a week and the school was also open on Sundays and three nights a week in winter. As a result, 'a considerable number of children are taught to read and write. The alterations to the building amounted to £700 (£65,000) of which £470 (£43,700) was still outstanding but he was optimistic of benefactors coming forward. One of the results which was spurring him on was that 'The children are cleaner, tidier, more obedient and less rude than they once were.'

He was also hoping for contributions from the Temperance movement as the staff and trustees of St Saviour's had 'swept away three public houses[37] ... two out of the three were about as unsatisfactory in every way as can be found in Preston.'

The parish also had a strong Band of Hope group (promoting temperance) which organised activities, such as in September 1878 when they put on a dissolving slide show (projected from a magic lantern with two lenses) depicting 'The Story of the Bottle' and 'The Drunkard's Children' to encourage abstinence from alcohol. The parish of St Saviour's and its mission in the area grew apace through the 1870s and 1880s. The *Herald* reported on 23 November 1889 that St Saviour's Bazaar had been held with the aim of raising the £700 (£78,940) needed to demolish 'half a dozen insanitary and tumbledown dwellings' which had got in the way of the school's 'effective working'. Pulling down these 'unsightly' buildings would provide an area for a playground and to rebuild the mission school. The takings on the first day came to a staggering £850 (£95,850).

In 1876, Joshua Williamson, a thirty-four-year-old grocer, had an encounter with two homeless children which spurred him to help poor children in the town

In 1876, Joshua Williamson, a thirty-four-year-old grocer, had an encounter with two homeless children which spurred him to help poor children in the town. At first, he set up a non-denominational mission which met in Rose Street and later in a building on the site of the old, notorious beerhouse, Liverpool House which became Shepherd Street Mission. The charity grew in strength from subscriptions and donations from Preston people. In 1900, Williamson, who had moved to the affluent Stanley Place in the 1880s, gave up his business to run the charity. He acquired further premises to accommodate children and adults in Berry Street, Laurel Street and Oxford Street where Crow Hill House became a children's home. As well as care and instruction, the children, numbering between 80 and 100, were taken out to the country and treated to parties at Christmas where they appeared 'with clean faces and their behaviour throughout was excellent'.[38]

The *Chronicle* reported on 13 January 1883 the end of a week-long set of evening meetings at the Mission. The Superintendent, Mr Williamson, gave a report on the Mission's workings in six areas – religious services, Sunday School, 'reclaiming unfortunate women, snatching lost and destitute children from the gutter', distributing tracts and temperance work. Numbers on the whole were said to be making 'a general increase'. Also tracts were distributed and twenty lodging houses were visited each Sunday morning. 'In these places are to be found between 300 and 400 of the lowest class'. In the same year, the Mission declared itself independent of financial input from religious authorities, notably the Dissenters, and became wholly supported by public and private donations.

Nearly seven years later, the *Chronicle* reported on 18 October 1890 that the Mission,

> ... situated as it is in the lowest part of the town, is doing excellent work and, during the past year, many children have been rescued from the drunkenness which surrounds them. As the Mission works on unsectarian principles, children of all creeds attend and are taught useful lessons. There are many sympathisers. Two hundred and fifty people attended the 14th Annual Tea Party.

A year later, at the Annual Tea Party, the Superintendent, Mr Jesse Chilman, reported, 'The great secret of success was for people to take the trouble to bend their backs in the ragged school and mission work and stoop to assisting to rescue children out of the dens of misery and immorality.'[39]

Crow Hill House continued to work through many transformations in the twentieth century and was sold in 1989. The mission continues as the Shepherd Street Trust (2020).

A church minister who was active in the early 1870s was Rev. Edmund Lee, the senior curate of the Parish Church under the Vicar, Canon Parr. In this period, the divisions between the Christian denominations in Preston were deep, though not quite as deep as in other towns and cities. Anthony Hewitson, whose allegiance was never made obvious, commented that Rev. Lee, Canon Parr, Rev. Thompson and Rev. George Alker were all anti-Catholic in their early years but tempered their feelings in later life. Lee and Thompson declared to Hewitson that they did not hate Catholic people just the Catholic hierarchy. This was possibly connected to the Catholic Emancipation Act of 1829 and the restoration of the Catholic hierarchy in 1850 after almost three hundred years' absence. The tempering of

Between 1870 and 1875 he preached in all the Anglican churches in the area on special days such as feast days, guild celebrations and jubilees.

attitude may have come from constant contact with Catholics, as they made up 33–35 percent of the town's 85,000 population. Rev. Lee held degrees from Trinity College, Dublin and Oxford and was very active during the Benzing Affair and after.[40] After repeated calls for more active church involvement in the town's moral and social problems in articles and correspondence in Preston's four newspapers, Lee seems to have taken up the challenge. Between 1870 and 1875 he preached, according to regular reports, in all the Anglican churches in the area on special days such as feast days, guild celebrations and jubilees. He was also active on committees, speaking when Canon Parr sat in as chairman or similar. When he gave charity sermons there was often a collection for the poor attached or the proceeds from the sale of tickets. In addition, he preached occasional, outdoor sermons on summer evenings on the fringe of the Sandhole.

The local newspapers caught up with him a few times in his efforts to 'reach the people themselves'. The first, on Tuesday 9 August 1870 when he delivered a sermon to a large crowd on Syke Hill, on the junction of Shepherd Street and Stoneygate. His theme of forgiveness of sins was taken from the Acts of the Apostles, Chapter 13 verses 38 and 39[41] 'which was listened to with much attention'.[42] The article previewed (though did not cover) a similar sermon for the following Thursday on mercy, forgiveness and healing using Christ's healing of the beggar, Blind Bartimaeus.[43] A year later, the *Herald* reported that Rev. Lee had been preaching in a house on Rose Street every Thursday evening during the summer. The theme of the latest sermon was the famine in the days of King Ahab and God's prophet, Elijah,

Rev. Lee had been preaching in a house on Rose Street every Thursday evening during the summer… 'on Thursday last, the weather being hot and his hearers not well provided with eau-de-cologne, he took his stand upon some steps in Syke Hill'

sustained by the widow woman in the first Book of Kings Chapter 17, delivered 'to a very select audience gathered from the cellars and lodging houses of the locality; but on Thursday last, the weather being hot and his hearers not well provided with eau-de-cologne, he took his stand upon some steps in Syke Hill.'

In the final lines of his article on St Augustine's, Hewitson, who could be a fearless critic and realist, states

> Taking the district in its entirety, it is industriously worked by the Catholics. They deserve praise for their energy. Their object is to push on Catholicism and improve the secular position of the inhabitants, and they do this with a zeal which is most praiseworthy.[44]

From the start of the parish in 1838, the clergy of St Augustine's must have realised what they were up against and the problems they faced. One of them, a huge, growing parish, was partly solved in 1860 when St Joseph's parish was established in Skeffington Road. There had been a great deal of time and effort put into that, raising money by every means a Victorian parish could employ, such as bazaars, special teas, collections, field days and charity sermons. The other immediate issues were poverty, the drink problem, especially in men and the education of the young. The schools were well established by 1860 and the numbers increased after the 1870 Education Act.

The local newspapers were mildly anti-Catholic, except when taking money for advertisements for parish events

The local newspapers were mildly anti-Catholic, except when taking money for advertisements for parish events. However, they were 'not consistent, with the generally anti-Catholic *Herald* occasionally reporting and even praising the activities of Roman Catholics.'[45] Apart from the events and dates recorded in the parish notice books, the pastoral work of the parish went unrecorded, but the strength behind much of the effort must have come from the consistency of its leadership; between 1840 and 1906, there were only five parish priests. Very occasionally, the work of these men and their curates was reported, albeit anonymously.

On 18 December 1857, when Mary Gaffer (aka Gaffery) was burned to death, she was visited by Fr Cookson or Fr Swarbrick who entered 'the miserable hovel' where she lived to give her the sacrament of Extreme Unction. The *Chronicle* added the tart comment 'to which persuasion she professed to belong' without bothering to find out anything of the miserable existence she had had until then. Almost twenty years later, in January 1875, a correspondent calling himself/herself 'Q' wrote to the editor of the *Chronicle* to complain about the state of morals in certain areas of the town and proceeded at great length on his/her perceived absence of Christian ministers 'from where they should be, in the worst areas ministering to sinners.' He/she continues, '... we must throw off the idea of caste, we must get among the people, we must go into the highways and hedges, the back slums to bridewell, all places where drinkers abound.'

Q professed to have a friend who was 'given to visiting the poor' of the Sandhole and said that he had never seen a Protestant minister 'visiting the wretched outcasts though he had often come across a Catholic priest'. He/she said another man from a Protestant family had become a Catholic because, he said

> I have lived near twenty years in yon miserable hovel and all that time I have never seen the face of any minister except a priest and at last came to the conclusion that the Catholic religion must be a pure Christian religion or its priests would not have come and cared for a poor, wretched creature like me.

At the end of a short report of a meeting on 7 December 1874, a *Chronicle* reporter remarked. 'Great praise is due to the Rev Canon Taylor (parish priest of St Augustine's) for the exertion and attention he is giving to the moral elevation of the poor people in this district.'

It is easy to forget that the old, the young, the poor and the sick were living cheek-by-jowl with the drinking dens and bawdy houses. The most direct way financial and material help was given was through the St Vincent de Paul Society, which is a global Catholic organisation, set up for helping the poor and deprived. Most parishes have volunteers working in them. The *Chronicle* reported on 8 October 1859 that on the previous Sunday there had been collections for the Society after each Mass which realised £21 (£295). A year later, a meeting of the parish Society was chaired by the Right Reverend Bishop Alexander Goss, second Bishop of Liverpool.[46] The reports which were read that day

> ... stated that the amounts of relief given to poor families in that year, in the shape of tea, bread, clogs and clothing as well as amounts of money in aid of different objects of the Society. Bishop Goss praised the efforts of the Society in making the welfare of the poor greater. He encouraged the wealthy to contribute more and assist the clergy and lighten their burden by visiting the poor.[47]

After this time, the Society held collections after Mass well into the next century. Among the papers from St Augustine's deposited at the Lancashire Archives[48] are two small notebooks. One is an account book bearing the legend 'St Augustine's SVP account book 1860– '. In it are recorded the mundane workings of the SVP group. The usual church door collections at the time amounted to ten shillings (£55). A float of three pounds (£328) was kept for any eventualities. Money was given to the needy in such areas as 'housecleaning, bedding and clogs'. During the Cotton Famine (1862–5) the Society gave soup and food to the poor and those put out of work. The other is a fragment of a record of the kind of relief given and to whom. The following is a selection showing people from the Sandhole receiving food from the parish SVP.

> 20 July 1871–18 January 1872 Alice Towers 15 Leeming Street
>
> 30 November 1871–18 January 1872 Mrs Dewhurst 8 Blelock Street
>
> 12 September 1872–15 May 1873 James Burns 21 Queen Street

3 April 1873–8 May 1873 James Holden 37 Queen Street

1 July 1875–19 August 1875 Cornelius Hogan 45 Queen Street

11 January 1877–18 October 1877 Alice Wainman 13 Leeming Street

29 March 1877–31 May 1877 Mary Salisbury 10 Back Leeming Street

A further note in the Parish Notice Book, from which news and information were read out at Mass, for the year 1881–2, 1,639 poor people (out of a parish population of 5,200) had been given four shillings (£22) each to relieve their situation.

Two other ways of 'reaching the people' are interconnected – the drive against alcohol and local enterprises to promote adult education. These two were bound up with the intention of enticing people, mostly men, away from the public house, drink and the consequences of drunkenness and immorality. In his social history of Lancashire, John Walton says that, for men, the public house was 'a social centre offering warmth, gossip, information, entertainment, meeting rooms and comradeship.'[49] One way to break this trend would be to create the same pleasures and pastimes in a safer environment.

Another reason why licensed premises were popular with men was put forward by Emma Griffin in an interview in June 2020.[50] Having studied the Victorian economy from the angle of men being the family's breadwinner, she suggests that, from her research, that men seem to have had the best out of the system, but delving more deeply she found that it was difficult for them too.

> A working man could be out of the house for fifty or sixty hours a week, so a lot of children saw their fathers as distant, remote figures. And because the house was so powerfully coded as a space for women and children, fathers often felt out of place there … This often ended up in a vicious circle where a father would start drinking because he

felt rejected by the family, but that made his children hate him even more.

It was cheaper to get a mug of alcohol than a cup of clean water and lax licensing laws meant that pubs were everywhere

Just as research for this Sandhole project has uncovered, 'alcohol was a very significant problem in the Victorian era. It was cheaper to get a mug of alcohol than a cup of clean water and lax licensing laws meant that pubs were everywhere.'[51]

To move forward, this vicious circle would need to be broken. Many on the doorstep of the Sandhole and its fringes could see what damage alcohol and the alehouse could do. Joseph Livesey, the famous Teetotaller, had taken the pledge in March 1832, totally abstaining from drinking alcohol for good, while the Temperance Society was established the following year. That group was made up of an amorphous membership; some favoured total abstinence while other were open to a controlled intake. Livesey wrote long, erudite letters to the newspapers, gave speeches in Preston and other Lancashire towns and produced many pamphlets. However, his impact in the Sandhole was hardly felt until the 1870s when St Saviour's and St Augustine's formed groups of temperance minded people who were determined to eradicate the evils of drink.

Father James Nugent,[52] the famous Catholic chaplain of Walton Prison and promoter of measures to help the poor in Liverpool, gave a lecture on temperance at St Augustine's in Lark Hill House School hall on 1 July 1874 to an audience of 1400 people. He said he had accepted the invitation because he had read in the Preston newspapers how 'easy to see the terrible hold intemperance had on the people. Drink is the source of all the vice and evils which beset society.' This vice, he stated, grew up in children from 'the bad example of drunken and debauched parents'. He said that the man who was a drunkard was a bad master, a bad servant, a bad husband and

... the man who was a drunkard was a bad master, a bad servant, a bad husband and a curse to his children; an intemperate woman was the source of humiliation and degradation of her children

a curse to his children; an intemperate woman was the source of humiliation and degradation of her children'. Too often, children were glad to escape from a home which was often the scene of misery and every degradation, which caused its own problems in the future. He accompanied this with evidence he had seen personally in Liverpool. However, he felt that Preston was better off because of the consistent and steady employment in the cotton mills. At the end, about 350 people took the pledge.[53]

Father Nugent was present when the Cardinal Archbishop of Westminster, Henry Manning,[54] gave a lecture on abstinence from alcohol at the Corn Exchange on 13 September 1876 to 1300 members of St Augustine's Temperance Association which was celebrating its second anniversary. He regarded Preston as 'a most Christian town', but he had heard after he had arrived at the Exchange that there was 'a public house in the town for every 132 persons and one which was frequented by six and seven hundred persons daily and between two and three hundred children under sixteen.' He said that 60,000 people from all classes died from drunkenness and parents were showing bad example, including the rich and well-off. 'Drunkenness [is] a shame and a scandal, a disease and a curse to our country'.

As a result of this lecture, at the next full meeting of the Temperance Association on 15 November, Canon Taylor voiced his fears about the young people of the parish, especially being so close to one of the worst parts of the town. He suggested that the Association should include members of the Boys' and Girls' Guilds and asked parents to cooperate in getting their children enrolled.

1877 saw the arrival of an enthusiastic young priest at St Augustine's called Patrick Kirwan. Still aged only twenty five he galvanised the Association and was given the floor as the main speaker at its third anniversary in the hall at Lark Hill School in front of 1100 people (*Chronicle* 23 June 1877). An admirer of Joseph Livesey and his work, Father Kirwan talked about the attraction of the public house for 'the drunkard'. If it was not the drink it was 'the agreeable company he found there'. In conclusion, his remarks echoed the sentiments and writings of Rev. John Clay, the Anglican prison chaplain, long before he was born. 'It was the drunken husband who made the home miserable, and if he had to become sober, there would be no unhappiness at home. Poverty, prisons, asylums and worse are the lot of drunkards.'

Before he finished his address, he urged people to take the pledge as many had already done at St Augustine's. He encouraged a 'more united front [and] the cause of Temperance would triumph.'

Less than three months later, Cardinal Manning returned to St Augustine's to speak about the evils of drink. He spoke in the same vein as Rev. Kirwan had previously and added that if there was anything worse than a drunken man or woman it was a drunken child. He called on as many people as possible to show good example and help others. 'If you, for the love of God and of your neighbour, for the sake of setting an example, to others, of giving strength to those who were partial or habitual drunkards … I believe that you would help the work of saving souls …'

He approved of drinking alcohol 'in temperate measure' but paid tribute to those priests and parishioners who had pledged total abstinence. In the same speech he said that Canon Taylor had asked him to announce that all the money from the evening, with its 'crowded and enthusiastic audience' (*Chronicle* 1 September 1877), would be put towards 'building a room … to be used for amusement and reading … [where] there would always be a plentiful supply of tea and coffee'. Canon Taylor said it would be primarily for men, presumably to keep them away from the alehouse.

This was very much a trend of the times. Every village, hamlet, parish and district wanted a reading room where magazines, newspapers and lending libraries would be available for the further and broader education of those who had only rudimentary schooling. In these places 'It would have been unusual to see anyone reading a paper by themselves and, regardless of reading ability, anyone interested in the news could have picked up the main points by listening to the paper being read ... Reading places were sociable places ...'[55]

A year later, at a meeting of the Association, a committee was formed to build the parish reading room and a coffee room. This venture was to cost two hundred pounds (£22,000) of which seventy-six pounds (£8,300) had already been collected. Four weeks later, at a new establishment called St Augustine's Men's Institute, a certain Mr Joseph Crombleholme said that the institutes and reading rooms set up by other agencies[56] worked side by side with Catholics and had interchanges of ideas in 'combatting attractions such as the bar parlour and singing room'. He added a further dimension to this which was the introduction of discussions and reading materials on general subjects for their influence on improving minds. After careful discussion, he added, that playing cards and dominoes could be played though 'they should not be the main objects'.

On Christmas Eve 1880, the *Chronicle* reported on the opening of a parish club at St Augustine's. St Saviour's had been developing their buildings (see above) and had moved their girls' school from premises in Vauxhall Road which St Augustine's bought and refitted as club premises. The large room was used as a reading and lecture room and for recreation and entertainment for members. The upper room was set aside for games and included two billiard tables. There were also modern and up to date 'lavatories and conveniences'. Canon Taylor hoped it might be 'the means of gathering within it the youths and men of the congregation so that they might receive proper recreation and go home in a proper and sober state at night'. Attached to this club was a refreshment room 'where members could be supplied with hot tea and coffee at all hours of the day and night'.

An example of the entertainments which were held there was one night when comedy and higher literature were performed in front of a large audience in the form of readings from Shakespeare and Tennyson. These included the lead up to, and assassination of, Julius Caesar and the first part of the famous poem, 'The May Queen'. Comic readings included Douglas Jarrold's 'Mrs Candle's Lecture on the Family Umbrella' and 'Faithless Sally Brown' by Thomas Hood.

Judging from St Augustine's Notice Books, the Temperance Association was holding well attended monthly meetings where there would be entertainments[57] or visiting speakers like Father Nugent, who was a guest annually between 1875 and 1878. By the end of October 1874 there were 865 members. In September 1878, an estimated 700 people attended a meeting at Lark Hill School where reformed drinkers talked about their lives of drunkenness. After this, fifty people took the pledge, bringing the total for the parish to well over a thousand. From 1877, the young Father Kirwan was a driving force in the Association, chairing its meetings and giving lectures at its larger gatherings. His drive and fervour must have been noted by many from other denominations and civic organisations, which resulted in him being asked to write a memorial for the Licensing Sessions of August 1882. In that he backed Anglican and Nonconformist petitioners who called on magistrates not to grant new licences or renew any for notorious establishments. Although it was read in the session by Mr Edward Edelston, it was the first time Catholics had been invited to present such a memorial.

In September 1878, an estimated 700 people attended a meeting at Lark Hill School where reformed drinkers talked about their lives of drunkenness

A few days later, in September, the 1882 Guild Merchant celebrations took place with its pageantry, ceremony and processions, the last of which used Church Street on the return section of their route, thereby skirting the northern edge of the Sandhole. In the Catholic procession on Thursday 7 September, St Augustine's Temperance Association walked with the Women's, Men's, Girls' and Boys' Guilds which indicates the strength of determination and dedication of those involved.[58] This drive to alcoholic abstinence on the very doorstep of the most drink sodden and degenerate area of the town starved it of many potential customers and victims.[59]

Missionary efforts were also made by people who were not affiliated to any organisation. On 3 October 1891, the *Lancashire Evening Post* reported that

> Two ladies of education have gone to work in the Water Street area to live 'humbly and helpfully' among the poor and fallen in the lowest parts of the town. No appeal has been made for money and neither accepts wages in their work with prostitutes. It is quite time that some help is given them. The mission could be doubled for £50 (£5,700) a year, and twice this ought to be found in a town which wastes its thousands on the follies and frivolities of the day. The good which has been done in Water Street and its unsavoury purlieus has been marked.

Added for good measure was a report that 'One woman who ran a brothel was found a job in the North. A letter has been received from her mistress referring to her as an example of faithful service and Christian conduct in the house.'

Although the area retained a poor reputation into the twentieth century, the area once known as the Sandhole gradually lost its grimy attraction and had 'disappeared' by 1890. Acts of Parliament such as the Licensing Act, the Habitual Criminals Act and the New Criminal Law Amendment Act undercut the means and immoral confidence of the area. The strengthening and the reorganisation of the police and the tacit admission of certain property owners that they did know what was going on in their houses further undermined those who were determined to make their money in such an unsavoury fashion. The work of two Christian parishes, St Saviour's and St Augustine's, who may never have held much of a dialogue with each other or cooperated with each other, worked tirelessly, in isolation, to break the attraction of the public house and the immorality which, almost irresistibly, followed. Some sympathy must be reserved, however, for those women who may have fallen, irretrievably, into the Sandhole way of life with no safety net of state benefits and only the workhouse and the inevitable pauper's grave to look forward to.

Notes

Chapter One

1 George Dangerfield, *The Strange Death of Liberal England*,1st ed 1937 (New York: Serif, 1997), 125.

2 *BBC History Magazine* (June 2020), 70.

Chapter Two

1 'Report on the State of the Irish Poor in Great Britain' *HMSO* (1835).

Chapter Three

1 Born 1841, the 1851 Census shows her as a pauper child called Mary Gaffery in the Penwortham Workhouse at Middleforth Green, in a school set up in 1847 for poor children. All of them have 'Unknown' entered in the column for Place of Birth. One six-year-old girl was just recorded as 'Foundling'.

Chapter Four

1 Steanson preferred an abbreviated form of his original surname, Stephenson. The main problem with this is that no-one knew how to spell it and so there are numerous versions of it. The spelling used in this study is 'Steanson', the one he used consistently while he was in Preston.

2 Catherine H. Rogers, Frank J. Floyd, Marsha Mailik Seltzer, Jan Greenberg, Jinkuik Hong, 'Long Term Effects of the Death of a Child on Parents' Adjustment in Midlife' (2010), *Journal of family psychology : JFP : journal of the Division of Family Psychology of the American Psychological Association*, vol. 22.2 (2008): 203–11.

3 Laura Nott, 'Grief and Substance Abuse: Coping After Loss', *Elements Behavioural Health* (2017).

4 Margaret Whiteside, aged 61, lived with her daughter's family at 23 William Street and was possibly one of a small army of Christian women in Anglican and Catholic parishes who tended the sick, assisted women in childbirth and laid out the dead long before any social care was instituted.

5 Hallie Rubenhold, *The Five: The Untold Lives of Women Killed By Jack The Ripper* (Cambridge: Black Swan, 2020).

6 Of the nine houses in Blelock Street five had steps, being those with half sunk cellars. Numbers 4, 5, 6 and 7 had three steps. Number 8 had one step.

7 Carl Wernicke discovered Wernicke Encephalopathy in 1881 which is brought on by alcohol abuse and causes paralysed eye movements and mental confusion. About the same time, Sergei Korsakoff discovered Korsakoff Syndrome which is a loss of memory caused by alcohol misuse. The two symptoms are usually diagnosed together because of their connection to alcoholism.

8 Mayo Foundation for Medical Education and Research, 2019.

Chapter Five

1 Heather Shore, Professor in History at Leeds Beckett University and author of *London's Criminal Underworlds c. 1720–c. 1930: A Social and Cultural History* (Basingstoke: Palgrave Macmillan, 2015).

2 'Gay' as in the Victorian sense of 1) lewd, dissolute, loose morals, sexual pleasure (*OED*); 2) prostitution (*The Slang Dictionary*, 1869).

3 He implies here that he will let the reader judge for him/herself in the articles, but he does more than 'watch' and actually investigates people and situations before making judgements himself.

4 A hop was an informal dance. Two pence or 'tuppence' in 1865 was the equivalent of 75 pence in 2018.

5 Orders to force fathers to pay towards the cost of their illegitimate offspring.

6 In the Book of Genesis, God put a mark on Cain after he had killed his brother Abel to make him stand out to others, saying 'You will be a restless wanderer on the earth.'

7 French for soliciting or touting for business.

8 Thomas Otway 1652–1685, English dramatist. The full line reads 'Villains that undervalue damnation, will forswear themselves for dinner and hang their fathers for half a crown.' (*The Soldier's Fortune*, 1678).

9 '...wide is the gate and broad the way that leadeth to destruction.' King James Bible, Matthew 7.13.

10 Kellow Chesney, *The Victorian Underworld* (London: Pelican, 1979), 112.

11 James Walvin, *A Child's World – English Childhood 1800–1914* (London: Pelican, 1992), 135–6.

12 Judith Flanders, *The Victorian City* (London: Atlantic Books, 2013), 180.

13 David Gange, *The Victorians* (London: Oneworld Publications, 2017), 48.

14 'Our Churches and Chapels', a collection of articles from the *Preston Chronicle*, published in this collection in 1869, pp. 11–12.

15 The reception attendant at the Lambeth Workhouse male section, mentioned in James Greenwood, *A Night in a Workhouse* (London: *Pall Mall Gazette*, 1866).

Chapter Six

1 Coincidentally, earlier that day, my great-great grandparents, John Garlington and Ellen Green, had got married at St Augustine's Church, not three hundred yards away from this place.
2 William Dobson, 'Preston in the Olden Time', lecture (Wm Dobson and Son, 1857).
3 Daniel Gillespie was sentenced to transportation to New South Wales at the Quarter Sessions at Lancaster and sailed on the *America* on 14 April 1829.
4 More than likely 'halloo!' which was a hunting call used to call attention.
5 The Census taken on 2 April shows them at 30 Shepherd Street.
6 A trick often used by prostitutes.
7 The 26 October 1876 edition of the *Burnley Express* states that Chester had just returned home after a fortnight in prison. Dr Geddie, the town surgeon, said the victim's nose was broken, her forehead cut open, her face swollen, and one eye was only partly open. There were bruises all over her body and on her throat. The case was sufficiently serious to be carried in other regional newspapers.
8 Possibly Alice Whittle of Knowsley Street.
9 Sailors were always a target for prostitutes and thieves as they were paid at the end of voyages and were therefore the richest working-class men around, at least for a few days.
10 Jane Almond had run a brothel in Bolton's Court (off Church Street) from 1840 to 1870.
11 The *Lancaster Guardian*, the *Wellington Journal*, the *Wrexham Gazette*, the *North Wales Chronicle*, the *Cheshire Observer* and the *Western Gazette*.
12 A gill (pronounced 'jill') was a quarter of a pint.
13 Round the corner from Shepherd Street, at the end of Stoneygate.
14 Tallent returned to the Sandhole after her imprisonment. In 1865 she was the victim of an assault by Thomas Quigley while ordering a drink in his beerhouse in Shepherd Street.
15 In October 1866: it says something of the stupidity of the thieves, William Moore and James Pratt, that they took the lead to Blackburn's marine store (nothing to do with the sea – more of a junk shop), round the corner in Leeming Street, who refused it and reported them to the police.
16 James Walvin, *A Child's World*, 17.

17 Rosa Maguire's Reformatory for Catholic Girls in Bedminster in Somerset, which had 72 girls between the ages of 9 and 19.
18 Thomas Archer, *The Pauper, The Thief and The Convict* (London: Groombridge and Sons, 1865) 98.
19 This all came to light when the girl told her older sister she was 'sore'.
20 Friargate was much frequented by prostitutes at this time, especially at night.
21 In the Victorian period, because of long skirts and petticoats, women and girls wore split drawers.

Chapter Seven

1 John Walton, *Lancashire: A Social History 1558–1939* (Manchester: Manchester University Press, 1987), 181.
2 *Ibid.*
3 In 1856 Proctor had tried to secure the licence for the Lodge Bank Tavern but it was refused.
4 A string instrument, similar to a violin or a viola where the strings are played by a fixed arm which is moved by a handle rather than a bow. At the present time (2020) a hurdy-gurdy can fetch between £500 and £1000.
5 Bastardy was an offence where a parent, usually the father, did not contribute to the upkeep of an illegitimate child.
6 *Preston Chronicle* 28 August 1869 – the figures given for licensed premises in this report were: 226 public houses and 274 beerhouses – 500 in total.
7 In 1870 the accommodation at the Rifleman was described as: Ground Floor – a vault, two small parlours and a kitchen; First Floor – Large dancing room, small refreshment room and a bedroom; Second Floor – small vault and five or six bedrooms.
8 Tom Sayers (1826–65) was an English bare-knuckle fighter who was only beaten once. (*Encyclopaedia Britannica* [1911]).
9 Short sentences were regarded by some prostitutes as a time to 'wash and brush up'.
10 Ben Wilson, *Decency and Disorder 1789–1837* (London: Faber and Faber, 2008), 190.
11 Shakespeare, *The Tempest*, 4.1, 188–9.
12 Chesney, *The Victorian Underworld*, 373.
13 A surety is an individual who takes legal responsibility for another person's debt or behaviour. If Dunderdale was wanting sureties, she could find no-one to vouch for her good behaviour]
14 Thomas Edelston (1830–99) was part of a law firm which had offices at 7 Winckley Street.
15 Robert Green Watson (1830–92) was part of a law firm which had offices at 8 Winckley Street.

16 Reflecting the interests of one party or one side.
17 The case came to nothing, but Pitcher was replaced in 1871.
18 James Dunn (1824–72) died at home at 15 Stephenson Terrace, Deepdale Road aged 48 on Tuesday 9 May of congestion of the lungs. Had suffered from acute rheumatism the previous year. Formerly worked in London, Birmingham and Swansea.
19 The Stanleys, the family of the Earls of Derby, left Preston shortly after the 1830 election when Edward Stanley was defeated by Henry 'Orator' Hunt. Their house adjacent to the stables, Patten House, had been demolished in 1830.
20 A strong, rather coarse fabric woven with a linen warp and a woollen weft, first used in the fifteenth century for bed ware and first associated with Linsey in Suffolk.
21 Saturday was market day for fruit, vegetables, butchers' meat and pigs.
22 A two-shilling piece.
23 Tuesday was market day for the buying and selling of hay and straw, which brought in men from the rural areas round Preston.
24 *Herald* 24 September 1870.
25 Margaret E. De Lacy, *Policing and Punishment in Nineteenth Century Britain* (London: Routledge, 1981), 204.
26 Watch Committees were composed of magistrates and local officials responsible for the efficiency of the local police force from 1835 to 1968.
27 Edward Swainson (1818–73) had donated a stained-glass window in the new Anglican church of St Saviour's.
28 This averages out at eightpence (£3) profit per pint. Taking in other sales this is still rather high for a Sandhole establishment.
29 This Act set up 'retreats' for the cure of what later became known as alcoholics.
30 Gourvish and Wilson, *Consumption of Beer in England and Wales* (Cambridge: Cambridge University Press, 1994), 127–8.
31 Boarders had food provided and washing done. Lodgers just rented a room or space.
32 *Encyclopaedia Britannica*, 1911.
33 Chesney, *The Victorian Underworld*, 110.
34 *Ibid.*
35 Cheese was not cheap and fluctuated in price. According to market prices in the Herald, the price of wholesale cheese in January worked out at an average of one shilling and ninepence a pound (£7.66). In December it had fallen to (£6.53).
36 Under the accumulation system. In the previous five years she had been in prison ten times, for a total of thirty months.
37 Born in 1836, Norton had a string of convictions from 1857 until 1871 including drunkenness, assault, theft and running a brothel.

38 Born in 1846, Parker had a number of convictions from 1861 up to this point for theft, receiving stolen money and assault.
39 Reported by the *Herald* on 15 November 1873.
40 A specialist type of iron with a large, raised handle.
41 Henry Marriott born Coventry 1820. He came to Preston as a private in the 6th (Royal Warwickshire) Regiment in 1844. Became the Nuisance and Sanitary Inspector for the Borough in 1846 and the Fire Brigade Superintendent in 1852, holding both offices concurrently. Died of chronic bronchitis in January 1883.
42 Under the miasma theory that disease was caused by bad air.
43 Taylor's was usually a busy house, usually accommodating thirty lodgers.

Chapter Eight
1 Figures taken from Pamela Horn, *Amusing the Victorians* (Stroud: Amberley, 2014), 92.
2 James Nicholls, *Last Orders: A Social History of Drinking* (London: History Today Ltd, 2012), 13.
3 Gourvish and Wilson, *Consumption of Beer in England and Wales*, 126.
4 Pamela Horn, *Amusing the Victorians*, 92.
5 Until 1974 both Manchester and Liverpool were policed by this force.
6 Born in Ireland in 1828. Retired as Vicar of St Mary's in 1904 after 47 years' service.
7 Until well into the twentieth century, St Mary's had the most populated parish in Preston. 2221 parishioners walked in the 1882 Guild Procession. At one time, Rev. Alker had five curates.
8 Born in Württemberg in 1834 – studied at Berlin University and St Bee's Theological College.
9 In 1871, 38,000 children under the age of 15 lived in Preston out of a total population of 85,427 – 40 percent.
10 There were serious attempts at this time to sell houses en bloc in Leeming Street, Shepherd Street, Blelock Street and Greaves Street.
11 Also held by the Chief Constable, Joseph Oglethorpe.
12 It is unclear whether the Alker/Benzing partnership was intended to be a lasting arrangement, but it ended in January 1873 when Rev. Benzing became involved in a paternity suit involving an eighteen-year-old woman, Lilly Woodhouse, the sister of Robert Woodhouse, the parish clerk. A constant visitor to the house in Avenham Road, sometimes four times a day, he 'became intimate' with Miss Woodhouse in April 1872 and she gave birth in January 1873. He left Preston finally in February. The *Chronicle* described him in April 1873 as arriving in September 1871 as 'a spiritual and moral reformer … with a consuming anxiety to save the lost and reform the godless' and left town 'a coward and a delinquent … an arrant rascal.'

13 Emma Griffin, author of *Breadwinner: An Intimate History of the Victorian Economy* (New Haven: Yale, 2020), in an interview with *BBC History Magazine*, June 2020.
14 Like Jane Rowley, Connolly was a long-time resident in the Sandhole. Born in 1825 and lacking any education, her usual crime was robbery, but she was also found guilty of assault (twice), drunkenness (nine times) and family neglect until she was given three years for housebreaking in Burnley in 1881.
15 Barbara Marchant was living here in 1861 (see earlier chapter on James Steanson).
16 Barbara Marchant and Ann Collett were living here in 1865 when Steanson died.
17 Also home to Jane Rowley.
18 Also home to Bridget Connolly.
19 Aged eighteen. Chief Constable Dunn remarked at Wallace's court case that there had been twelve cases in the previous fortnight of girls keeping brothels under 20 years of age – three had been sent to Sessions and given 12 months' imprisonment, two of which had been under twenty.
20 In 1875, Mary Jane Pearson received six months' hard labour in Lancaster Castle for her third offence.
21 The 'Other Purposes' provision criminalised 'gross indecency' between males in Section 11 which was added only a week before the Act became law. It was this Act by which Oscar Wilde was convicted in May 1895.
22 Published by the *Chronicle* on 24 December 1869.
23 Page 3.
24 Article first published in the *Chronicle* on 8 May 1869.
25 Page 39.
26 Page 42.
27 First published in the *Chronicle* on 18 September 1869.
28 A reference to Charles Dickens' travels round Seven Dials in London in the 1830s.
29 Pages 142–3.
30 Page 39.
31 The Ragged School movement began in 1844, supported by the Evangelical philanthropist, Anthony Ashley Cooper, seventh Earl of Shaftesbury who was its first President. It began with the intention of teaching poor children how to read the Bible, but by 1850 it had the aim of 'removing every ragged, destitute child from our streets and to placing that child in the path of industry'. After the 1870 Education Act, the movement rapidly declined. Shaftesbury wrote, 'The godless non-Bible system is at hand … Everything for the flesh and nothing for the soul. Everything for time and nothing for eternity.' Rev.

Richard Turnbull, *Shaftesbury: The Great Reformer* (Oxford: Lion Hudson, 2010), 151.

32 *Chronicle* 15 October 1859.

33 The school moved because the new parish of St Saviour wanted the old chapel, temporarily, for conducting services.

34 Because of the Cotton Famine caused by the American Civil War.

35 It must be remembered that this area was adjacent to the Parish Church of St John and fell nominally under its jurisdiction until 1860, and that St Augustine's had been ministering in the district since 1838.

36 Page 145.

37 The Foundry Arms, the Lodge Bank Tavern and the Garden Gate.

38 *Chronicle* 31 December 1881.

39 *Chronicle* 24 October 1891.

40 Rev. Dr Edmund Lee (1831–84) was described by a correspondent to the *Chronicle* as a 'hard working pastor, an excellent preacher, a talented lecturer, a profound teacher and a ripe scholar'. Not in complete agreement with teetotalism he occasionally gave talks on the wines of the New Testament. In 1875 he turned down the incumbency of Holy Trinity Church in Preston after being strongly recommended. Hewitson had found the parish very unappealing. The Bishop of Manchester 'found' for him the tiny, sparse village parish of Esh in County Durham where he later died from ill health.

41 'I want you to realise that it is through him that forgiveness of your sins is proclaimed. Through him justification of all sins which the Law of Moses was unable to justify is offered to every believer.' (Jerusalem)

42 *Chronicle* 13 August 1870.

43 Mark 10: 46–52 Christ heals the blind beggar and forgives his sins.

44 Page 44.

45 Andrew Hobbs, *A Fleet Street In Every Town: The Provincial Press in England, 1855-1900* (Cambridge: Open Book Publishers, 2018), 46.

46 Born in 1814, Bishop Goss constantly toured the then massive Liverpool diocese from 1856, visiting parishes as far north as Carlisle and as far west as Bolton. It is thought that he died of exhaustion in 1872 aged 58.

47 *Chronicle* 15 December 1860.

48 RCPA 1–22.

49 *Ibid.*, 181.

50 *BBC History Magazine*, 72.

51 *Ibid.*, 72.

52 James Nugent 1822–1905 was a pioneer for the rights and welfare of the poor by encouraging people of wealth and standing to help. He opened a ragged school, a night shelter, a refuge, a certified industrial

school and was the first Catholic chaplain at Walton Prison where he worked for 22 years.

53 It was possible to take a partial pledge to abstain from spirits or on certain days such as weekends.

54 Henry Manning (1808–92) was ordained as an Anglican priest in 1833 and ordained as a Catholic priest in 1851.

55 Andrew Hobbs, 73.

56 Including St Saviour's.

57 Such as Professor Smith of Lincoln who performed 'Magic and Mystery' for two hours in October 1877.

58 St Saviour's Band of Hope had walked the day before in the Church of England Procession.

59 Nine months after the Guild, The Bishop of Liverpool, Rev. Bernard O'Reilly, who had said the sung a Guild High Mass at St Augustine's on Guild Monday, took the very unusual step of moving all three priests at once from the parish. Canon Taylor was moved to St Peter's, Lytham to replace his brother who had died. Fr Kirwan was moved to Blackburn where he worked in various parishes until his death in 1922. The senior curate, Fr John Chapman was also moved to Blackburn where he died in 1886 aged 40.

Bibliography and Sources Consulted

Acton, William, *Prostitution Considered in Its Aspects* (Churchill 1857)

Anderson, Michael, *Family Structures in 19th Century Lancashire* (Cambridge: Cambridge University Press, 1971)

Archer, Thomas, *The Pauper, The Thief and The Convict* (London: Groombridge and Sons, 1865)

Aspin, Chris, *The First Industrial Society: Lancashire* (Lancaster: Carnegie Publishing, 1995)

Berry, A. J. *The Story of Preston* (London and Bath: Sir Isaac Pitman and Sons. Ltd, 1912)

Brand, Emily, *The Georgian Bawdy House* (Shire Publications, 2015)

Brandwood, Davison and Slaughter, *Licensed to Sell* (English Heritage 2006)

Burnett, John, *Liquid Pleasures* (London: Routledge, 1999)

Burroughs, Peter (contr), *History of the British Army* (Oxford: Oxford University Press, 1996)

Chesney, Kellow, *The Victorian Underworld* (Pelican, 1979)

Clark, George Thomas, 'Report on the Health of the Borough of Preston 1849'

Clay, Rev. John, 'Preston Prison Chaplain's Reports 1841–1850'

Clay, Rev. John, 'Report on Sanatory (sic) Condition of Preston 1843'

Clemesha, H. W., *A History of Preston* (Manchester: Manchester University, 1912)

DeLacey, M. E., *Policing and Punishment in 19th Century* (Routledge, 1981)

Dennis, Richard, *English Industrial Cities of the Nineteenth Century* (Cambridge: Cambridge University Press, 1984)

Dobson, Bob (ed), *A Preston Mixture* (Landy Publishing, 2007)

Eastoe, Jane, *Victorian Pharmacy* (Pavilion, 2010)

Ensor, R. C. K., *England 1870–1914* (Oxford: Oxford University Press, 1936)

Fishwick, Henry, *History of the Parish of Preston* (Aldine Press, 1900)

Flanders, Judith, *The Victorian City* (Atlantic Books, 2013)

Flintoff, Thomas R., *Preston Churches and Chapels* (Lancaster: Carnegie Publishing, 1985)

Foakes-Jackson, F. J. *Social Life in England 1750–1850* (Macmillan, 1916)

Frazer, W. M., *History of Public Health* (Baillière, Tindall, Cox, 1950)
Freethy, Ron, *Lancashire Privies* (Countryside Books 1998)
Gange, David, *The Victorians* (Oneworld, 2017)
Gardiner, J. and N. Wenhorn (eds), *Companion to British History* (Collins 1995)
Gayler, Roberts & Morris, 'Sketch Map of Economic History of Britain 1975'
Goodman, Ruth, *How To Be A Good Victorian* (Penguin Viking, 2013)
Gourvish and Wilson, *Consumption of Beer in England and Wales* (Cambridge: Cambridge University Press, 1994)
Greenwood, James, *A Night in a Workhouse* (London: *Pall Mall Gazette*, 1866)
H.M.S.O., 'Markets and Fairs in England and Wales 1928'
Halliwell, Stephen, 'Preston Pubs blog' (for dates)
Harrison, J. F. C., *Early Victorian Britain* (Fontana, 1979)
Harvey, A. D., *Sex In Georgian England* (Phoenix Press, 2001)
Hemyng, Bracebridge, *London Underworld* (Mayhew) (*Morning Chronicle* 1861)
Hewitson, Anthony, *History of Preston* (*Chronicle* Office, 1883)
Hewitson, Anthony, *Preston Court Leet Records* (*Guardian* Printing, 1905)
Hindle, David John, *Life in Victorian Preston* (Amberley, 2014)
Hindle, John David, *From a Gin Palace to a King's Palace* (Tempus, 2007)
Hobbs, Andrew, *A Fleet Street in Every Town* (Open Book Publishers, 2018)
Hope, E. W., *Health at the Gateway* (Cambridge: Cambridge University Press, 1931)
Horn, Pamela, *Amusing the Victorians* (Amberley, 2014)
Hunt, David, *A History of Preston* (Lancaster: Carnegie Publishing, 2009)
Jones, Steve, *Capital Punishments* (Wicked Publications, 2000)
Jones, Steve, *Lancashire Lasses: Their Lives and Crimes* (Wicked Publications, 2001)
King, J. E., *Richard Marsden and the Preston Chartists 1837–48* (Lancaster: Lancaster University, 1981)
Kirby, Dean, *Angel Meadow* (Pen and Sword, 2016)
Kuerden, Richard, *Brief Description of the Burrough and Town of Preston 1818*
May, Trevor, *Victorian and Edwardian Prisons* (Shire, 2010)
Morgan, Nigel, *Deadly Dwellings* (Mullion Books, 1993)
Morgan, Nigel, *Housing in Victorian Preston* (Preston CDC, 1982)
Morgan, Nigel, *Vanished Dwellings* (Mullion Books, 1990)
Nicholls, James, *Last Orders: A Social History of Drinking* (London: History Today, 2012)
Picard, Liza, *Victorian London* (Phoenix, 2006)
Preston Chronicle 1831–85
Preston Electoral Roll, 1835–6

Preston Herald 1864–85
Roberts, Robert, *The Classic Slum* (Pelican, 1983
Rubenfold, Hallie, *The Five: The Untold Lives of The Women Killed by Jack the Ripper* (Black Swan, 2020)
St. Augustine's Parish Notice Books 1855–1882
Steinbach, Susie, *Women in England 1760–1914* (Phoenix, 2005)
Stone, Lawrence, *Family, Sex and Marriage in England 1500–1800* (Penguin, 1979)
Strong, Roy, *England in the Eighteenth Century* (Penguin, 1989)
Sweet, Matthew, *Inventing the Victorians* (Faber, 2001)
The Builder Volume XIX Nos 983/4, 'Condition of our Towns'
Thomas, Donald, *The Victorian Underworld* (John Murray, 2003)
Thompson, F. M. L., *The Rise of Respectable Society 1830–1900* (Fontana, 1988)
Timmins, Geoffrey, *Preston: A Pictorial History* (Phillmore & Co, 1992)
Timmins, J. G., *Handloom Weavers' Cottages* (Lancaster: Lancaster University, 1977)
Tulket, Marmaduke OSB, 'An Account of the Borough of Preston 1821'
Turnbull, Richard, *Shaftesbury* (Lion Hudson, 2010)
Walsh, Tom and Gregg Butler, *The Old Lamb and Flag* (Lancaster: Carnegie Publishing, 1992)
Walton, John K., *Lancashire: A Social History 1558–1939* (Manchester: Manchester University Press, 1987)
Walvin, James, *A Child's World 1800–1914* (Pelican 1992)
Webb, Beatrice and Sydney, *Liquor Licensing in England* (Longmans, 1903)
Wilson, Ben, *Decency and Disorder 1789–1837* (Faber, 2008)
Woodward, Llewellyn, *The Age of Reform 1815–1870* (Oxford: Oxford University Press, 1962)

Information about syphilis was gleaned from the Shire/Red Planet/BBC television production of 'History Cold Case – Crossbones Girl' first broadcast in 2010.

I would also like to acknowledge the friendly and efficient assistance given to me by the staff of the Lancashire Archives in Bow Lane, Preston, during my hours of research into uncharted waters.
I would also like to thank my former pupil, Capt. Doctor Sam Green R.A.M.C. for his valuable advice on medical matters.
I am also grateful for access to material in the Local History Studies Department of the Harris Library.